Communications in Computer and Information Science 1664

More information about this series at https://link.springer.com/bookseries/7899

Richard J. Barnett · Daniel B. le Roux ·
Douglas A. Parry · Bruce W. Watson (Eds.)

ICT Education

51st Annual Conference of the Southern African Computer Lecturers' Association, SACLA 2022
Cape Town, South Africa, July 21–22, 2022
Revised Selected Papers

Springer

Editors
Richard J. Barnett
Stellenbosch University
Stellenbosch, South Africa

Daniel B. le Roux
Stellenbosch University
Stellenbosch, South Africa

Douglas A. Parry
Stellenbosch University
Stellenbosch, South Africa

Bruce W. Watson
Stellenbosch University
Stellenbosch, South Africa

ISSN 1865-0929 ISSN 1865-0937 (electronic)
Communications in Computer and Information Science
ISBN 978-3-031-21075-4 ISBN 978-3-031-21076-1 (eBook)
https://doi.org/10.1007/978-3-031-21076-1

This Springer imprint is published by the registered company Springer Nature Switzerland AG
The registered company address is: Gewerbestrasse 11, 6330 Cham, Switzerland

Preface

SACLA 2022, the 51st annual conference of the Southern African Computer Lecturers' Association, was hosted by the Department of Information Science, Stellenbosch University, during July 21–22, 2022, at the Protea Hotel Cape Town, Waterfront Breakwater Lodge in Cape Town, South Africa. It was the first time since 2019 that members of the Southern African computer education community could come together in person to share research findings and engage with colleagues from across the Southern African and international communities. In 2022, SACLA was also collocated, for the first time, with the annual research conference of the South African Institute for Computer Scientists and Information Technologists (SAICSIT), which gave delegates an additional opportunity to network with other academics in related fields.

In seeking to bring together computing lecturers, the organizing committee invited authors to submit research papers on a wide variety of computer education disciplines, including, but not limited to, the following:

- education-oriented research or classroom experience;
- innovative teaching techniques or pedagogical tools;
- curricular innovations or initiatives;
- curriculum adaptations for relevance to discipline/students;
- innovative industry-education collaboration interventions;
- program/curriculum design to address local opportunities and challenges;
- didactics and methods of teaching and assessment;
- ethical problems related to teaching and learning;
- transition of newly graduated school pupils;
- transition of newly graduated students into industry;
- international comparability of degrees and levels of knowledge/skills/performance;
- separation or combination of teaching and research; and
- post-hoc analysis of successes and failures in teaching and learning.

The international Program Committee consisted of 45 members, of which almost half were international (from outside South Africa). A rigorous double-blind refereeing process was followed for all submissions, where each submission was reviewed by at least three members of the Program Committee. Each paper was reviewed by at least one Program Committee member from outside South Africa. A total of 31 full paper submissions were received for consideration and, following review, 10 papers were selected for presentation at the conference and publication in this volume. This represents a 32% paper acceptance rate which is consistent with prior volumes in this series. Authors of accepted papers received constructive criticism from both the reviews and the conference audience to improve the papers prior to inclusion in this volume.

Additionally, the program chairs selected one paper and reviewer to receive awards for being the best submission and best reviewer, respectively. By placing emphasis on not only the best research work but also the best review, the program chairs acknowledge the hard work the Program Committee put into making the conference possible. The best paper was awarded to the paper "I feel like I am teaching myself": An Exploratory Study of the Factors and Implications of Online Learning co-authored by Malcolm Garbutt, Pitso Tsibolane and Tristan Pillay. For the consistent high quality of her reviews, the award for best reviewer was issued to Lisa Seymour from the University of Cape Town.

In addition to the 10 papers accepted for publication, the organizing committee invited two keynote speakers to deliver talks at the conference. These keynote speakers engaged the audience on topics relevant to computer education in practice and the publication landscape in South Africa. Joe Newbert presented a keynote entitled "Learning, Unlearning and Relearning Business Analysis" in which he outlined the gaps between higher-education graduates and industry expectations of them. Johann Mouton's keynote was entitled "A Scientometric Assessment of the State of Computer Sciences in South Africa" in which he illustrated the state of the computing sciences field within the South African scientific community. Both these keynotes were invaluable to the conference audience. In addition to these keynotes, Dan Wells from EskomSePush presented an invited talk on how the popular loadshedding app EskomSePush was built and is maintained. With loadshedding a major current event in South Africa, this was well received by the audience. It was also good for computing educators to see the fruits of top graduating students in practice.

The conference also had an international panel led by Adriana Steyn which focused on the after effects of the COVID-19 pandemic and illustrated how different academic institutions around the world are adapting to a post pandemic world. This panel, in the spirit of new international collaboration, was presented via Zoom.

The organizing committee would like to thank all the speakers, delegates and authors for making SACLA 2022 a great success, and we wish the SACLA 2023 organizing committee the best for their conference.

July 2022

Richard J. Barnett
Daniel B. le Roux
Douglas A. Parry
Bruce W. Watson

Organization

The 51st Annual Conference of the Southern African Computer Lecturers' Association (SACLA 2022) was organized by the Department of Information Science, Stellenbosch University, South Africa.

Executive Committee

Conference Chair

Richard J. Barnett	Stellenbosch University, South Africa

Program Chairs

Daniel B. le Roux	Stellenbosch University, South Africa
Douglas A. Parry	Stellenbosch University, South Africa
Bruce W. Watson	Stellenbosch University, South Africa

Program Committee

Millicent Agangiba	University of Mines and Technology, Ghana
Shirley Atkinson	University of Plymouth, UK
Shaun Bangay	Deakin University, Australia
Dewald Blaauw	Stellenbosch University, South Africa
Alan Chalmers	University of Warwick, UK
Loek Cleophas	Technische Universiteit Eindhoven, The Netherlands
Marian Daun	Universität Duisburg-Essen, Germany
Sigrid Ewert	University of the Witwatersrand, South Africa
Leila Goosen	University of South Africa, South Africa
Stefan Gruner	University of Pretoria, South Africa
Pieter Hartel	TU Delft, The Netherlands
Marie Hattingh	University of Pretoria, South Africa
Michaela Huhn	Ostfalia Hochschule für angewandte Wissenschaften, Germany
Barry Irwin	Noroff University, Norway
Nobert Jere	Walter Sisulu University, South Africa
Eduan Kotze	University of the Free State, South Africa
Jan Kroeze	University of South Africa, South Africa

Herbert Kuchen	Westfälische Wilhelms-Universität Münster, Germany
Horst Lichter	RWTH Aachen University, Germany
Janet Liebenberg	North-West University, South Africa
Christiaan Maasdorp	Stellenbosch University, South Africa
Linda Marshall	University of Pretoria, South Africa
Machdel Matthee	University of Pretoria, South Africa
Greg Michaelson	Heriot-Watt University, UK
Matthew Mullarkey	University of South Florida, USA
Liezel Nel	University of the Free State, South Africa
James Njenga	University of the Western Cape, South Africa
Thomas Noll	RWTH Aachen University, Germany
Kwete Nyandongo	University of Johannesburg, South Africa
Peter Ölveczky	University of Oslo, Norway
Tania Prinsloo	University of Pretoria, South Africa
Helen Purchase	University of Glasgow, UK
Rayne Reid	Noroff University, Norway
Petrus Schoonwinkel	Stellenbosch University, South Africa
Monika Seisenberger	Swansea University, UK
Lisa Seymour	University of Cape Town, South Africa
Hussein Suleman	University of Cape Town, South Africa
Estelle Taylor	North-West University, South Africa
Pitso Tsibolane	University of Cape Town, South Africa
Thomas van der Merwe	University of South Africa, South Africa
Lorna Uden	Staffordshire University, UK
Walter Uys	University of Cape Town, South Africa
Janis Voigtländer	Universität Duisburg-Essen, Germany
George Wells	Rhodes University, South Africa
Olaf Zukunft	Hochschule für angewandte Wissenschaften, Germany

Contents

Pandemic Pedagogy

Curriculum

Relevant Cybersecurity: Curriculum Guidance for the South African Context

Robin Brink[1], Jacques Ophoff[1,2(✉)], and Zainab Ruhwanya[1]

[1] University of Cape Town, Cape Town, South Africa
BRNROB030@myuct.ac.za, zainab.ruhwanya@uct.ac.za
[2] Abertay University, Dundee, UK
j.ophoff@abertay.ac.uk

Abstract. Cybersecurity is vital to most organisations, and it is important that Higher Education institutions ensure the relevance of degrees to meet industry needs. It is desirable to minimise any gap in the skills graduates obtain compared to what organisations expect when hiring a cybersecurity professional. This research examines the cybersecurity tasks, knowledge, and skills that are sought by South African organisations. Content analysis was used to compare job advertisements from five well-known online job portals with the knowledge areas, units, and topics from the Cybersecurity Curricula 2017. The results indicate that knowledge in organisational security is most needed, specifically relating to identifying and protecting organisations against risk. Some areas are shown to be less relevant in the sample of advertisements, such as component security. The results of the analysis can be used by Higher Education institutions, as well as other training providers, to ensure an industry-relevant cybersecurity curricula in the South African context. The research also demonstrates a replicable approach that can be used to ensure cybersecurity education-industry alignment in the future.

Keywords: Cybersecurity curricula · Knowledge areas · Content analysis · South Africa

1 Introduction

There is a worldwide shortage of cybersecurity professionals, and it is projected that by the year 2022 there will be approximately 1.8 million cybersecurity-related positions unfilled worldwide [2]. The demand for skilled cybersecurity professionals continues to outpace the supply, with suitably qualified graduates being highly sought after by industry [11,16]. Indeed, many countries view this as an area of national priority [5].

Like other countries around the globe, South Africa faces a shortage of skilled cybersecurity professionals [13,14]. Higher Education institutions should adapt to the increasing demand by leveraging frameworks that suggest skills needed in the cybersecurity field. These frameworks include: the Organising Framework of

R. J. Barnett et al. (Eds.): SACLA 2022, CCIS 1664, pp. 3–19, 2022.
https://doi.org/10.1007/978-3-031-21076-1_1

Occupations (OFO) [3]; Skills Framework for the Information Age (SFIA) [19]; Workforce Framework for Cybersecurity (NICE Framework) [15]; and the Cybersecurity Curricula 2017 (CSEC2017) [9]. It has been found that especially the NICE Framework and CSEC2017 represent a baseline for improving the cybersecurity field through skills development and educational training [7]. However, these frameworks are broad, and it can be challenging to determine the most relevant parts to meet industry requirements in the local context.

The purpose of this research is to identify the most relevant cybersecurity knowledge areas in the South African context. This is achieved through a comparison of the CSEC2017 with local job advertisements, to determine which areas are most sought after in industry. An assumption which underpins this approach is that organisations list the most critical skills for a role in such advertisements, to ensure suitable candidates are identified during the recruitment process. In this research content analysis was used to analyse a sample of 60 job advertisements in a systematic manner. The results can be used by Higher Education institutions to ensure the relevance of cybersecurity curricula to address local opportunities and challenges.

2 Background

Governments and industry bodies are aware of the need to increase the number of cybersecurity professionals and actively attempt to do so [7,10]. Cybersecurity builds on the core fields of information security and information assurance, and can be defined as: "A computing-based discipline involving technology, people, information, and processes to enable assured operations in the context of adversaries. It involves the creation, operation, analysis, and testing of secure computer systems. It is an interdisciplinary course of study, including aspects of law, policy, human factors, ethics, and risk management." [9, p. 16]. In developing countries, such as South Africa, this is especially important for the protection of online services and data, as more businesses and consumers go online [8,13]. To ensure relevance, industry is often consulted to determine what skills are deemed necessary for cybersecurity professionals [6,10]. However, it is not clear which skills are more sought after and whether these are adequately addressed in curricula guidance.

To produce skilled cybersecurity professionals academic institutions need to establish viable curricula and learning environments which enable the delivery of targeted cybersecurity programs. Such programs must address current cybersecurity issues and any emerging problems arising from cybercrime and cyberattacks. Curricula are formed by looking at the knowledge, skills, and abilities (KSA) that are theoretically needed, the needs of the cybersecurity community, and accreditation standards for cybersecurity professionals. A viable cybersecurity program needs to include content that supports computer-based knowledge, interdisciplinary topics, as well as practical components that support the application of theoretical content [2]. Traditionally there has been minimal industry input, as curriculum requirements have been created without investigating the needs of local businesses [10]. To bridge this gap the use of Industry Advisory Boards is one method to ensure that curricula remain aligned with industry needs in the long-term [20].

2.1 Industry Requirements

It is the norm that even competent graduates need additional training before they are job ready. One explanation for this is a mismatch between what is taught in Higher Education and what is expected in industry [2]. In a case study representative of this problem, the Boeing Company found that the skills which graduates have are inconsistent with what is needed within the cybersecurity industry. To ensure relevant skills the company aligned itself with academic partners to create a viable curriculum using the CSEC2017 and NICE Framework. The result was that the company had increased hiring flexibility and access to competent professionals [2]. The resulting growth in the overall pool of cybersecurity professionals is also beneficial to other companies.

From an academic perspective there is relatively little research focusing on whether the taught KSAs are relevant to what is needed by the cybersecurity workforce [10]. Researchers have attempted to identify skills that cybersecurity professionals need through the analysis of job advertisements. In the Australian context Potter and Vickers [16] collected 33 security-related job advertisements and identified six main categories of jobs. Subsequently they used questionnaires to explore relevant skills for cybersecurity professionals. In the South African context Parker and Brown [14] adopted the roles, descriptions, and skills needed for the various roles from [16]. They collected 196 security-related job advertisements and identified a wider range of work roles and skills required in this context. However, the results from these studies are not sufficiently structured in terms of topics and knowledge areas to be applied to cybersecurity program development. It is therefore clear that a framework is needed to align the process of curriculum development with what is needed by industry (e.g. to structure an analysis of cybersecurity job advertisements).

2.2 Theoretical Frameworks

Various frameworks seek to improve the pool of professionals by suggesting skills that are needed in the field. These range from general frameworks, such as the OFO and SFIA, to those focused on cybersecurity, such as the NICE Framework and CSEC2017.

Organising Framework of Occupations (OFO). The South African OFO is an occupational classification system that provides a framework for the identification, articulation, reporting, and monitoring of skills demand and supply in the South African labour market. The OFO focuses on jobs and occupations: a job is said to be a set of tasks and duties to be carried out by an individual, while an occupation is a set of jobs or a category that extends to several jobs with similar tasks and duties. The OFO provides detailed definitions and a common language when speaking about occupations, which is needed in the diverse South African context [3]. However, it only lists the high-level tasks that should be performed by an individual (e.g. "Overseeing the security of ICT systems") and is thus of limited value in determining relevant KSAs.

Skills Framework for the Information Age (SFIA). SFIA is a global framework (formally launched in 2000 and currently in its eight revision) that describes the skills and competencies required by professionals in digital work roles, such as information and cyber security. It provides a globally accepted language for the skills and competencies needed in the digital world [19]. SFIA consist of seven levels of responsibility which is characterised by generic attributes, along with descriptions of professional skills and competencies belonging to the level. The framework provides a clear description of the activities and skills needed as levels of responsibility progress. One of the key themes is information and cyber security, which is further divided into several categories. While SFIA is not specific to cybersecurity it can provide a useful indication of how activities and skills progressively become more sophisticated.

Workforce Framework for Cybersecurity (NICE Framework). The NICE Framework was created via a partnership between government, academia, and the private sector. It seeks to uplift the cybersecurity workforce through education, training, and workforce development. More specifically, it defines cybersecurity work and provides a starting point for formulating career paths and educational programs. The framework is structured into a hierarchy of work roles, competencies, and tasks, knowledge, and skills (TKS) statements. Tasks describe the work within an organisation, while knowledge and skills describe the learner (e.g. students, job seekers, and employees). These building blocks allow organisations to describe their cybersecurity work and workforce [15]. The NICE Framework can be used by educators to develop a curriculum, or degree program, covering the core knowledge and skills to perform cybersecurity tasks.

Cybersecurity Curricula 2017 (CSEC2017). The CSEC2017 was created by a joint task force of major international computing societies. It sets a standard for the content a cybersecurity curriculum should contain, aiming to grow the pool of qualified cybersecurity professionals by providing guidelines on how to structure a viable Higher Education (university-level) cybersecurity curriculum [2,9]. However, to date there are few examples of guidance, resources, and application of the CSEC2017 to develop curricula [4,10].

The CSEC2017 defines eight knowledge areas (KAs), as summarised in Table 1. It is structured in a hierarchy of knowledge areas, knowledge units (KUs), topics, and learning outcomes. According to the framework "each knowledge area is made up of critical knowledge with broad importance ... [representing] the full body of knowledge within the field of cybersecurity." [9, p. 20]. Within these knowledge areas, "knowledge units (KUs) are thematic

Table 1. CSEC2017 Knowledge Areas [9]

Knowledge Area	Description
Data Security	Protection of data throughout its life-cycle
Software Security	Development and use of software that reliably preserves the security properties of information and systems
Component Security	Design, procurement, testing, analysis and maintenance of components integrated into larger systems
Connection Security	Security of the physical and logical connections between components
System Security	Security aspects of systems that use software, consisting of components and connections
Human Security	Protecting the individual's data and privacy in the context of organisations
Organisational Security	Protecting organisations from cybersecurity threats and managing risk to support the successful accomplishment of the organisation's mission
Societal Security	How cybersecurity impacts society as a whole, both positive and negative

groupings that encompass multiple, related topics; the topics cover the required curricular content for each KU." The framework also acknowledges that topics and learning outcomes may be influenced by a disciplinary lens and institutional properties (e.g. program length, geographic location, etc.).

This structure should feel familiar to Higher Education academic staff. It can be noted that there is a link between the CSEC2017 learning outcomes and TKS statements (formerly referred to as KSAs) in the NICE Framework. This allows academic institutions to link CSEC2017 curricular recommendations to work and workforce requirements that may be specified using the NICE Framework [9].

Due to its focus on cybersecurity and post-secondary degree programs this research adopted the CSEC2017 framework. The analysis in Sect. 4 thus aligns with the knowledge areas and knowledge units defined by this framework.

3 Research Design

This research adopts an interpretivist philosophy, and it is acknowledged that the interpretation of the data may be subjective. However, by following a structured approach to data collection and analysis it is believed that research quality and rigour was ensured.

3.1 Data Collection

Details from cybersecurity job advertisements were collected over a period of three months. Five South African online job portals were used: Careers24,

Indeed, LinkedIn, PNet, and SimplyHired. These were chosen due to being well-known and comparable with similar studies [14]. A variety of search terms were used, consisting of 'cyber security', 'cybersecurity', 'IT security', and simply 'security' to ensure wide coverage. Thus a purposive sampling approach was employed. Job advertisements were manually collected and reviewed weekly by one of the researchers. This ensured that possibly relevant data was not lost due to an advertisement being removed once the position was filled.

Each advertisement was screened for relevance to a cybersecurity role and duplicate advertisements across portals were removed, keeping the most detailed version. Advertisements that were not relevant (e.g. outside South Africa or for positions such as 'security guard') were noted and excluded from further analysis. In addition, those that did not contain sufficient detail were excluded. For example, some advertisements consisted of only a single instruction for the applicant to send a curriculum vitae to a specific contact. This screening process ensured that only relevant job advertisements were used in the subsequent analysis. A total of 60 job advertisements were retained for analysis.

3.2 Data Analysis

Data analysis was guided by the KAs, KUs, and topics defined in the CSEC2017. Content analysis was used to analyse the content of job advertisements and compare this against the CSEC2017. According to Neuendorf [12] "Content analysis may be briefly defined as the systematic, objective, quantitative analysis of message characteristics." In this study the type of content analysis was human-coded analysis, performed by one of the researchers. The approach can be defined as descriptive as the analysis describes characteristics of the sample of job advertisements.

During the analysis each job advertisement's content was categorised into the various KAs, KUs, and topics of the CSEC2017. The specific focus was the area of cybersecurity a role represents, and the TKS that the employer connects to it. During the analysis no double-counting was performed and a TKS was only allocated to one topic/KU per KA. Example extracts from advertisements were retained to substantiate points within the analysis process.

4 Analysis and Findings

This section presents the content analysis of the sample of cybersecurity job advertisements (referred to as Jxx where xx presents the job advertisement number in the dataset). It starts by describing general characteristics of the data, after which the data is categorised according to KAs and KUs.

4.1 General Characteristics

Jobs were initially sorted into roles based on the title or job description. This resulted in the identification of 15 distinct roles within the data. The three most occurring roles were: IT Security Specialist (14 cases); Security/Cyber Analyst (8 cases); and Cyber Security Officer (5 cases). These roles are quite generic and don't correspond to standard roles as described by the NICE Framework. While cases did include more specific roles, it appears that industry is not following the 'common language' defined by frameworks.

In terms of experience required, most jobs desired 5+ years of experience (24 cases). This was followed by 3–5 years of experience (21 cases) and 1–3 years of experience (12 cases). Possessing a technology-related Bachelor's degree (30 cases) or higher certification or diploma (14 cases) was a general requirement. A range of certifications were also desirable, with the three most occurring certifications being: CISSP (17 cases); CISM (13 cases); and CISA (11 cases). The analysis identified reference to 13 different certifications across all cases, showing that these are sought after and that collaboration between Higher Education institutions and such training providers could be beneficial for learners [2].

It's suggested that competent cybersecurity professionals need to have both technical and non-technical (soft) skills [9,16]. However, in the sample of job advertisements there was infrequent reference to soft skills, with a more prominent focus on duties to be performed and experience/qualifications needed. The most sought-after soft skill was 'communication' (14 cases) which aligns with previous research [10,14]. Following this the 'ability to work in a team' was sought (8 cases). Representative example extracts are: *"good written, oral, and interpersonal communication skills"* [J33] and *"work effectively with team members"* [J39]. While more reference to soft skills may have been expected, this confirms the importance of expanding curricula to include social and emotional learning which develops intrapersonal, interpersonal, and cognitive skills [1].

4.2 Knowledge Areas

Job advertisements were analysed according to the KUs and topics, which link to a KA. The overall coverage of KAs by job advertisements is illustrated in Fig. 1. This figure shows the relative importance of each KA based on the number of KUs counted within each area. It can be observed that the most frequently encountered KA is 'Organisational Security' (31%) while 'Component Security' (2%) occurs the least. In the following sections each KA will be analysed in more detail.

Organisational Security. There are nine KUs within this KA. This was by far the most referenced KA, accounting for almost a third of all content. However, it is acknowledged that this KA contains the most KUs (as defined by the CSEC2017) which contributes to its high coverage within the data.

The 'Risk Management' and 'Security Governance & Policy' KUs occurred most frequently (54 cases each). This indicates that 90% of organisations see these as issues that need to be addressed. The industry data aligns with security literature, which has a long history recognising the importance of effective security governance. An important management topic is managing cyber risk within

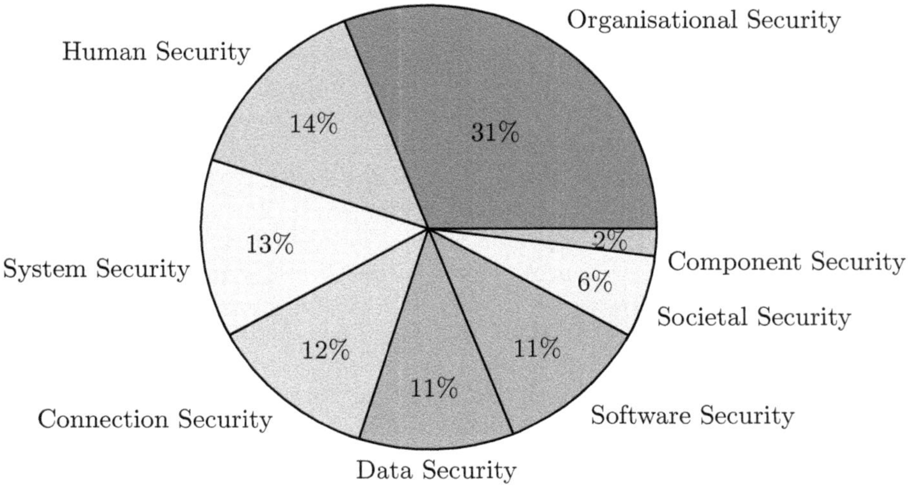

Fig. 1. Distribution of knowledge areas (N = 60)

an organisation. The topic 'Risk assessment and Analysis' was referred to in 22 cases, showing its importance. Examples of this requirement are:

> *"Knowledge of risk assessment tools, technologies and methods."* [J03] and *"Perform regular risk assessments and keep management aware of threats."* [J39]

The topic 'Security Governance' was referenced in 15 cases, with an example of this requirement being:

> *"Responsible for monitoring the governance aspects related to the Security within company to ensure the standards are maintained."* [J24]

Other prominent topics which relate to the above mentioned areas include 'Strategic Planning' (14 cases) and ' Performance Measurements (metrics)' (11 cases). These activities can help to support key stakeholders with decision making and organisational strategies which rely on security.

From an operational perspective, 'System Hardening' (21 cases) and 'Incident Response' (19 cases) were desirable skills. This aligns with previous findings highlighting key cybersecurity skills [10,14]. While these topics focus on systems and processes, it was also seen that 'Security Awareness, Training and Education' (14 cases) was a common topic. This relates to the Human Security KA which is discussed below. An example of this requirement is:

> *"Educates management & staff on security risk through reporting and presentations. Monitors Information Security industry trends and educates the organization of critical information."* [J51]

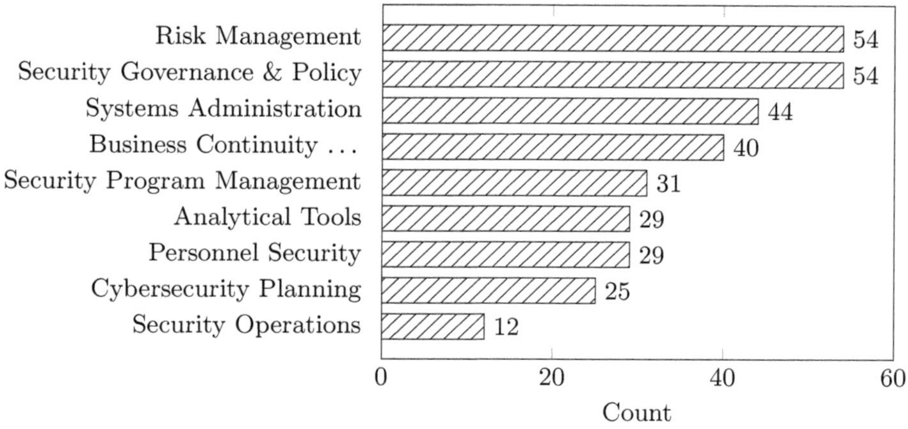

Fig. 2. Knowledge units within organisational security

Lastly, it was noticeable that 'Project Management' ability and experience (18 cases) was a desirable soft skill. This is also recognised by computing curricula and previous research [2,10]. A summary of the KUs mentioned in job advertisements is shown in Fig. 2.

Human Security. There are seven KUs within this KA. The 'Awareness and Understanding' KU featured most prominently (38 cases) and links closely with organisational security. Specific topics which featured more prominently include 'Cyber vulnerabilities and threats awareness' (14 cases) and 'Cybersecurity user education' (7 cases). There is large body of research in these areas, with organisational case studies in the South African context [18]. It has also been shown that cyber situational awareness is strongly linked to implementation of security measures [17]. Thus this KA has an important influence on others. An example of this requirement is:

> *"Develop an awareness and communications plan for the technology and greater business and executives that is aligned with strategy and considers a range of risks and themes."* [J02]

Another prominent topic is 'Enforcement and rules of behaviour' (21 cases). This refers to methods and techniques to ensure compliance with security policies, using both positive and negative behavioural enforcement. An example of this requirement is:

> *"Ensure that all Information Security policies and procedures are followed according to the [organisation] requirement."* [J42]

As this topic deals with individuals and their behaviour it has an interdisciplinary nature very different to other areas in computing. The CSEC2017

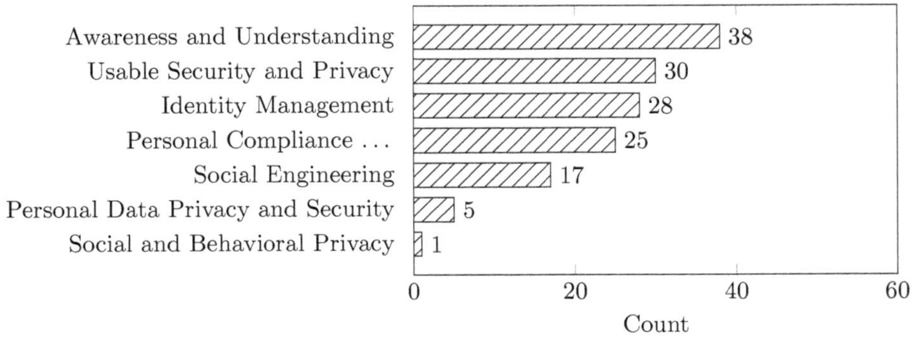

Fig. 3. Knowledge units within human security

emphasises that cybersecurity is an interdisciplinary course of study, and that an awareness and understanding of human-centred security is important [9]. A summary of the KUs mentioned in job advertisements is shown in Fig. 3.

System Security. There are seven KUs within this KA. Two KUs were more prominent, namely 'System Control' (50 cases) and 'System Management' (37 cases). Within system control, 'Audit' is a prominent topic which featured in 19 cases. This topic focuses on logs (logging and log analysis) and their use for intrusion detection. This was also found to be important in previous research [14].

The topic 'Penetration Testing' (13 cases) was also commonly seen. This relates to a cybersecurity professional's ability to proactively protect the organisation and as such was found to be needed by previous researchers [10,14]. Examples of this requirement are:

> *"Participate in the design and execution of vulnerability assessments, penetration tests, and security audits."* [J33] and *"Perform mobile, complex application, infrastructure, as well as social engineering assessments and penetration testing."* [J32]

Within this KA consideration of the system as a whole, rather than just connected components (i.e. systems thinking), was also emphasised. This aligns well with most computing curricula. A summary of the KUs mentioned in job advertisements is shown in Fig. 4.

Connection Security. There are eight KUs within this KA. The 'Network Defence' KU had the most references (48 cases). A prominent topic is 'Implementing Firewalls and Virtual Private Networks (VPN)' which featured in 20 cases. Examples of this requirement are:

> *"Direct experience with anti-virus software, intrusion detection, firewalls and content filtering."* [J03] and *"Daily administration of firewall rules, IPS Policies and Filters via change control procedures."* [J34]

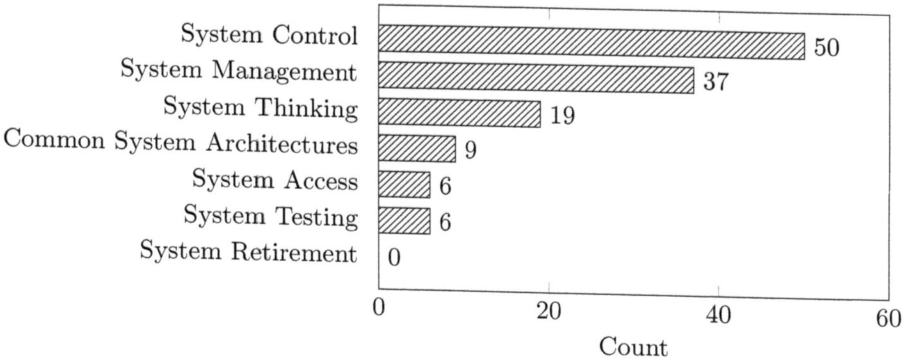

Fig. 4. Knowledge units within system security

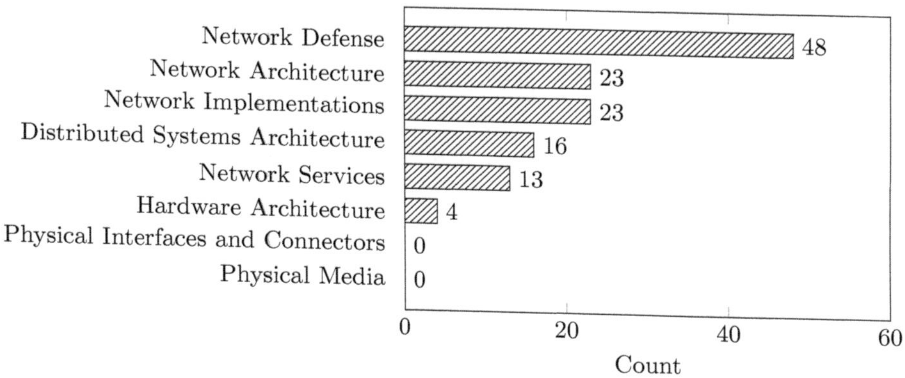

Fig. 5. Knowledge units within connection security

It is acknowledged that keeping track of emerging trends and maintain currency of knowledge are important aspects of a cybersecurity role [10]. The 'Emerging trends' topic was also visible in the data (9 cases), for example to *"Investigate, document, and report on information security issues and emerging trends."* [J29]. A summary of the KUs mentioned in job advertisements is shown in Fig. 5.

Data Security. There are eight KUs within this KA. The most frequently occurring KU was 'Digital Forensics' which featured in 50 cases. A topic which featured prominently was 'Reporting, incident response and handling' (24 cases). An example of this requirement is:

> *"Perform daily information security monitoring, reporting and verifying the integrity and availability of business-critical resources, systems and key processes, reviewing system and application logs, and verifying completion of scheduled jobs within the Information Security portfolio."* [J05]

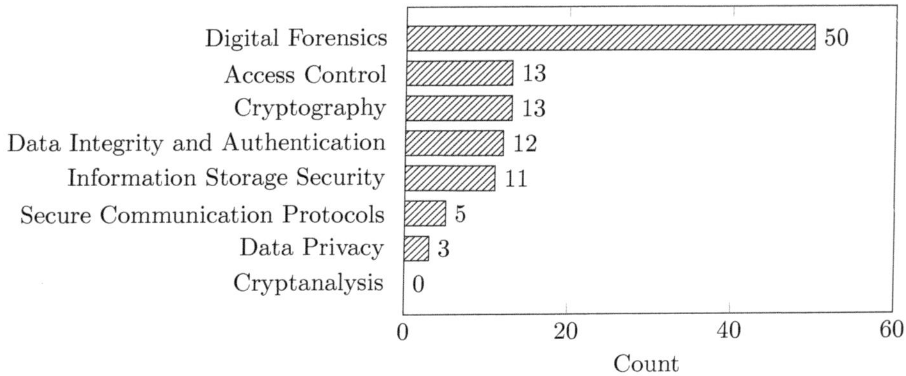

Fig. 6. Knowledge units within data security

Another important topic was the 'Investigatory Process' (11 cases). An example of this requirement is:

> *"Participate in incident response planning and investigation of security breaches, and assist with disciplinary and legal matters associated with such breaches as necessary."* [J46]

It could be observed that the requirements were often linked to security governance and risk management, through monitoring and reporting of security metrics. It was somewhat surprising that the 'Data Privacy' KU did not feature more prominently. This could be attributed to data being collected before the POPIA commencement date, or the search terms used. It would be expected that data privacy is an important topic in the current South African context. A summary of the KUs mentioned in job advertisements is shown in Fig. 6.

Software Security. There are seven KUs within this KA. There was demand for all KUs, with 'Deployment and Maintenance' and 'Design' featuring most prominently (20 cases each). Within deployment and maintenance the most important topic was 'Patching and the vulnerability lifecycle' (16 cases). This aligns with previous research which emphasises patch management and vulnerability assessment as important skills within cybersecurity [10,14].

The importance of documentation was also seen, with the topic 'Security Documentation' featuring in 10 cases. An example of this requirement is:

> *"Document technical issues identified during security assessments."* [J32]

This confirms the importance of communication as a soft skill for cybersecurity professionals. A summary of the KUs mentioned in job advertisements is shown in Fig. 7.

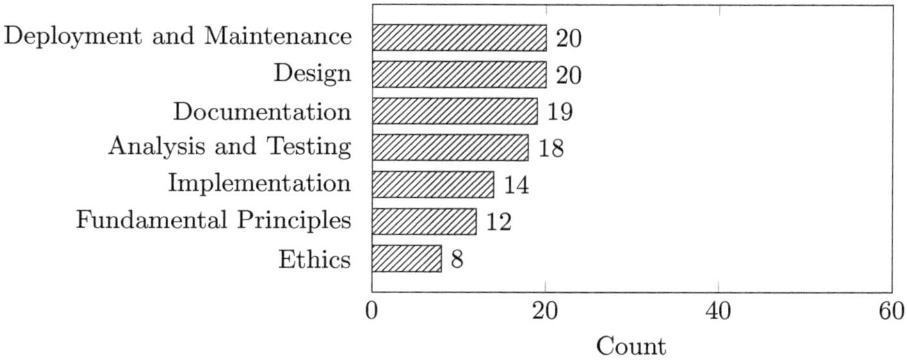

Fig. 7. Knowledge units within software security

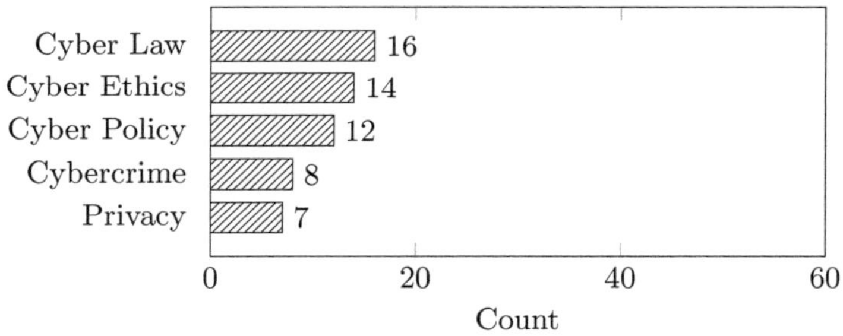

Fig. 8. Knowledge units within societal security

Societal Security. There are five KUs within this KA. There was relatively little mention of tasks, knowledge, and skills related to this area. The most frequently occurring KU was 'Cyber Law' (16 cases). Job advertisements rarely asked for applicants to be aware of specific laws, but to monitor and ensure compliance with applicable cyber legislation, for example:

> *"Evaluate security exposures, misuse or non-compliance to law or legislation and ensure implementation of security controls to address these."* [J41]

Knowledge of 'Privacy laws' as a topic was only relevant to 3 cases. Here reference was to data privacy laws, in general. More broadly, the 'Cyber Ethics' KU was referred to in 14 cases, with specific mention of the topic 'Ethical Hacking' in 7 cases. In general job advertisements also emphasised the importance of high ethical standards and trustworthiness for a cybersecurity professional. A summary of the KUs mentioned in job advertisements is shown in Fig. 8.

Component Security. There are four KUs within this KA, which had the least coverage in the job advertisements. The 'Component Design' KU was most

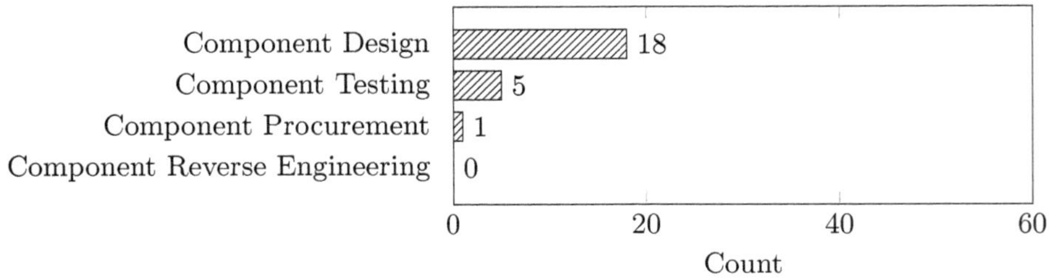

Fig. 9. Knowledge units within component security

referred to (18 cases), with the topic 'Principals of secure component design' featuring most often (9 cases). An example of this requirement is:

> *"Test, install, configure and upgrade new and existing network components to ensure optimal performance."* [J48]

While this KU features specialised topics, such as reverse engineering and supply chain issues, it also includes common software engineering tasks such as unit testing and security testing. Thus this is an important KA for the software development lifecycle. A summary of the KUs mentioned in job advertisements is shown in Fig. 9.

4.3 Summary of Findings

The content analysis highlights the CSEC2017 KAs, KUs, and topics which were most frequently found in the sample of job advertisements. A total of 1015 TKS statements were identified and mapped to KUs, an average of 127 per KA or 17 per job advertisement. The discussion provided a visual indication of how frequently each KU was encountered. However, to get a better understanding of the relative importance of KAs, Table 2 provides a ranking based on the average KU count.

Table 2. Ranking of knowledge areas

Knowledge Area	KU Count	Average (KU Count/KUs)
Organisational Security	318	35.33
Human Security	144	20.57
System Security	127	18.14
Connection Security	127	15.88
Software Security	111	15.86
Data Security	107	13.38
Societal Security	57	11.4
Component Security	24	6

There were 11 KUs that were identifed in at least half of the job advertisements: Risk Management (54); Security Governance & Policy (54); System Control (50); Digital Forensics (50); Network Defense (48); Systems Administration (44); Business Continuity, Disaster Recovery, and Incident Management (40); Awareness and Understanding (38); System Management (37); Security Program Management (31); and Usable Security and Privacy (30). It could be argued that these are core aspects of the discipline.

On the other hand, there were five KUs that were not identified at all during the analysis: System Retirement; Physical Interfaces and Connectors; Physical Media; Cryptanalysis; and Component Reverse Engineering. While it is beyond the scope of the paper to comment on possible reasons for this, these areas should be carefully examined for relevance. Within South Africa, Higher Education academic staff could use these collective findings to guide curriculum development which matches local industry needs.

5 Conclusion

This research used a content analysis of a sample of job advertisements to identify the most relevant cybersecurity KAs in the South African context. It ranked these areas according to the frequency with which they were encountered in the data, thus helping to prioritise TKS that are in high demand. It was found that organisational security, and several related KUs, were most frequently encountered. The findings also highlighted communication, the ability to work in a team, and project management as soft skills which are important in the cybersecurity domain.

Since cybersecurity is a vast, interdisciplinary domain these findings have value in guiding Higher Education institutions in the development of cybersecurity programs. It can help academic staff to make the most efficient use of their time to prepare content. An additional benefit is that graduates who successfully assimilate the identified TKS will be better prepared to meet industry requirements. This could lead to increased graduate employability and the fostering of closer collaboration between academia and industry.

The findings from this study present a snapshot of data, and to maintain relevance data collection and analysis should be repeated with regular frequency. It is acknowledged that human-coded content analysis may raise reliability concerns, despite being conducted in a systematic manner. A similar investigation using topic modeling techniques could be useful to confirm the results. It is also possible to focus more on specific roles, such as those related to privacy, by employing suitable search terms. Naturally the methodology can also be repeated in other countries and contexts.

References

1. Armstrong, K., Parmelee, M., Santifort, S., Burley, J., van Fleet, J.: Preparing tomorrow's workforce for the fourth industrial revolution. Technical report, Deloitte Global and the Global Business Coalition for Education (2018). https://www2.deloitte.com/global/en/pages/about-deloitte/articles/gx-preparing-tomorrow-workforce-for-the-fourth-industrial-revolution.html
2. Burley, D., Lewis, A., Jr.: Cybersecurity curricula 2017 and Boeing: linking curricular guidance to professional practice. Computer **52**(3), 29–37 (2019). https://doi.org/10.1109/MC.2018.2883567
3. Department of Higher Education and Training: Organising Framework for Occupations (2021). https://webapps.dhet.gov.za/OFORegister
4. Emmersen, T., Hatfield, J., Kosseff, J., Orr, S.: The USNA's interdisciplinary approach to cybersecurity education. Computer **52**(3), 48–57 (2019). https://doi.org/10.1109/MC.2018.2883605
5. Gcaza, N., von Solms, R.: A strategy for a cybersecurity culture: a South African perspective. Electron. J. Inf. Syst. Dev. Countries **80**(1), 1–17 (2017). https://doi.org/10.1002/j.1681-4835.2017.tb00590.x
6. Haney, J., Lutters, W.: Skills and characteristics of successful cybersecurity advocates. In: Workshop on Security Information Workers, Symposium on Usable Privacy and Security (2017). https://www.usenix.org/conference/soups2017/workshop-program/wsiw2017/haney
7. Hudnall, M.: Educational and workforce cybersecurity frameworks: comparing, contrasting, and mapping. Computer **52**(3), 18–28 (2019). https://doi.org/10.1109/MC.2018.2883334
8. Irons, A., Ophoff, J.: Aspects of digital forensics in South Africa. Interdisc. J. Inf. Knowl. Manag. **11**(2014), 273–283 (2016). https://doi.org/10.28945/3576
9. Joint Task Force on Cybersecurity Education: Cybersecurity Curricula 2017: Curriculum Guidelines for Post-Secondary Degree Programs in Cybersecurity. Association for Computing Machinery, New York (2018). https://doi.org/10.1145/3184594
10. Jones, K., Namin, A., Armstrong, M.: The core cyber-defense knowledge, skills, and abilities that cybersecurity students should learn in school: results from interviews with cybersecurity professionals. ACM Trans. Comput. Educ. **18**(3), 11:1–11:12 (2018). https://doi.org/10.1145/3152893
11. McGettrick, A.: Toward effective cybersecurity education. IEEE Secur. Priv. **11**(6), 66–68 (2013). https://doi.org/10.1109/MSP.2013.155
12. Neuendorf, K.: The Content Analysis Guidebook. SAGE Publications Inc., Thousand Oaks (2017). https://doi.org/10.4135/9781071802878
13. van Niekerk, B.: An analysis of cyber-incidents in South Africa. African J. Inf. Commun. **20**, 113–132 (2017). https://doi.org/10.23962/10539/23573
14. Parker, A., Brown, I.: Skills requirements for cyber security professionals: a content analysis of job descriptions in South Africa. In: Venter, H., Loock, M., Coetzee, M., Eloff, M., Eloff, J. (eds.) ISSA 2018. CCIS, vol. 973, pp. 176–192. Springer, Cham (2019). https://doi.org/10.1007/978-3-030-11407-7_13
15. Petersen, R., Santos, D., Wetzel, K., Smith, M., Witte, G.: Workforce Framework for Cybersecurity (NICE Framework). Technical report, NIST Special Publication (SP) 800–181 Rev. 1, National Institute of Standards and Technology (2020). https://doi.org/10.6028/NIST.SP.800-181r1

16. Potter, L., Vickers, G.: What skills do you need to work in cyber security? A look at the Australian market. In: Proceedings of the 2015 ACM SIGMIS Conference on Computers and People Research, pp. 67–72 (2015). https://doi.org/10.1145/2751957.2751967
17. Renaud, K., Ophoff, J.: A cyber situational awareness model to predict the implementation of cyber security controls and precautions by SMEs. Organ. Cybersecur. J. Pract. Process People **1**(1), 24–46 (2021). https://doi.org/10.1108/OCJ-03-2021-0004
18. Scrimgeour, J.-M., Ophoff, J.: Lessons learned from an organizational information security awareness campaign. In: Drevin, L., Theocharidou, M. (eds.) WISE 2019. IAICT, vol. 557, pp. 129–142. Springer, Cham (2019). https://doi.org/10.1007/978-3-030-23451-5_10
19. SFIA Foundation: Skills Framework for the Information Age (SFIA 8) (2021). https://sfia-online.org/en
20. Taylor, E., Calitz, A.P.: The Use of industry advisory boards at higher education institutions in Southern Africa. In: Tait, B., Kroeze, J., Gruner, S. (eds.) SACLA 2019. CCIS, vol. 1136, pp. 244–259. Springer, Cham (2020). https://doi.org/10.1007/978-3-030-35629-3_16

Experiences, Motivations and Plans of Humanities Students Pursuing a Major in Information Systems in South Africa

Temoso L. R. Masilo(✉) and Gwamaka Mwalemba(✉)

Department of Information Systems, Faculty of Commerce, University of Cape Town, Rondebosch, Cape Town 7700, South Africa
temoso.masilo@alumni.uct.ac.za, gt.mwalemba@uct.ac.za

Abstract. In recent years, there has been emphasis on the need for graduates and professionals with skillsets that span beyond one domain or discipline. This study explores the motivations, experiences and plans of students pursuing a multidisciplinary degree combining majors from the Humanities with Information Systems. This was accomplished through a qualitative, exploratory case study at a South African University. The findings indicate that students are motivated by a broad range of factors including their personal attributes, individuals close to them and the employability/financial prospects of a degree. One of the significant findings in terms of the experiences of students is that students sometimes feel like because their degrees are from the Faculty of Humanities, peers and potential employers in the technology industry doubt their Information Systems related skills. After completing their studies, students have a wide variety of plans such as pursuing Information Systems related careers or starting a business. Some students expressed a desire to make an impactful difference. The outcomes of this study can inform other universities that wish to implement similar degree programmes as well as students looking to pursue such programmes.

Keywords: Multidisciplinary degree · Student experiences · Student motivations · Student plans · Humanities · Information systems · Informatics · South Africa

1 Introduction

The role of Information Systems (IS) as an academic discipline, has been under discussion for the past two decades (Mwalemba 2019). There is ongoing debate regarding the field as a discipline and its research agenda (Scheuermann and Kroeze 2017). Currently, the main outlook on IS is that it is there, solely, to increase an organisation's revenue by enhancing productivity and efficiency (Mwalemba 2019). Additionally, Mwalemba (2019) mentions that evidence of IS playing a transformative role is minimal. However, recent literature reflects that researchers and other individuals in the field of IS are realizing that the focus of IS needs to become wider and should start to consider greater societal issues (Scheuermann and Kroeze 2017). One of the ways which this can occur

R. J. Barnett et al. (Eds.): SACLA 2022, CCIS 1664, pp. 20–42, 2022.
https://doi.org/10.1007/978-3-031-21076-1_2

is through multidisciplinary degree programmes that combine IS with subject matter from the Humanities. Pairing IS with subject matter from the Humanities would be ideal as the Humanities are known to grapple with issues in society and ways in which these societal issues could be addressed (Fecher et al. 2021).

Within the South African context, degree combinations which combine the Humanities/Arts and IS (a.k.a. Informatics) are relatively new, especially at the South African university where this study takes place. This exploratory study is significant as it seeks to unearth initial ideas regarding the motivations, experiences and plans of students within this domain. This information may be useful to those designing or enhancing multidisciplinary degrees (that are similar to the degrees that this study focuses on) especially in terms of the alignment between the objectives of multidisciplinary degrees and the goals of students.

The primary question of this study is **"What are the motivations, experiences and plans of students pursuing a major in the Humanities with a major in Information Systems?".**

Insights from the students pursuing these degrees, more specifically Humanities degrees with a major in Informatics (H/IS degrees), could bring awareness on their motivations and whether they plan to contribute towards addressing society's challenges and nurturing the development of their country. This study could also serve as an indicator of whether the experiences of students, align with the experiences which these degrees intend to facilitate. Insights from this study can also help researchers and other individuals in the IS education space to better position IS as an academic discipline. This is valuable as education has great potential to facilitate sustainable, systemic changes within our society (Mwalemba 2019).

2 Related Works

2.1 Tertiary Education and Its Approach to Challenges

Undergraduate ICT education and the role that education can play in the national or regional development of developing countries is a research area that has received little attention (Mwalemba 2019). This is despite the rapid rate of progressions within the field of IS that give rise to many opportunities for agile, relevant research. This creates the need for interdisciplinary work (Scheuermann and Kroeze 2017).

A holistic, multidisciplinary approach is required to overcome challenges, more specifically those faced by Information and Communications Technology for Development (ICT4D). This holistic, multidisciplinary approach would go beyond Computer Science (CS), Information Technology (IT) and IS by also encompassing Developmental Studies (Mwalemba 2019). An example of a multidisciplinary approach is Humanities-enriched IS, which is still in its pre-disciplinary phase. It can be described as the use of Humanities approaches to aspects of computing and IS (Kroeze et al. 2011).

2.2 The Humanities and IS

It is said that "the scope of the Humanities is the experience of the world, the expression of these experiences and the understanding of these expressions" (Scheuermann and

Kroeze 2017, p. 1). Scheuermann and Kroeze (2017) go on to further conclude that the IS discipline can be seen as the Humanities of the digital field because IS deals with the human experiences with computer systems and the expression of the world through digital media. They suggest that there should be a focus on the theoretical and practical applications within both fields as this can help achieve a synergy between these two disciplines.

2.3 Factors Influencing the Choice of Study and Career Choices

Factors influencing study choice are sometimes intertwined, which makes the decision-making process complex (Kazi and Akhlaq 2017). Having a genuine interest in a subject has been consistently found to be one of the most important factors which influence a student's choice of majors (Wei Zhang 2007).

Students draw a significant portion of influence in their career choice from socio-demographic factors including family and peers (Shumba and Naong 2012). Students not only draw inspiration and listen to the advice from close peers and family but also feel a sense of obligation to please or inspire the people closest to them, who in most cases are parents and siblings (Laming et al. 2019). Edwards and Quinter (2011) acknowledge the existence of a link between study choice and peer influence but argue that as students progress through tertiary institutions and interact with their peers, the advice of peers becomes less important, especially when compared to the advice provided by family, teachers and career counsellors. Much like parents, teachers are also viewed as key stakeholders in the career choices that students eventually pursue (Shumba and Naong 2012).

In the modern and rapidly changing world, students are typically more inclined to careers that eventually guide them towards good income and societal status (Sharif et al. 2019). Gyamera (2018) found that the greatest motivation for students seeking tertiary education was employment opportunities and job security. Ahmed et al. (2017) mention that within the South African context, financial factors, more specifically anticipated benefits from a career (such as the opportunity for higher earnings in the future and promotions) have a big impact on the career choices of students. In the short-term, IT students seem to desire to be software developers/programmers, however, in the long-term, this transitions into a desire to start a business or work in higher management (McKenzie et al. 2017).

2.4 Student Experiences

According to Temple et al. (2014), student experiences can be defined as the entirety of a student's interplay with their educational institution. Student experiences can be influenced by the expectations of the students, based on their university choice and field of study, and are thus largely subjective (Gyamera 2018). Some students have unrealistic expectations that admittedly were inspired by television and film, while others have little to no expectations and just plan to take it day by day (Laming et al. 2019).

In terms of academic experiences, Gyamera (2018) defined the academic experience as how students understand the state of the curriculum, especially in connection with fulfilling the individual academic expectations of the student.

When students describe their most enjoyed aspect of university, it almost always boils down to the social experience - the ability to interact, socialize and network. Further than just surface interactions and potential future networks, Gyamera (2018) also noted that peer-to-peer learning from friends and colleagues was also a big part of the student's social experience. Despite this, Laming et al. (2019) noted that not all students have a positive experience outside of academics with a student stating "School was terrible, the people were terrible. Not a good learning environment.". Thus, it is safe to conclude that the social experience of university goers is largely specific and different from student to student.

3 Methods

This exploratory study is interpretive, inductive and cross-sectional. The qualitative case study research strategy is used as it can facilitate the gathering of in-depth, multi-faceted insight into a specific matter, within its natural real-life context (Crowe et al. 2011).

3.1 Data Collection and Analysis

The data was collected until saturation was achieved, through semi-structured interviews, a video, documents and websites that are related to the H/IS degree. An interview protocol which included prompting questions was used during the semi-structured interviews. Questions relating to the background of participants were asked before questions which were in alignment with the research questions were asked. The research questions are as follows:

- What motivates students to study Information Systems alongside their Humanities majors?
- What are the experiences of Informatics students while they pursue their degrees?
- What plans, goals and aspirations do Informatics students have for after they obtain their degrees?

The interviews had a conversational approach, with additional questions being formulated based on the responses of participants.

Due to the variety of sources used, data triangulation was achieved, which aligns with the case study approach of this study. Thematic analysis based on the systematic step-by-step process outlined by Braun and Clarke (2006) was then performed on the collected data through the NVivo software.

3.2 Sample

A South African university is the focus for all data collected in this study. The sample population for this study included senior undergraduate students or recent graduates (who graduated within 1 year or less of when the study was conducted) who were registered in the Faculty of Humanities with a major in IS. An academic staff member who helps facilitate the relevant academic programmes was also interviewed to get a different perspective based on their overall experience with a variety of students and the objectives of the academic programmes. The convenience approach was used to sample the population as the researchers were a part of the Department of Information Systems at the South African university.

3.3 Case Description

University and Degree Programme Description

This study was conducted at a South African university that is highly ranked and widely considered to be a top university on the African continent. Students in the Faculty of Humanities can study either a Bachelor of Arts (BA) degree or a Bachelor of Social Sciences (BSocSci) degree that is structured or flexible. Typically, students in these degree programmes need to major in two subjects or fields. One major has to be from the Faculty of Humanities while the other can be from a different faculty. This study is focused on Humanities students who have IS (referred to as Informatics in the Faculty of Humanities) as one of their majors. Informatics is offered by the Department of Information Systems which is housed in the Faculty of Commerce.

For a student to qualify with a major in Informatics, they are required to study one 1st year level course (an introduction to IS course), four 2nd year level courses (a programming course, a systems analysis/design course, a database design course and a systems development course) and two 3rd year level courses (an IT project management/software development course and an electronic commerce course). They also must select one additional course which is either on 2nd year level or 3rd year level (an IT infrastructure course or a course about the management of business processes). All these courses are offered by the Department of Information Systems.

Participant Description

Seventeen participants from a South African University were interviewed for this study. Eight were current students who were in their 3rd academic year, eight were graduates and one participant was a professor/lecturer. Six graduates were pursuing an Honours in IS, one graduate was pursuing an Honours in Gender Studies and one graduate had already graduated with an Honours in IS and was pursuing a career in User Interface (UI)/User Experience (UX) design. The professor was interviewed because they played a critical role in the formulation of the H/IS degree at the specific South African University where this study was conducted. They also lecture in IS and advise students during registration.

The table below profiles the degree programme (excluding Participant Q who is the professor), classification and activity of the participants at the time of the study (Table 1).

Table 1. Participant profile

Participant	Participant degree programme (excl. participant Q)	Classification	Current activity
A	BSocSci in Economics & Informatics	Student	3rd Year
B	BA in Informatics & Digital Media: Media & Writing	Graduate	Honours in IS
C	BSocSci in Politics and Governance & Informatics	Student	3rd Year
D	BSocSci in Psychology & Informatics	Graduate	Honours in IS
E	BSocSci in Anthropology & Informatics	Graduate	Honours in IS
F	BA in Informatics & Spanish	Graduate	Part time work (Honours in IS Complete)
G	BSocSci in Politics and Governance & Informatics	Student	3rd Year
H	BSocSci in Informatics & Industrial Sociology	Student	3rd Year
I	BSocSci in Informatics & Industrial Sociology	Graduate	Honours in IS
J	BSocSci in Economics & Informatics	Student	3rd Year
K	BSocSci in Politics and Governance & Informatics	Student	3rd Year
L	BSocSci in Informatics & Industrial Sociology	Graduate	Honours in IS
M	BA in Informatics & Digital Media: Media & Writing	Student	3rd Year
N	BA in Informatics & Digital Media: Media & Writing	Student	3rd Year
O	BA in Film & Media Production: Digital Media & Informatics Stream	Graduate	Honours in Gender Studies
P	BSocSci in Informatics & Industrial Sociology	Graduate	Honours in IS

(continued)

Table 1. *(continued)*

Participant	Participant degree programme (excl. participant Q)	Classification	Current activity
Q	Professor in the Department of Information Systems	Professor, Researcher & Student Advisor	Helps to convene the degree, advises students and lectures

4 Results

4.1 Overview of Findings

Various themes emerged relating to the motivations, experiences and plans of Humanities students pursuing a major in IS. The themes outline the primary outcomes from the data that was collected through the semi-structured interviews and analysis of documents, websites and a video. Some themes have sub-themes. The appendix (Table 2) gives an overview of the key findings. A column which contains examples of quotations has been included.

4.2 Motivations

Students are motivated by a wide spectrum of factors to pursue a H/IS Degree. In general, students felt that the multidisciplinary aspect of the H/IS Degree allowed them to get the best of both worlds, with Participant M, stating that they felt that through this combined degree, they had found their place in university. Several participants were influenced by close family to pursue a major in IS while others were influenced by factors that relate to the tertiary institution, such as academic staff. Participants considered their personal attributes and their desires for their own individual futures, when deciding to study a major in IS.

Personal Attributes

The attributes and abilities of a student played a significant role in their choice to pursue a Humanities degree with a major in IS. Students considered whether the chosen degree programme would provide them with the opportunity to express their innate traits. Examples of traits they felt they could express in the IS major were analytical prowess, leadership and problem-solving. For the Humanities major, students felt they could be empathetic and could exercise their critical thinking, listening and people skills. Creativity was a prominent trait amongst participants with most saying that they get to express it on the Humanities side while others felt that IS is where their creativity could be expressed. Several students felt that a multidisciplinary degree such as the H/IS degree met their needs best and made them feel fulfilled.

The Influence of Family

Students constantly referenced family members as the reason why they enrolled in one of their majors, especially IS. Participant Q, a student advisor, mentioned that they observed that one of the reasons why students had an interest in pursuing a major in Informatics was due to the pressure parents placed on them. A key observation is that these individuals who recommended IS to participants, had experience in IS or were professionals within the IS or broader technology field. These individuals held positions such as a Business Analyst, Software Developer, Systems Architect, etc.

Tertiary Institution Related Motivations

Students pursued a H/IS degree due to advice from academic staff, a lack of interest in other degrees, interest in the subject matter of the H/IS degree or due to not meeting the entry requirements for their first option.

Advice from Academic Staff

Students usually are certain about one major but often need guidance regarding their second major. In this instance they sometimes turn to student advisors or other knowledgeable academic staff. In other instances, students get this exposure during orientation week when brief sessions are held to introduce them to different majors.

Entry Requirement Barriers or a Lack of Interest in Other Faculties

The flexibility of the Faculty of Humanities is valuable as it gives students the opportunity to pursue studies and careers in other fields beyond the Humanities. This is highly beneficial for students who did not meet the entry requirements of other faculties or were not interested in enrolling into other faculties.

The lack of interest in pursuing IS through other faculties, more specifically the Faculty of Science and the Faculty of Commerce is something that the Department of Information Systems and Participant Q took note of when the Informatics major was not available in the Faculty of Humanities. The following words by Participant Q who is a professor that played a key role in the process of making Informatics available as a major in the Faculty of Humanities show this:

> *"so some of them (students) are just passionate about technology and [for] some of them it's something they've always wanted to do. They're not interested in science and they're not interested in business. ...[so] they end up in Humanities, but they want to do technology." [Participant Q]*

The IS department accommodated this by offering Informatics as a major in the Faculty of Humanities.

Future-Related Motivations

There are three kinds of motivations that are related to the future of students. They are the career prospects of the degree/major, the perceived demand for the skills that a major imparts on a student and whether the major can enhance the societal awareness of a student.

Career Prospects
Several students cited employability and financial prospects as a significant factor that led to their decision to pursue IS. Students felt that a major in IS put them in a better position in terms of job security as they were not confident about the opportunities in the Humanities field. Participant M, who has dreams of pursuing a career in IS that will enable them to apply the knowledge and skills attained from both their majors, is an example of such a student as they said:

> *"...I am a little bit nervous about graduating with a Humanities degree, and not finding job security in South Africa. I took Information Systems because I was interested in it, but also, because it was a little bit of a safety blanket for me, ...to know that I had something that would let me work in any country, anywhere in the world, that I was going to be very sort of employable with the skills that I had" [Participant M]*

This sentiment correlated with what an IS professor said in a video on the university's School of IT (SIT) website, which was that Humanities students who have a major in Informatics, have a high chance of getting a job.

However, the above sentiments expressed about Informatics being pursued as a major because a degree specialising in Humanities alone is not promising (in terms of career prospects) is in direct contradiction with what the Faculty of Humanities website outlines as one of the reasons why a student should pursue their studies in their faculty which is that *"Humanities graduates are sought after in the workplace"*.

Skills Demand
Certain participants stated that there is a high demand for IS skills and that they were happy and felt privileged to be able to pursue this degree. This shows that offering IS to students in other faculties is valuable as they get the opportunity to gain skills in other fields. The idea that skills in technology (including IS) are highly sought after is in alignment with what an IS professor stated in a video on the university's SIT website which was that *"all careers need technology"*.

Societal Awareness
It emerged that becoming acquainted with societal matters is a motivating factor for students. A degree in the Faculty of Humanities has the potential to enhance the societal awareness of students. This can be said because in an overview given for undergraduate studies, on the Faculty of Humanities website, one of the goals for Humanities courses is to foster *"social sensitivity"* and for Humanities degrees to *"encourage students to seek out new ways of viewing today's complex world and society"*.

Participant O (who indicated that their pronouns are they/them/their) expressed that they are concerned that people who study IS alone and are not well versed in social issues contribute to the creation of systems that are not inclusive. They said:

"there wasn't a moment to sit and pause about, the fact that when people create systems, [they're] genuinely impacting lives. [They're] making limiting assumptions about what the world is and how it works and if the system doesn't allow, the system doesn't allow. But the system is built by people. But which kinds of people? People who are not well versed in social science issues, and that's why we have these problems." [Participant O]

Technology students that are grounded in societal matters were said to possibly have an edge over other students and could possibly make a positive impact. In a video on the university's SIT website, an Associate Professor from the Centre of Film and Media studies in the Faculty of Humanities made a profound statement that highlights the importance of societal awareness:

"there is a sense that technology is responsible for very many exciting opportunities, which people who understand society and understand people [and] understand communication; they're the most likely to be able to exploit those opportunities. The creators of new technology are also the creators of new societies." [Associate Professor, Centre of Film and Media studies]

In the same video a Chief Executive Officer (CEO) of an Animation and Gaming company said that *"it's about a well-rounded understanding about people and humanity and technology and how it influences them".*

It can therefore be said that individuals who have a multidisciplinary background such as an academic degree in both the Humanities and IS can be considered as being well-rounded.

4.3 Experiences

The experiences of students are multi-faceted. Some experiences are unique to an individual, while others relate to the institution where a student is pursuing their studies or to the academic content and how it is delivered. The final facet of a student's experience relates to their interactions with peers or the technology industry and the perceptions that students believe exist.

The Individual Experience

When students expressed their experiences, some mentioned that it was challenging, while others focused on how their experience was engaging and enjoyable as they found their studies interesting. It was interesting to hear Participant D express that they would switch to different sides of themselves as they navigated their studies in their two majors. Participant G expressed that it was an eye-opening experience as they had limited exposure and engagement with societal issues, due to their personal background and the environment in which they grew up in.

Academic Experiences

The academic experiences that participants shared touched on the academic content, the requirements of their academic courses and on the learning contexts.

Campus vs Online Learning

After the COVID-19 pandemic hit in 2020, the university moved operations to online. Teaching and learning was still conducted online during the data collection phase of this study. Since participants were senior students, they had the opportunity to experience both contexts. A number of them expressed that online learning impacted their experience negatively because of the limited social interactions. Participant N expressed that they felt isolated and outlined the following:

> *"that interaction with other people, other classmates and stuff, makes a huge difference ... I feel like I haven't had a lot of interaction with people in my field or in my majors where I can bounce ideas off" [Participant N]*

Subject Matter & Academic Demands

The issues that came up were mostly related to the Humanities subject matter as it was said to be repetitive and content heavy. Some students felt that the H/IS degree was high pressure due to their experiences with deadlines being close to one another. It is noteworthy that when participants felt under pressure, they prioritised their IS major.

Institutional Experiences

The key institutional experiences have been divided into two categories, namely 'Administration' and 'Gaps'. Administration is centred around the experiences students had, that were due to the administration of the H/IS degree, while Gaps highlights some areas where students felt there could be an improvement.

Administration

Timetable clashes, incomplete exam timetables and the previous exclusion of the IS major in the Faculty of Humanities handbook were administration issues that came up. The previous exclusion of the Informatics major in the Faculty of Humanities handbook was an issue as a number of students consider taking Informatics as a major, after encountering it in the Humanities handbook.

Gaps

One of the participants mentioned that more support is required for projects that involve external sponsors. A gap that was pointed out a number of times is the lack of exposure to careers that accommodate the multidisciplinary aspect of a H/IS degree. One of the participants stated the following:

> *"there was never any acknowledgement from anyone or the curriculum, other than myself of how the two [majors] can actually complement each other." [Participant D]*

Relations with People and Industry

As participants interact with their peers and with the broader technology industry, participants formed certain perceptions based on their experiences. These have been outlined in the following subthemes:

Observations Regarding Students from Different Faculties

Participants mentioned that they noticed differences between other students who they interacted with, who were coming from different faculties. The following words put this into focus nicely: *"you're interacting with people with completely different mindsets. So I guess that can be interesting at times." [Participant B]*

Outlook on Humanities Students

A concerning theme that emerged amongst students was the way in which their peers viewed them or the perception that they believe the technology industry has of them. Participants expressed how they were looked down upon, undermined and sometimes doubted in terms of their IS capabilities. Some also mentioned that they would experience imposter syndrome in the Department of Information Systems. In IS classes, Participant O felt they were taken less seriously and even undermined by students from other faculties. Participant O described how they felt like they were viewed as not being *"intellectually rigorous"* like other students or as not being able to *"keep up with them"*.

However, Participant F's sentiments contrasts the above as they said that their experience with peers wasn't negative but that it was more of intrigue because the peers were unfamiliar with the H/IS degree.

In terms of the technology industry, more specifically employers in the IS space, participants expressed concerns about being excluded from IS job opportunities or being viewed as inadequate since they pursued their major in IS through the Faculty of Humanities. The following words by Participant N illustrate this:

> *"I don't feel like I'm qualified enough to apply for a job as an Information Systems specialist as yet because I don't have that background [from] the Commerce faculty." [Participant N]*

This motivated some students to pursue an Honours degree in IS as it is offered by the Faculty of Commerce and would result in the student having a Bachelor of Commerce (Honours) conferred upon them when they complete their Honours studies. Participant I cited this as a motivating factor for pursuing an Honours in IS. They said:

> *"I knew that for me to be taken seriously, I have to have an Honours degree...it has to be BCom (Bachelor of Commerce) something, you know. It doesn't have to be [a] Bachelor [of] Social Science because they just don't take you seriously when you have a social sciences degree." [Participant I]*

4.4 Plans

The plans that participants have for after they have obtained their degrees are very diverse and multi-layered. Several participants desired to further their studies in IS. A similar phenomenon emerged when students expressed the kinds of formal employment or businesses they would like to pursue. Some participants highlighted how they desired to be a part of making a positive change in our world, while others were uncertain regarding their future.

Making a Difference

As participants shared their plans, underlying reasons emerged. These reasons are the driving force behind the plans a participant has for the future. Participants can use the underlying reason as a criterion to help decide where they invest their time and effort in the future. A reason that stood out was the desire to make a difference. The desire to be an agent of change in a certain aspect.

Participant O, who said they would like to pursue a career in education as a teacher, also expressed that they would like to make a change, specifically in terms of the social dynamics in society. They said:

> *"I'm quite concerned about the social dynamics of our society...You spend most of your time at school...[therefore] the politics and values that the school espouses, will directly correlate to the politics and value system that the students will have. So I want to create a school that has, like, this radical idea of just, I don't know, just caring about [each other and] people." [Participant O]*

Further Study

Pursuing further studies is one of the options that students considered for after they obtained their degrees. A desire that was expressed several times by third year students was to study their Honours in IS. This aligns with what an Associate Professor (from the Centre of Film and Media studies in the Faculty of Humanities) said in a video on the university's SIT website which is that an Honours in IS is *"highly sought after"*.

Third year students who want to pursue Honours, want to pursue it for reasons such as not feeling ready to work, having no plans for the year after completing their current studies or to gain a better understanding of their chosen major. Others want to explore the option of short courses in an effort to enhance their employability and competitiveness in the job market.

Business

Some students expressed an interest in starting their own ventures. This could be in the short term or in the long term. These businesses could possibly be within the IS domain. The desire to start a business, that some students have, correlates with what Participant Q, a Professor in the IS department, mentioned which is that *"more and more people do need to create their own jobs...not necessarily work for a company."*

Formal Employment
Job roles within the IS domain were dominant. Participants had an interest in different employment opportunities such as Business Analyst, Software Developer, UI/UX Designer, Consultant, Teacher, Political Analyst, Project Manager, Senior Level Management Positions (e.g. CEOs), etc.

Uncertainty
Other participants mentioned that they were still uncertain about their future and what they intend to do. This was an interesting observation as the students interviewed are penultimate students. The uncertainty was due to a variety of reasons. One of the reasons was stated by Participant J as follows: *"I don't think I've thought that far"*. Participant K mentioned that they would like to take more time to explore their options and try to identify what it is they would like to do. Despite the uncertainty, Participant A did make it known that they would like to do something that incorporates both their majors, namely Economics and IS.

5 Discussion

5.1 Motivations

The first goal of this study was to explore the motivations of Informatics students. Themes relating to student motivations are the personal attributes of a student, the influence of their family, tertiary institution related motivations and future-related motivations. Participants in this study mentioned that they either looked into IS or pursued it as a major due to the advice of family or academic staff. It is interesting to note that students did not cite their peers as an influence. This aligns well with what Edwards and Quinter (2011) argued which was that, as students progress through tertiary institutions, the advice of peers becomes less significant in comparison to the advice provided by family and educational staff such as career counsellors. A potential reason for this is that students trust their family and academic staff. The trust that they have in their family can be because students know that their loved ones have their best interests at heart. The trust in academic staff could be because of the experience and superior knowledge that they are perceived to have. Interestingly, the family members that influenced students in this study were in a similar position to staff as they were found to be professionals within the technology arena. Another possible reason for students heeding the advice of family could be what Laming et al. (2019) mentioned, which is that students tend to feel a sense of obligation to please or inspire the people closest to them.

Another theme that stood out among participants was the future-related motivations. Edwards and Quinter (2011) and Gyamera (2018) pointed out that the greatest motivation for students seeking tertiary education was employment opportunities and job security. As highlighted in the 'Career Prospects' sub-theme, sentiments related to employment opportunities and job security were consistently expressed amongst participants, with students taking Informatics as a major due to the anticipated job opportunities in the IS field. Students were not confident about the employment prospects of their Humanities major despite the Faculty of Humanities website claiming that their graduates are highly sought after locally and abroad. A possible reason for this misalignment is that the Faculty of Humanities has not sufficiently made students aware of the opportunities available to them. Another possible reason is that there are a limited number of opportunities available, even though Humanities graduates from the South African university are highly sought after for the opportunities that are available. The study found that there is a perception that skills in the field of technology, specifically IS, are highly in demand, especially in South Africa.

Lastly, it was very interesting to note that certain participants felt that technology professionals need to be well-versed with societal matters and that courses in the Humanities can awaken societal awareness within students. Instilling social sensitivity in students is one of the goals of the Faculty of Humanities. Social awareness amongst students is important as Mwalemba (2019) mentioned that a holistic, multidisciplinary approach, that includes developmental studies, is required in order to address the challenges that are faced by ICT4D and developing countries. A CEO mentioned that a well-rounded understanding of humanity and technology is important for the future world of work, especially when considering that the creators of technology could possibly be considered as the creators of societies, according to an Associate Professor from the South African university. This study found indications that students have the desire to make a difference by contributing towards positive change in business and society and by considering the people affected by technology.

5.2 Experiences

The second goal of this study was to get a general overview of the experiences of students. Themes around student experiences as it relates to the individual, academics, the tertiary institution and their relations with peers and the technology industry were developed from participant responses gathered in the study. When looking at the individual experience of students, it was repeatedly expressed by participants that it was enjoyable, interesting and engaging to study their Humanities major alongside Informatics. In this case, interest in the subject seems to have emerged after the student had already decided to study the selected subjects and had already had some experience with the subject matter. A possible explanation for this is that students were not familiar with Informatics prior to taking it as a major, which is why they only had an interest in trying it out, but not necessarily an interest in the subject matter. This is slightly different from what Wei Zhang (2007) put forward which was that students have an interest in the subject, which influences their choice regarding subjects/majors (i.e. the interest is more of a motivation than an experience). Perhaps one could conclude that interest in subject matter is a motivation that encourages students to continue pursuing a major.

Within the theme of 'Academic Experiences' and the subtheme of 'Campus vs Online Learning', it emerged that students are not happy about online learning as it deprives them of the social interactions that they would have had on campus. A possible reason for this could be because, according to Gyamera (2018), the social experience is what students enjoy most about university. It also came to light that due to the limited interactions amongst students, students are missing out on the opportunity to share and hear career ideas from one another. This is something that Gyamera (2018) highlighted when they stated that peer-to-peer learning forms a big part of a student's social experience.

Within the theme 'Institutional experiences' it came up that H/IS degree students have a lack of exposure to careers that integrate the two fields that a student specialises in. This could be due to a variety of reasons. One of these could be that each department that offers a major, only focuses on giving exposure to careers directly related to the major which they teach. Another possibility is that because of the many possible combinations for majors within the Faculty of Humanities, it might not be easy to ensure that there is direct exposure to careers that match up with each of the different possible combinations of majors. It is left to students to identify connections and uncover possible careers based on their majors.

Lastly, within the theme of 'Relations with people and industry', a concerning subtheme emerged which is about the outlook which peers and industry have on Informatics students. This study found that some Informatics students feel like their IS capabilities are doubted merely because they are from the Faculty of Humanities. A similar sentiment came up in terms of industry, specifically the IS workplace, as students felt like their Informatics major is not enough to secure a job within the field of technology. Due to the looming fear experienced by students, which is that a BA or BSocSci can disadvantage them when applying for jobs, it became important to some students to pursue an Honours in IS as it is a BCom degree. A possible reason for this outlook that students pointed towards, is the lack of awareness regarding the availability of Informatics as a major within the Faculty of Humanities. A number of factors could have contributed to this, such as the fact that it is only within the last 5 years (2017–2021) that the Informatics major started to appear in the Humanities handbook and it is only from last year (2020) that more than 10 students completed an H/IS degree within the same year. Another possible contributing factor to this outlook on Informatics students is the connotations that the Faculty of Humanities has, such as being non-technical and having lower academic requirements for entry into a Humanities degree.

5.3 Plans

The third and final goal of this study was to explore the plans, goals and aspirations that Informatics students have for after they have obtained their degrees. The themes which emerged that relate to the plans of Informatics students are about making a difference, studying further, starting a business, securing formal employment and uncertainty as some students were still figuring out the next step for their lives. The uncertainty that some students experience could be due to the overwhelming number of options available to them.

The desire to make a difference, that some students had, may be due to their social awareness that has been heightened by their Humanities studies as the goal of Humanities courses, at the South African university, is to foster *"social sensitivity"* and for Humanities degrees to *"encourage students to seek out new ways of viewing today's complex world and society"*. This aligns with what Fecher et al. (2021) stated which is that the Humanities are known to grapple with issues in society and ways in which these societal issues could be addressed.

Based on this study, a lot of students' plans are related to the Informatics major, largely because students feel that there are more opportunities in the technology arena. The availability of the Informatics major in the Faculty of Humanities is valuable as if students do not have the opportunity to pursue an Informatics major, they would not be able to directly pursue technology opportunities with ease. Students are interested in a diverse set of roles that are in business analysis, consulting, UX/UI design, software development, etc. It is however noteworthy that the job roles that Informatics students desire are not concentrated on software development/programming roles like in McKenzie et al.'s (2017) study. This could be due to the multidisciplinary nature of the H/IS degree which is not solely focused on IT like the participants in McKenzie et al.'s (2017) study. However, the long-term aspirations that McKenzie et al. (2017) encountered, align with some of the student plans which came up in this study, such as the desire to work in higher management or to start a business.

6 Conclusion

This study focused on exploring and gathering insights regarding the motivations, experiences and plans of Humanities students who have a major in IS. Students feel that their personal attributes are suited for a H/IS degree. Some students took Informatics as a major due to the advice of family or academic staff. A key motivating factor for students to study IS is the associated career prospects and the perception that IS skills are in demand. Other motivating factors that the study revealed are tertiary institution related motivations. Societal awareness is an additional motivation that is related to the future of a student as it was identified that technology professionals who are well-versed in societal matters are needed for the future world of work and for overcoming the challenges currently faced in the world.

The experiences of students are multi-faceted. Students have individual experiences but also have experiences in terms of their academics, their institution and their interactions with peers and industry. As individuals, some students completely enjoy studying a multidisciplinary degree such as the H/IS degree, while others occasionally find it challenging. Students do not really like learning online as they value the social experience which comes with learning on campus. They are sometimes irritated by administration challenges which they encounter and believe that there are areas where the South African institution, in this study, needs to improve. Students sometimes feel like their H/IS degree is not enough to compete for employment opportunities within the technology industry and feel like their peers sometimes doubt their technical abilities.

In terms of the plans that Informatics students have for the future, some are uncertain of the path which they shall follow while others are driven to make a positive difference in the world. Frequently, students desire to study to Honours level, while a few consider Masters studies. Students consider a wide variety of formal employment opportunities that are primarily in the technology field. Examples of possible careers include UI/UX design, business analysis, software development, consulting, project management, education etc. Starting a new business, likely in the IS domain, is an aspiration that some have.

The insights gathered in this study can aid the enhancement of Humanities-IS curricula by helping those who administer or plan to administer multidisciplinary degrees (similar to the H/IS degree). These individuals could align the overall objectives of these degrees, with what appeals to students, student goals/plans and the key factors (e.g. career prospects, societal awareness) that students take into consideration when deciding to pursue a degree programme similar to the H/IS degree. Based on some of the findings in this study, it is recommended that institutions consider ensuring that their multidisciplinary degrees are well marketed to students and industry. This can help with preventing or eradicating a negative outlook in terms of the capabilities of students and the skills acquired during their studies. Additionally, it could be of value to students enrolled in multidisciplinary degree programmes if they get exposure to career options that accommodate all the disciplines that they major in. The distribution of resources or facilitation of guest lectures are some of the ways that this could be approached. This could help students see the value of their multidisciplinary degree. It is suggested that an institution tries to minimise occurrences of administration issues such as timetable clashes. Delivering the subject matter in an engaging manner helps students to find the work interesting and enjoyable.

On a deeper level, this study gives researchers and other individuals in IS education the opportunity to reflect and become aware of whether the experiences of students align with what the Humanities-IS education curricula intend to facilitate. IS leaders can also evaluate whether the plans of students align with the intended outcome and impact of degree programmes similar to the H/IS degree. Furthermore, the insights gathered regarding the experiences of students provide a practical glimpse of the dynamics that exist between the Humanities and IS. This can aid attempts to understand the nature of the current relationship that exists between the two fields of study.

Appendix

(See Table 2).

Table 2. Overview of findings

Broad category	Theme	Sub-theme	Quotations
Motivations	Personal attributes	–	*"I really love a challenge...IS is very challenging...And at the same time, I'm like a huge empath, I love people, I love thinking of ways to help people. I think I fulfilled both of those needs that I have" [Participant D]* *"...sociology was the creative side, the understanding people, the critical thinking and analysis, things like that. Then the IS was technical, design, coding and things like that." [Participant P]* *"...we did that basic HTML and the web designing and for me, it was something about taking a line of words, and it creates something. That creative element just really hooked me." [Participant E]*
	The influence of family	–	*"My parents are software developers. So I did do a little bit of programming here and there. And I guess you could say, that is a bit of why I took that route, they did influence me a bit..." [Participant B]* *"So we looked through the handbook and we saw Information Systems and my dad's in IT so my parents were like, maybe you should try that." [Participant E]*
	Tertiary Institution related motivations	Advice from academic staff	*"...she (course convener) said, 'Okay, you can actually do Information Systems.' And yeah, that's how I got on to doing Information Systems." [Participant I]* *"So one of the curriculum advisors, or like mentors...suggested that I do a language... I think taking Spanish was the best, best decision I had ever made" [Participant F]*
		Entry requirement barriers or a Lack of interest in other faculties	*"I applied in Commerce and Humanities and they didn't accept me in Commerce. I got accepted in the Humanities faculty." [Participant I]* *"I realized that I didn't really like any of the Commerce courses that I was doing." [Participant C]* *"So I knew I want to do Information Systems. But I didn't want to do it through the [Commerce] faculty" [Participant P]*

(*continued*)

Table 2. (*continued*)

Broad category	Theme	Sub-theme	Quotations
	Future-related motivations	Career prospects	*"you [are] basically guaranteed work after your degree, it (Information Systems) is very in demand and there's money" [Participant H]* *"I find it slightly odd for us as Humanities students to find job opportunities in the market...I need to look for a job for myself, and that job can only possibly come from the Commerce related major." [Participant G]*
		Skills demand	*"IT is one of the most high demand career professions in South Africa at the moment. So having done IT ...you become really privileged to have done something that's in high demand." [Participant I]* *"it's quite a sought-after skill...it's looked for when it comes to jobs and careers and stuff. I'm quite happy that I've got that to my name" [Participant N]*
		Societal awareness	*"I think any professional needs to be well versed in the current times that we're living in and the social issues that we face. And sociology did a lot of that" [Participant I]* *"I tend to think they'll be very special, very exceptional students, because of their way of thinking. These are students who have a very solid grounding in human affairs, understanding the social issues, but they now also have some technical knowledge." [IS Senior Lecturer in a video]*
Experiences	The individual experience	–	*"it was just fun...I started enjoying the course like I told you. I like theory...so I started enjoying it a lot more than just thinking about money" [Participant H]* *"it was difficult and challenging, yes, but I could actually see that I was understanding the work, I was engaging with the work and I enjoyed it" [Participant P]* *"I was always in like two minds...like, switch between thinking like this, and thinking like that, like, nothing kind of came together. I kind of had to find how I felt they came together." [Participant D]*

(*continued*)

Table 2. (*continued*)

Broad category	Theme	Sub-theme	Quotations
	Academic experiences	Campus vs Online learning	*"I didn't appreciate the online, I still don't appreciate the online learning...I prefer to be back on campus interacting with people and stuff like that." [Participant G]* *"it was definitely unfortunate that we couldn't be on campus. So that was a bummer." [Participant B]*
		Subject matter & Academic demands	*"there were times where I felt like we were being pressured. Maybe not intentionally but some of the courses put the deadlines so close to each other" [Participant E]* *"there's always that one major that you need to put more effort into, and for infos (Information Systems), that would definitely be my priority." [Participant F]*
	Institutional experiences	Administration	*"So the times would often clash...but I was doing a structured degree program that should work out from a timetable point of view. That's not my fault." [Participant O]* *"in second year, my exams didn't even come up on my exam timetable, because I was registered for a completely different combination of courses...So that was kind of annoying" [Participant F]* *"when I saw Informatics on the Humanities guideline back in like, before first year, I said okay, yeah, that's cool." [Participant A]*
		Gaps	*"I think it would be great if more, different kinds of fields could be introduced into the undergraduate degree because they kind of focused a lot on software development and not everyone wants to do that." [Participant P]* *"I think they need to offer students a little bit more support when it comes to dealing with external projects." [Participant K]*
	Relations with people and industry	Observations regarding students from different faculties	*"you get a very different type of person that you will find in the Commerce faculty compared to what you would find in the Humanities faculty" [Participant F]* *"Everyone (Humanities students) kind of butted heads because everyone wanted their work to be shown...They want their input to show through and they were kind of more against making something cohesive" [Participant D]*

(*continued*)

Table 2. (*continued*)

Broad category	Theme	Sub-theme	Quotations
		Outlook on Humanities students	*"Sometimes you feel maybe a bit of imposter syndrome being in the Information Systems department when you have a Humanities background." [Participant B]* *"I thought I'd be more employable if I was a BCom student as opposed to being in Humanities or any other faculty" [Participant C]*
Plans	Making a difference	–	*"my idea of making change and making good change…in the business world. I think that's something I really want to do." [Participant L]* *"that would be the dream, if I could do something that was sort of also considering the people that were using the technology and not just the technology." [Participant M]*
	Further study	–	*"I mean, I would love to do masters, if I could" [Participant G]* *"I was actually looking at getting some…short course certifications as well, just to add onto the IS side." [Participant K]*
	Business	–	*"I do want to one day start a business where I can start helping SMEs (Small and Medium-sized Enterprises) …with software solutions and build my own software business." [Participant C]*
	Formal employment	–	*"I'm looking into Junior Project Manager positions, because I tend to lean more to the people side of technology." [Participant J]* *"I want to be a Business Analyst." [Participant H]*
	Uncertainty	–	*"I don't really know where I want my career to be…it can be a little bit overwhelming to think about the future, which is why I want to postpone my future by doing an Honours." [Participant N]* *"…in terms of jobs, I'm pretty much uncertain, because I would like to do something that, obviously, I can use both of my majors for." [Participant A]*

References

Ahmed, K.A., Sharif, N., Ahmad, N.: Factors influencing students' career choices: empirical evidence from business students. J. Southeast Asian Res. **2017**, 1–15 (2017)

Braun, V., Clarke, V.: Using thematic analysis in psychology. Qual. Res. Psychol. **3**(2), 77–101 (2006)

Crowe, S., Cresswell, K., Robertson, A., Huby, G., Avery, A., Sheikh, A.: The case study approach. BMC Med. Res. Methodol. **11**(1), 100 (2011). https://doi.org/10.1186/1471-2288-11-100

Edwards, K., Quinter, M.: Factors influencing students career choices among secondary school students in Kisumu municipality, Kenya. J. Emerg. Trends Educ. Res. Policy Stud. **2**(2), 81–87 (2011)

Fecher, B., Kuper, F., Sokolovska, N., Fenton, A., Hornbostel, S., Wagner, G.G.: Understanding the societal impact of the social sciences and humanities: remarks on roles, challenges, and expectations. Front. Res. Metrics Anal. **6**, 1–14 (2021)

Gyamera, G.O.: I just want to be somebody: exploring students' motivations and experiences in universities. South Afr. J. High. Educ. **32**(3), 154–171 (2018)

Kazi, A.S., Akhlaq, A.: Factors affecting students' career choice. J. Res. Reflect. Educ. (JRRE) **11**(2), 187–196 (2017)

Kroeze, J.H., et al.: ECIS 2010 panel report: humanities-enriched information systems. Commun. Assoc. Inf. Syst. **28**(1), 24 (2011)

Laming, M.M., Morris, A., Martin-Lynch, P.: Mature-Age Male Students in Higher Education: Experiences, Motivations and Aspirations. Springer, Cham (2019). https://doi.org/10.1007/978-3-030-24478-1

McKenzie, S., Coldwell-Neilson, J., Palmer, S.: Informing the career development of IT students by understanding their career aspirations and skill development action plans. Aust. J. Career Dev. **26**(1), 14–23 (2017)

Mwalemba, G.: Information systems education for development: a typology of ICT4D pedagogies. In: Nielsen, P., Kimaro, H.C. (eds.) ICT4D 2019. IAICT, vol. 552, pp. 337–348. Springer, Cham (2019). https://doi.org/10.1007/978-3-030-19115-3_28

Scheuermann, L., Kroeze, J.H.H.: Digital humanities and information systems: innovating two research traditions. Presented at the Twenty-Third Americas Conference on Information Systems. Association for Information Systems, Boston (2017)

Sharif, N., Ahmad, N., Sarwar, S.: Factors influencing career choices. IBT J. Bus. Stud. **15**(1), 33–46 (2019)

Shumba, A., Naong, M.: Factors influencing students' career choice and aspirations in South Africa. J. Soc. Sci. **33**(2), 169–178 (2012)

Temple, P., Callender, C., Grove, L., Kersh, N.: Managing the student experience in a shifting higher education landscape. High. Educ. Acad. **1**(1), 1–25 (2014)

Zhang, W.: Why IS: understanding undergraduate students' intentions to choose an information systems major. J. Inf. Syst. Educ. **18**(4), 1–14 (2007)

Assessment

Towards an Automated Assistant for Generating Mathematics Problems

Zola Mahlaza(✉)

Department of Informatics, University of Pretoria, Pretoria, South Africa
z.mahlaza@up.ac.za

Abstract. High school learners in low-income countries are negatively impacted by the SARS Covid-19 pandemic. Consequently, university lecturers of mathematics will have to offer remedial classes to bridge the gap. Since they cannot create practice problems at scale for each student's needs, there is a need for computational tools to do so. There are no existing and published formalisations of mathematical problems that abide by the South African curriculum to allow the automatic generation of problems. We aim to address this gap by formalising exam problems written by grade 12 South African learners in the period 2008–2020. We evaluate the problem types by demonstrating 65% coverage of the 74 matric rewrite problems from the years 2011–2018. The presented problem formalisations allow the generation of maths problems to be used for student-led remedial practice.

Keywords: Mathematics education · Mathematical formalisation · Controlled natural language · Natural language generation · Digital educational tools

1 Introduction

Secondary education was negatively impacted in low-income countries after governments announced lockdowns in response to the Covid-19 pandemic. When the South African government announced relaxations to its first lockdown, the department of Basic Education considered three models for re-opening schools to avoid losing the entire year:

1. "two separate sets of teachers and pupils use the same school building [but] one set [uses] in the morning [and another set] in the afternoon" [8]
2. "groups/grades of learners alternate classes/lessons on different days of the week" [8]
3. "bi-weekly rotational attendance" [8]

All these considered models required that learners spend less time at school and may require additional effort from high school teachers. This is likely to lead to cohorts of first-year university learners who do not have the proper mathematics

R. J. Barnett et al. (Eds.): SACLA 2022, CCIS 1664, pp. 45–57, 2022.
https://doi.org/10.1007/978-3-031-21076-1_3

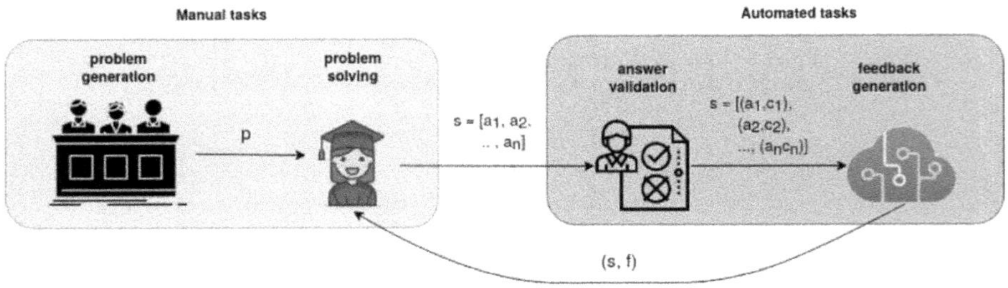

Fig. 1. Existing framework for validating and feedback provision. Abbreviations and symbols used: p = problem, a_i = answer step i, c_i = correctness of answer step i, and f = feedback.

foundation. Consequently, university lecturers will have to offer remedial classes. A more attractive solution is the development and introduction of computer-based education technologies to assist university lecturers.

Existing technology can already be used by university lectures to assist learners in accordance with the framework depicted in Fig. 1. In this framework, an educator(s) manually creates a maths problem (**p**) and when a student is given the problem, they produce a solution (**s**) that has multiple steps ($\{\mathbf{a_1}, ..., \mathbf{a_n}\}$). The validity of each step can be automatically checked by an answer validation service and the validated answer ($\{(\mathbf{a_1}, \mathbf{c_1}), ..., (\mathbf{a_n}, \mathbf{c_n})\}$), where $\mathbf{c_1^n}$ denote the correctness of each step, is then used by the feedback generator to produce feedback (**f**). This feedback is often limited to specifying that the answer is correct/incorrect. The biggest challenge with this framework is that it requires significant effort from the educator. We take the position that in order for these remedial classes to be effective, the problems must take into account each student's proficiency and these must be produced in large volumes in order to cater for large numbers of learners (e.g., Mathematics I at the University of Cape Town had more than 458 learners in 2011 [4]). As such, we propose to modify the architecture presented in Fig. 1 and introduce a module for automatically generating mathematics problems that abide by the South African curriculum. Such an approach would reduce effort from the educator and also allow learners to have greater control over the types of problems that they need additional practice on. For this paper, we focus only on the task of problem generation and leave out answer validation and feedback generation for future work.

To the best of our knowledge, the only information system that has the capability to generate mathematics problems geared to the South African curriculum is a proprietary product created by Siyavula[1]. Currently, it is not possible to build a system that is open to all learners because there are no published models of South African high school maths problems and the existing government-issued curriculum statements[2] are designed for humans and are not detailed so as to allow the automatic generation of problems. There is also no

[1] https://www.siyavula.com/.
[2] https://wcedeportal.co.za/eresource/106331.

controlled natural language for authoring such problems and no algorithms that can automatically generate problems. In this paper, we propose to address this gap by developing novel archetypes of high mathematics problems which we use together with a novel controlled natural language (CNL) to create the Computer Assistant for High School Mathematics (COMPAH). We have chosen to limit the scope of COMPAH to the first topic that grade 12 learners find challenging, namely *sequences and series*, after analysing the department of basic education's diagnostic reports from 2012–2020. To develop the assistant and its underlying resources, we began by creating a corpus of sequences and series problems from grade 12 exams papers from 2008–2020, analysing the corpus and formalising the problems, extracting the archetypes for the various problem types, creating templates for supported archetypes, and creating a tool that uses those resources to generate problems. We evaluated the resources by demonstrating their coverage over a held-out portion of the created corpus and showed that the identified problem types support 65% of the test set's problems. If we do limit each problem type to a specific sequence and series type, where appropriate, then coverage is 73%.

The rest of the paper is structured such that Sect. 2 examines existing work on the generation of mathematics problems, Sect. 3 introduces the problem and controlled natural language, Sect. 4 evaluates and discusses the coverage of the extracted problem types, and Sect. 6 concludes.

2 Related Work

The only information system that can generate mathematical problems for the South African curriculum is proprietary; hence, we can not determine the precise nature of how it is able to achieve this task. The company that develops the system only states that it relies on the Python programming language and custom exercise templates[3] to generate problems. As such, we have to look at the broader research community for related work. There are two strands of work that generate mathematical problems, namely, those that come from the Natural Language Processing (NLP) and educational psychology research communities.

NLP research has investigated the use of recurrent neural networks [10], answer-set programming and traditional natural language generation techniques [5], and pre-trained language models [9] to generate word problems, which may sometimes be personalised to each student. The input to such systems varies depending on the goal of their respective authors. For instance, Zhou et al.'s [10] focus is generating problems that differ in style but test the same mathematical knowledge. As such, the input to their model is a topic/style and equation—the equation is not automatically generated. The goal of Polozov et al.'s [5] work is to generate personalised maths problems and expect tutor/teacher and student requirements as input. The tutor provides the properties of the equations that underlie the problem to be generated. Specifically, they enter the operators that can be used in the equation and also provide a template for the equations.

[3] https://www.siyavulaeducation.com/technology-components.html.

The student specifies the features that drive the narrative style of the problem. For instance, they enter the theme of the story (e.g., fantasy) and the names, genders, and relationships between the story's characters. All the work on generating mathematics from the NLP community is not suitable for generating problems for South African learners, especially number patterns and sequences, since it mostly focuses on narrative generation for arithmetic and linear equation problems.

Research on the topic from the educational psychology field largely relies on templates for maths problem generation (e.g., [1–3]). The focus of such work is creating computer-adaptive tests (i.e., test items that are tailored to the learners' proficiency) and developing reliable scores for discriminating between learners of various proficiency. The major focus on such work is the latter and it uses test item theory since its models provide coefficients of test item difficulty. The only work in this area that is directly linked to the task at hand is the Adaptive Content for Evidence-based Diagnosis (ACED) prototype [6,7] that was built to support learners learning sequences and patterns at the grade 8 level in the United States (US). The system's architecture is appealing as it includes a model of the student's proficiency and the knowledge required to solve tasks, a method of updating learners' proficiency from their performance on tasks, and a model of the various tasks. However, the major limitation of the work for our task is that it is geared towards the US curriculum and its methods for problem generation are not publicly available.

Overall this means that while existing work has attractive properties from an architectural perspective, they are not sufficient to generate mathematics problems that abide by the South African mathematics curriculum.

3 COMPAH: Computer Assistant for High School Mathematics

In creating the problem archetypes, we analyse existing problems so as to create open and precise formalisation of mathematics problems.

We downloaded *sequence and series* problems from the South African Department of Basic Education's website[4] for the years 2008–2009 and 2011–2020. The year 2010 is not included because the website did not have the exam paper that was written in that year. We used the exam papers written in the November cycle to form the data to be used to formalise the problem types, build the archetypes, and create a controlled natural language. Henceforth, we shall refer to this corpus as the *development set*. We also used the papers written in the Feb/March cycle to create the *test set*. Specifically, these are the matric rewrite exam papers from 2011–2018 (inclusive).

We then analysed the problems presented in the training set in order to develop formal models of what the problem looks like. Prior to development, we first introduce some preliminaries to explain what we mean by "model".

[4] https://www.education.gov.za/.

3.1 Preliminaries

Developing models that are specific to sequence and series problems requires a general definition of what mathematical problems and solutions are. This is important because we want to distinguish between a maths problem and its description as we are not interested in only characterising problems at the linguistic-level. We take the position that a maths problem is a consistent axiomatic system (the problem setting) and a proposition (the answer). A student's solution can be defined as a proof, possibly inconsistent, of the problem's proposition. In order to demonstrate these components, consider the problem that was taken from [10]: "Joan found 70 seashells on the beach. She gave Sam some of her seashells. She has 27 seashells. How many seashells did she give to Sam?". This problem can be formalised using the axioms labelled A1-A5, the Peano axioms[5], and answer P1. The student is expected to provide a proof of proposition P1.

A1 $\forall x, y\ possesses(x, y) \rightarrow Person(x) \wedge Seashell(y)$
A2 $\forall x, y, z\ gave(x, y, z) \rightarrow Person(x) \wedge Person(y) \wedge Seashell(z)$
A3 $\forall x, y(\exists^{a} p\ possesses(x, p) \wedge \exists^{b} q\ gave(x, y, q) \wedge \exists^{c} r\ possesses(y, r)) \rightarrow$
$\exists^{a-b} s\ possesses(x, s) \wedge \exists^{c+b} t\ possesses(y, t)$
A4 $\exists^{a} s_1\ possesses(p_1, s_1) \wedge \exists^{b} s_1\ possesses(p_1, s_1) \rightarrow a = b$
A5 $\exists^{a} y\ possesses(sam, y) \wedge \exists^{70} y\ possesses(joan, y) \wedge \exists^{x} z\ gave(joan, sam, z) \rightarrow$
$\exists^{27} y\ possesses(joan, y) \wedge \exists^{a+x} y\ possesses(sam, y)$
P1 $x = 43$

Due to space limitations, we do not include a proof of the above problem. Using the above intuitive view as a basis, we present Definitions 1 and 2 in order to be precise on what problems and solutions are.

Definition 1 (Maths problem). *Let MP denote the set of maths problem and A denote the set of answers to a maths problem. We define a maths problem as the quadtruple* $\langle AS, \alpha, p, q\rangle \in MP$ *where the following conditions are met:*

- $AS \subseteq S_{FOL}$ *is a finite and consistent set of First Order Logic sentences*
- $AS = DA \cup PA$ *where DA are domain/theory axioms and PA are axioms of the problem*
- $\alpha_1, ..., \alpha_n \in A \subseteq S_{FOL}$ *are tautologies. They are the solutions to the problem*
- *p is a natural language description of the premise of the problem*
- *q is a natural language description of the question of the problem*

Definition 2 (Maths solution). *Let SO denote the set of solutions for a maths problem. We define a solution for some maths problem* $p \in MP$ *as the finite ordered list* $\langle s_1, s_2, ..., s_m\rangle \in SO$ *where* $s_m = \alpha_p$ *and* $\forall 1 \leq j \leq m\ s_j$ *one of the following conditions hold:*

[5] Omitted here for brevity.

- *α_p is a solution to the problem*
- *$s_j \in AS_p$ where AS_p is the problem's set of FOL sentences*
- *s_j is a tautology*
- *$\exists\ 1 \leq g, h < j$ such that $s_g \wedge s_h \rightarrow s_j$ can either be true or false*

Given the above definitions, we define a problem archetype as a template of a maths problem. Archetypes are formed by taking a problem $\langle AS, \alpha, p, q\rangle$ and its solutions A and modifying the sentences in AS and A such that there are statements have place-holders that can take different values. That allows one to create different instances of the same problem type. With these definitions in hand, we now turn to how we categorise sequences and series' in order to have a manageable organisation of the formalised problem types.

3.2 Categorisation of Problems

The development set initially had a total of 111 sequences and series problems but we filtered out 23 problems. The 23 problems were filtered out because they were either multimodal (i.e., text and images), the premise used a very specialised narrative that would necessitate the creation of a lexico-syntactic CNL[6], the sequence or series type could not be determined, or the question is judged to be unlikely to be repeated in the future.

Analysis of the remaining 88 sequences and series problems in the training set showed that there are four types of sequences, and series based on them, that are examined in the papers and we present the first three in Definition 3.

Definition 3. *Let G and A denote geometric and arithmetic geometric sequences, respectively. We define each of the possible sequence types as ordered sets in the following manner:*

- $G = \{x \mid x = (\{x_1\} \cup \bigcup_{i=2}^{\infty} \{x_i = f(i)\}, O_i)\}$ *where* $f(i) = x_1 r^{i-1}$
- $A = \{x \mid x = (\{x_1\} \cup \bigcup_{i=2}^{\infty} \{x_i = f(i)\}, O_i)\}$ *where* $f(i) = x_1 + (i-1)d$ *and* $d \in \mathcal{N}$ *is a constant*
- $Q = \{x \mid x = (\bigcup_{i=1}^{\infty} \{f(i)\}, O_i)\}$ *where* $f(x) = ax_1^2 + bx_1 + c$

The above sequence types have also been used in exams papers to form a sequence type that possesses an interleaving constant. For instance, the quadratic sequence (2, 3, 10, 23, ...) and the constant 0 can be used to form the new sequence type (0, 2, 0, 3, 0, 10, 0, 23, ...). We call this an interleaving sequence and define it in the following manner:

Definition 4. *Let I denote the interleaving sequence type. We define interleaving sequences in the following manner:*

[6] A design decision was taken to not have lexico-syntactic patterns in the current version to reduce complexity.

- $S = A \cup G \cup Q$
- $CI = \{y \mid y = \{(1-\alpha^i)k + \alpha^i x_i\}, O_i)\}$ *where* $i \in [1, \infty)$, $\alpha^i = i \mod 2$, $k \in \mathcal{N}$, *and* $x_i \in X \subseteq S$
- $SI = \{y \mid y = \{(1-\alpha^i)x_i + \alpha^i y_i\}, O_i)\}$ *where* $i \in [1, \infty)$, $\alpha^i = i \mod 2, y_i \in Y \subseteq S, x_i \in X \subseteq S$
- $I = CI \cup SI$

Using the sequence and series types we then analysed and formalised problems along these categories. We then formalised the remaining 88 problems by identifying the axioms that make up the problem setting and their answers, following from Definition 1.

3.3 Problem Types

After examining the axioms and solutions of the 88 formalised problems in the *development set* that use the various sequences and series types, we found a total of 64 archetypes or problem types. We present them here using a mixture of natural language and mathematical notation for ease of reading. We decided against only listing the formal problem (i.e., as quadruples of the form $\langle AS, \alpha, p, q\rangle$ following from Definition 1) for the benefit of human readers.

Archetypes for arithmetic sequences and series

1. Given $s_1 = f(x), s_2 = g(x), s_3 = h(x)$ for some $s \in A$. Show that $s_n = f(x) + (n-1)(h(x) - g(x))$
2. Given $s_1 = f(x), s_2 = g(x), s_3 = h(x)$ for some $s \in A$. Show that $s_i = \alpha$ for $i > 3$
3. Given $s_1 = f(x), s_2 = g(x), s_3 = h(x)$ for some $s \in A$. Show that $\sum_{i=1}^{n} s_i = \alpha$ for $n > 4$
4. Given $s_1 = \alpha, s_2 = \beta$ for some $s \in A$. Show that $s_i = \eta$ for some $i > 2$
5. Given $s_1 = \alpha, s_2 = \beta$ for some $s \in A$. If $\sum_{i=1}^{n} s_i = \pi$, show that $n = \zeta$.
6. Given $s_1 = \alpha, s_2 = \beta, s_3 = \gamma, ..., s_i = \eta$ for some $s \in A$. Show that $s_n = \alpha + (n-1)(s_{i+1} - s_i)$ for some i.
7. Given $s_1 = \alpha, s_2 = \beta, s_3 = \gamma, ..., s_i = \eta$ for some $s \in A$. If $s_i \equiv x \mod a$ for $i \in [start, end]$, show that $x \in \{x_1, ..., x_n\}$
8. Given $s_1 = \alpha, s_2 = \beta, s_3 = \gamma, ..., s_i = \eta$ for some $s \in A$. If $s_i \equiv x \mod a$, show that $\sum_{i=1}^{n} s_i = \pi$.
9. Given $s_1 + s_2 + s_3 + ... + s_k$ for some $s_n \in A$. Express the series using sigma notation.
10. Given $s_1 + s_2 + s_3 + ... + s_k$ for some $s_n \in A$. Show that $l = |\{s_i \mid s_i \equiv \omega \mod \lambda\}|$
11. Given $s_1 = \alpha, s_2 = \beta, s_3 = \gamma, ..., s_{i-1} = \delta, s_i = \epsilon, ..., s_j = \zeta$ for some $s_n \in A$. Show that $k = |\{s_i \mid s_i \equiv \pi \mod \lambda\}|$
12. Given $s_1 = \alpha, s_2 = \beta, s_3 = \gamma, ..., s_{i-1} = \delta, s_i = \epsilon$ for some $s_n \in A$. Show that $i = \eta$.

13. Given $s_1 = \alpha, s_2 = \beta, s_3 = \gamma, ..., s_{i-1} = \delta, s_i = \epsilon$ for some $s_n \in A$. Show that $\sum_{k=1}^{i} s_k = \eta$ for $s_k < 0$
14. Given $s_1 = \alpha, s_2 = \beta, s_3 = \gamma$ for some $s_n \in A$. If $\sum_{i=1}^{n} s_i = \pi$, show that $n = \zeta$
15. Given $s_1 = \alpha, s_4 = \beta$ for some $s_n \in A$. Show that $s_2 = \zeta$ and $s_3 = \eta$.
16. Given $s_n = f(n)$ for some $s_n \in A$. Show that $s_i = \alpha, s_{i+1} = \beta$, and $s_{i+2} = \gamma$.
17. Given $s_n = f(n)$ for some $s_n \in A$. Show that $\sum_{i=1}^{n} f(i) = \alpha$
18. Given $s_1 = \alpha, s_2 = f(x)$, and $s_3 = \beta$ for some $s_n \in A$. Show that $x = \gamma$.
19. Given $s_1 = \alpha$ and $d = s_{i+1} - s_i, \forall i \in \mathcal{Z}^+$. Show that $s_n = \frac{n}{2}(2\alpha + (n-1)d)$
20. Given $s_i = f(x), s_{i+1} = g(x)$, and $s_{i+2} = h(x)$ for some $s_n \in A$. Show that $x = \alpha$.
21. Given $s_1 + s_2 + s_3 + ... + s_k = \pi$ for some $s_n \in A$. Show that $s_i = \mu$ where $3 < i < k$.
22. Given $s_1 + s_2 + s_3 + ... + s_k$ for some $s_n \in A$. Show that $\sum_{i=1}^{k} = \mu$

Archetypes for geometric sequences and series

1. Given $s_1 = \alpha, s_2 = \beta, s_3 = \gamma$ for some $s_n \in G$. If $s_n = \alpha r^{n-1}$, show that $r = \zeta$
2. Given $s_1 = \alpha, s_2 = \beta, s_3 = \gamma$ for some $s_n \in G$. Does $\sum_{i=1}^{\infty} s_i$ converge?
3. Given $s_1 = \alpha, s_2 = \beta, s_3 = \gamma$ for some $s_n \in G$. Specify reasons why $\sum_{i=1}^{\infty} s_i$ converges?
4. Given $s_1 = \alpha, s_2 = \beta, s_3 = \gamma$ for some $s_n \in G$. Show that $\sum_{i=1}^{\infty} s_i = \zeta$
5. Given $s_1 = \alpha, s_2 = \beta, s_3 = \gamma$ for some $s_n \in G$. Show that $\sum_{i=1}^{n} s_i = \zeta$
6. Given $s_1 = \alpha, s_2 = \beta, s_3 = \gamma$ for some $s_n \in G$. Show that $\sum_{i=1}^{\infty} s_i - \sum_{i=1}^{n} s_i = ab^n$ for some a, b.
7. Given $s_1 = \alpha, s_2 = ks_1, ..., s_j = ks_{i-1}, ...$ for some $s_n \in G$. Show that the proposition $s_1 = \sum_{i=2}^{j} s_i$ is true/false.
8. $s_1 = \alpha, s_3 = f(x), s_3 = \beta$ for some $s_n \in G$. Show that $x = \eta$.
9. Given $s_1 = \alpha, s_2 = \beta, s_3 = \gamma$ for some $s_n \in G$. Show that $s_i = \eta$ for some $i > 3$
10. Given $\sum_{i=1}^{n} f(x, i)$ for some $f(x, i) \in G$. Show that $\sum_{i=1}^{n} f(x, i) = \zeta$ if $x = \alpha$.
11. Given $\sum_{i=1}^{n} f(x, i)$ for some $f(x, i) \in G$. If $\sum_{i=1}^{\infty} f(x, i)$ converges, show that $x \in \{x_1, ..., x_n\}$.
12. Given $s_1 = \alpha, r = \beta, \sum_{i=3}^{\infty} s_i = \gamma$ for some $s_i \in G$. If $s_i + s_{i+1} = \delta$, show that $s_i + s_{i+1} = f(a, r)$

13. If $\sum_{i=1}^{k} \alpha_1 \beta_1^{f(k)} = p$, Show that $\sum_{i=1}^{k} \alpha_2 \beta_2^{g(k)} = f(p)$
14. Given $s_n = f(n)$ for some $s_n \in G$. Show that $s_i = \alpha$.
15. Given $s_1 = \alpha, s_2 = \beta, s_3 = \gamma$, and $s_4 = \delta$ for some $s_n \in G$. Show that $s_i = \pi$ for $i > 4$.
16. Given $r = \frac{s_{i+1}}{s_i}$ and $\sum_{i=1}^{\infty} s_1 r^{i-1} = \alpha$. Show that $s_i = \alpha$.
17. Given $s_n = f(n)$ for some $s_n \in G$. If $\sum_{i=1}^{n} s_i = \alpha$, show that $n = \beta$.

Archetypes for quadratic sequences and series

1. Given $s_n = f(n)$. Show that $s_i = \alpha, s_{i+1} = \beta, s_{i+2} = \gamma$
2. Given $s_n = f(n)$. If $s_j = min(f(n))$, show that $j = \alpha$.
3. Given $s_n = f(n)$. If $d_i = s_i - s_{1+1}$ and $d_{i+1} = s_{i+2} - s_{i+3}$, show that $d_1 - d_2 = \alpha$.
4. Given $s_n = f(n)$. If $s_i < \alpha$, show that $i \in i_1, ..., i_n$
5. Given $s_1 = \alpha, s_2 = \beta, s_3 = \gamma$. Show that $s_i = \eta$ for some $i > 3$.
6. Given $s_1 = \alpha, s_2 = \beta, s_3 = \gamma$. Show that $s_n = an^2 + bn + c$ for some a, b, c
7. Given $s_1 = \alpha, s_2 = \beta, s_3 = \gamma$. If $s_{i+1} - s_i = \psi$ for some i, show that $s_{i+1} = \eta$ and $s_i = \zeta$.
8. Given $s_1 + s_2 + s_4 + ...$ where $s_n \in Q$. Show that $s_n = an^2 + bn + c$ for some a, b, c
9. Given $s_1 + s_2 + s_4 + ...$ where $s_n \in Q$. Express the series using sigma notation.
10. Given $s_1 + s_2 + s_4 + ...$ where $s_n \in Q$. Show that the proposition $\sum_{i=1}^{n} s_i = f(n)$ is true/false.
11. Given $s_1 = \alpha, s_2 = g(x), s_3 = \beta, s_4 = f(x)$ for some $s_n \in Q$. Show that $x = \zeta$.
12. Given $s_1 = \alpha, s_2 = g(x), s_3 = \beta, s_4 = f(x)$ for some $s_n \in Q$. If $d_i = s_{i+1} - s_i$ and $\sum_{j=1}^{n} d_j > \mu$, show that $n \in \{n_1, ..., n_m\}$
13. Given $s_1 = \alpha, s_2 = \beta, s_3 = \gamma, s_4 = \delta$ for $s_n \in Q$. If $d_i^1 = s_{i+1} - s_1$ and $d_i^2 = d_{i+1}^1 - d_i^1$, show that $d_1^2 = \zeta$
14. Given $s_1 = \alpha, s_2 = \beta, s_3 = \gamma, s_4 = \delta$ for $s_n \in Q$. If $s_i = \eta$, show that $i = \zeta$.
15. Given $s_1 = \alpha, s_2 = \beta, s_3 = \gamma, s_4 = \delta$. If $d_i = s_{i+1} - s_i$, show that $\sum_{i=1}^{n} d_i = f(n)$ is true/false.
16. Given $s_1 = \alpha, s_2 = \beta, s_3 = \gamma, s_4 = \delta$. If $\sum_{i=1}^{n} d_i = \eta$, show that $n \in \{n_1, ..., n_m\}$
17. Given $\sum_{i=p}^{\infty} \alpha \beta^{f(i)} = k$. Show that $p = \eta$.
18. Given $s_1 = \alpha, s_2 = \beta, s_3 = \gamma, s_4 = \delta$, and $s_5 = \epsilon$ for some $s_n \in Q$. If $d_i = s_{i+1} - s_i$, show that $d_n = f(n)$.
19. Given $s_i = \alpha, s_{i+1} = \beta$, and $s_{i+3} = \gamma$. If $d_i^1 = s_{i+1} - s_i$ and $d_i^2 = d_{i+1}^1 - d_i^1$, show that $d_i^2 = \eta, \forall i \in \mathcal{Z}^+$
20. Given $s_i = \alpha, s_{i+1} = \beta$, and $s_{i+2} = \gamma$ for some $s_n \in Q$. Show that $s_j = \eta$.
21. Given $s_1 = \alpha, s_2 = f(x), s_3 = \beta$, and $s_4 = h(x)$. Show that $x = \mu$.

Archetypes for interleaved sequences

1. Given $s_1 = \alpha, s_2 = \beta, ..., s_{11} = \lambda$ for some $s_n \in I$. Show that $s_i = eta$ for some $i > 11$.
2. Given $s_1 = \alpha, s_2 = \beta, ..., s_{11} = \lambda$ for some $s_n \in I$. Show that $\sum_{i=1}^{n} s_i = \eta$ for some $n > 11$.
3. $s_1 = \alpha, s_2 = \beta, s_3 = \gamma, s_4 = \delta, s_5 = \epsilon$, and $s_6 = \zeta$ for some $s_n \in I$. Show that $s_i - sj = \eta$ for some $i, j \in \mathcal{Z}^+$.
4. $s_1 = \alpha, s_2 = \beta, s_3 = \gamma, s_4 = \delta, s_5 = \epsilon$, and $s_6 = \zeta$ for some $s_n \in I$. Show that $s_i \equiv a(mod\ b), \forall i \in \mathcal{Z}^+$.

The mathematical formalisations are useful for being precise on the structure of mathematics problems. We now turn to the evaluation of the scope on the test set.

4 Evaluation of Scope

Analysis of the 74 questions found in the test set showed that 48 (65%) fell within the scope of the problem types extracted from the development set. Six of the other 26 questions were not directly covered by the extracted problem types but they were testing knowledge that is covered by the extracted problem types. For instance, question 3.2.1 from 2011 asked learners to calculate the sum of the first 20 items of geometric series and it was not captured by the extracted problem types, however, the same kind of question was asked in the building set in the context of an arithmetic series. This means that the external problem types cover 73% of the problems in the test set if we do not limit each problem type to a specific sequence or series type.

5 Utility of Archetypes

To demonstrate utility, we extracted templates to construct a CNL and used Python and the symbolic mathematics package SymPy[7] to capture the archetypes for the first fifteen arithmetic sequence and series problem types and developed a prototype assistant that makes use of the archetypes and templates to generate text. The prototype currently uses the architecture shown in Fig. 2. In the rest of section, we discuss these components and how they work together to generate a natural language problem description.

The problem generation module in Fig. 2 takes an identifier of a problem type, selects and populates the place-holders found in the archetype axioms using random values, and produces an instance of an abstract representation of the problem. For instance, when the module is given the identifier 4, it retrieves the archetype shown in Listing 1.1. The module then generates random values for s_1, s_2, and i the place-holders found in line 2 of Listing 1.1. Those values are

[7] https://www.sympy.org/en/index.html.

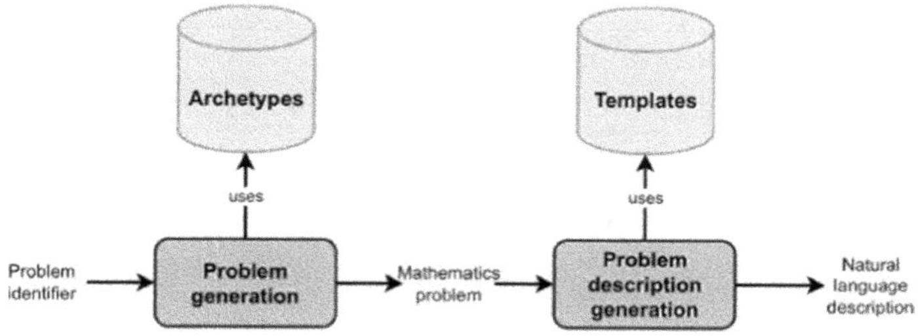

Fig. 2. Architecture used by prototype assistant

then used to create concrete values for the premises of the problem (lines 11–13) and the solution (line 16). The resulting mathematics problem is then fed to the question generation module.

```
1  class ArithmeticArchetypeFour(Archetype):
2      def __init__(self, s1, s2, i):
3          super().__init__()
4          s1_symbol = Symbol('s1')
5          s2_symbol = Symbol('s2')
6          i_symbol = Symbol('i')
7
8          prem1 = Eq(s1_symbol, s1)
9          prem2 = Eq(s2_symbol, s2)
10         prem3 = Eq(i_symbol, i)
11         self.premises.append(prem1)
12         self.premises.append(prem2)
13         self.premises.append(prem3)
14
15         self.seq = ArithmeticSequence(s1, s2 - s1, 's')
16         self.solution = self.seq.get_function()(i)
```

Listing 3.1. Archetype that can be used to generate arithmetic sequence problems of type 4

The problem description module takes in the maths problem, fetches the associated templates from the CNL, and then inserts the slot values in the templates using the information found in the Python archetype. For instance, for the problem created using the archetype in Listing 1.1, the module can select the templates `Consider the sequence: [sequence]` and `If the pattern continues in the same manner, determine [seqItemLabel]` for the premise and question respectively. In the premise template, the slot `[sequence]` is a place-holder for s_1 and s_2. In the question template, the slot `[seqItemLabel]` is a place-holder for the label for the ith element. The module can then used those premise and question templates to generate problems of the form:

```
Consider the sequence: 5, 17
If the pattern continues in the same manner, determine s_62.
```

The python archetypes, controlled natural language, and prototype implementation are released as supplementary material at https://zenodo.org/record/6927550.

6 Conclusion

This paper presented the first formalisation of mathematical problems that high school leaving learners are expected to master. This formalisation is based on the analysis of problems from a corpus of problems covering approximately 12 years of South African grade 12 exams. We evaluated the coverage of our formalisations on problems taken from the Matric rewrite exam papers from 2011–2018 (inclusive). We have found that the formalised problems cover 65% of the problems in the test set. Moreover, when we do not limit each problem formalisation to a specific sequence and series type, where appropriate, then we see that our formalised problem types cover 73% of the problems. We have also built a prototype assistant that relies on archetypes based on the formalised problem types and a controlled natural language to demonstrate the utility of the formalisations. The created artefacts can be used by lecturers to enable student-led revision of high school mathematics thus improving students' mathematics background. Other researchers may find the artefacts useful in investigating the diversity of maths problems over the years, how differences in the curriculum impact the actual problem posed to students, etc.

As current and future work, we focus on extending the archetypes and the controlled natural language to cover other problem types, introducing models of student proficiency, and investigating the impact of the assistant on educational outcomes.

References

1. Deane, P., Graf, E.A., Higgins, D., Futagi, Y., Lawless, R.: Model analysis and model creation: the task-model structure of quantitative item domains. ETS Research Report Series 2006, no. 1, pp. i–63 (2006)
2. Embretson, S.E., Kingston, N.M.: Automatic item generation: a more efficient process for developing mathematics achievement items? J. Educ. Measur. **55**(1), 112–131 (2018)
3. Holling, H., Bertling, J.P., Zeuch, N.: Automatic item generation of probability word problems. Stud. Educ. Eval. **35**(2), 71–76 (2009)
4. Jawitz, J.: The Challenge of Teaching Large Classes in Higher Education in South Africa?: A Battle to be Waged Outside the Classroom, vol. 4. African Sun Media, Cape Town (2013)

5. Polozov, O., O'Rourke, E., Smith, A.M., Zettlemoyer, L., Gulwani, S., Popovic, Z.: Personalized mathematical word problem generation. In: Yang, Q., Wooldridge, M.J. (eds.) Proceedings of the Twenty-Fourth International Joint Conference on Artificial Intelligence, IJCAI 2015, Buenos Aires, Argentina, 25–31 July 2015, pp. 381–388. AAAI Press (2015)
6. Shute, V.J., Graf, E.A., Hansen, E.G.: Designing adaptive, diagnostic math assessments for individuals with and without visual disabilities. ETS Research Report Series 2006, no. 1, pp. i–37 (2006)
7. Shute, V.J., Hansen, E.G., Almond, R.G.: An assessment for learning system called aced: Designing for learning effectiveness and accessibility. ETS Research Report Series 2007, no. 2, pp. i–45 (2007)
8. Subban, A.: Guidelines for the development of the school timetables - reopening for schools Covid-19. Technical report, Department of Basic Education (2020). https://wcedeportal.co.za/eresource/131181
9. Wang, Z., Lan, A.S., Baraniuk, R.G.: Math word problem generation with mathematical consistency and problem context constraints. In: Moens, M., Huang, X., Specia, L., Yih, S.W. (eds.) Proceedings of the 2021 Conference on Empirical Methods in Natural Language Processing, EMNLP 2021, Virtual Event/Punta Cana, Dominican Republic, 7–11 November 2021, pp. 5986–5999. Association for Computational Linguistics (2021)
10. Zhou, Q., Huang, D.: Towards generating math word problems from equations and topics. In: van Deemter, K., Lin, C., Takamura, H. (eds.) Proceedings of the 12th International Conference on Natural Language Generation, INLG 2019, Tokyo, Japan, 29 October–1 November 2019, pp. 494–503. Association for Computational Linguistics (2019)

The Use of Binary Scales in Rubrics to Evaluate Computer Science Assessments

Jacqui Muller(✉) and Japie J. Greeff

School of Computer Science and Information Systems, Unit for Data Science and Computing, North-West University, Vanderbijlpark, South Africa

jacqui.muller@outlook.com, japie.greeff@nwu.ac.za

Abstract. Creating a rubric for project based assessment in ICT modules is a complex process and can be quite subjective if the wrong scales are used for rubric elements. The aim of this paper is to present a framework for developing rubrics that use binary scales for the rubric elements which will both lessen the risk of subjectivity (with focus on objective criteria) entering into the marking process and also create an opportunity for automation to be used for the marking of parts of the assessment. The framework and process used to develop a rubric are explained and an example is presented of what the final result would look like if created in this way. The framework was developed using a Design Science Research approach which is also the suggested approach to be used in the creation of a rubric. It is believed that this approach, once automated, could lead to a more dynamic approach to assessment where students can submit their work partially and get feedback immediately and lecturers can track in real time the progress of the class.

Keywords: Rubric development · Binary scale · Project-based assessment

1 Introduction

A large part of education systems is the ability to measure the growth in knowledge around the concepts that have been taught within the applicable system or environment. There are multiple different ways to measure knowledge development, some of which include evaluations and assessments (Novita 2017). Novita (2017) suggests that an assessment is used to evaluate the attainment of learning outcomes which can be conducted as formal or informal assessments. The learning outcomes that an assessment aims to assess can be measured through the use of a rubric (Zano 2015).

Alves et al. (2020) defines a rubric as a tool used as a measurement in performance-based assessments. Rubrics can be used to measure individual portions (or items) of an assessment, referred to as rubric elements. Rubrics are good at assessing algorithms and programming concepts in the context of Information Systems, Computer Science or Information Technology project-based assignments and tests. A rubric is made up of elements that have a weighting of marks associated to each element being assessed or measured. In this paper a proposed framework is presented for creating rubrics for project-based assessments in computer science or information systems modules using rubric elements that are comprised of binary scales.

R. J. Barnett et al. (Eds.): SACLA 2022, CCIS 1664, pp. 58–72, 2022.
https://doi.org/10.1007/978-3-031-21076-1_4

2 Literature Review

According to Janse van Rensburg and Goede (2019) the kind of work graduates will do when employed in the Information Technology space will most likely be more akin to project-based assessment than to traditional assessments found in tertiary education. In project-based assessments there is a recognition that subjectivity can enter into the evaluation of work even with a rubric as can be seen by the work of Mustapha et al. (2016) where, even with a standard rubric that is employed for all assessments, there is still some risk of subjectivity. A well-designed rubric however can guard against this risk, provided that the criteria is defined in enough granular detail to reduce subjective interpretation as far as possible. Dawson (2017) puts forward 14 rubric design elements obtained from the literature to assist in the creation of well-designed rubrics. The problem with creating a single rubric though that applies to all assessments is that it does need to be very general, removing the ability to test specific skills in different assessments.

Jones and Tadros (2010) put forward that the weighting of marks in a rubric can be assessed using different scales, some of which could include categorical scaling, sliding scaling and binary scaling. These scales are considered in turn to indicate their characteristics.

2.1 Categorical Scale

Jones and Tadros (2010) position categorical scaling as the mark allocation of each rubric element being split up into categories with numerical values associated to each category. An example of this would be measuring each element in terms of the following categories:

- Not acceptable (attached to the numerical value of 1): The students' approach to addressing the rubric element in question is way below the standard or expectation. This could be because the element is not addressed at all within the assessment or that the students' approach displays a complete misunderstanding of the element.
- Below expectation (attached to the numerical value of 2): The students' approach to addressing the rubric element does not meet the standard results that were expected as an outcome of the assessment.
- Meets expectation (attached to the numerical value of 3): The students' approach to addressing the rubric element meets the standard results expected as an outcome of the assessment.
- Exemplary (attached to the numerical value of 4): The students' approach to addressing the rubric element exceeds the standard results expected as an outcome of the assessment.

The South African basic education system comprising of the foundation phase (grades R to 3), intermediate phase (grades 4 to 6), senior phase (grades 7 to 9) and FET phase (grades 10 to 12) curriculums governed by the Curriculum and Assessment Policy Statement (CAPS), divides the term results of students into categories based on the marks they received for the term (Education 2021). According to Morolong (2009), these categories are:

7 (80%–100%): Outstanding achievement
6 (70%–79%): Meritorious achievement
5 (60%–69%): Substantial achievement
4 (50%–59%): Adequate achievement
3 (40%–49%): Moderate achievement
2 (30%–39%): Elementary achievement
1 (0%–29%): Not achieved.

2.2 Sliding Scale

Park and Yan (2019) present the concept of a sliding scale as the consideration of different factors when deriving an overall score. These factors may vary between rubric elements and may not even be formally declared before the rubric is used to evaluate an assessment. Often these factors that need to be considered are determined by the assessor as they evaluate the assessment (Imbault et al. 2018). The objective of a sliding scale is to allow room for interpreting different influencing factors as part of the mark awarded for each rubric element. This is supported by Imbault et al. (2018) who suggest that data obtained through the use of sliding scale evaluations are, by their nature, interval.

2.3 Binary Scale

Jones and Tadros (2010) position the binary scale as the use of 1 and 0 to determine whether an element has been addressed adequately within an assessment or not. Where the sliding scale and categorical scale allows for some level of subjectivity and interpretation of elements between students, the binary scale aims to remove the level of subjectivity and only focus on whether the element is present/addressed or not. Haghdoost (2012) shows how the binary scale can be used to distinguish between two levels of evaluation. In the case of their research, Haghdoost (2012) used 0 to denote illiteracy and 1 to denote literacy. Park and Yan (2019) support the use of binary scale to segregate categories through 0 denoting 'no' and 1 denoting 'yes' as answers to the questions posed as rubric elements. Dimitrov (2016) presents an argument for the benefits of binary scale scoring with large-scale assessments. In this paper the binary scale is used to create rubric elements so as to remove the subjectivity (as far as possible) inherent in the other scales as well as to lay the groundwork for a higher level of automation in the assessing of project-based work.

3 Research Design

In this paper a framework is presented that can be used to develop a rubric with binary scaled elements for project-based assessments. This framework was developed using the Design Science Research (DSR) approach which is not only applicable to the creation of the framework but can also be used to iteratively develop rubrics for project-based assessments. It is likely that, once defined, a rubric can be further refined over a number of years each time the assessment is presented in a module.

Simon (1996) and Hevner (2007) propose Design Science Research as the introduction of new and innovative artefacts that motivate the desire to improve an environment. Lukka (2003) expands on this by stating that DSR can be used to solve real-life problems by making a contribution to the applied theory.

Hevner (2007) also supports using DSR to introduce new knowledge, executed in three cycles, namely relevance, design and rigour. The development of theories and artefacts will accept environmental needs (of people, processes and technologies) as inputs, utilising any applicable knowledge from the available knowledge base. The relevance cycle will represent the flow of all environmental needs and environmental application between the environment and the information system (IS) research. The rigour cycle will represent the flow of knowledge between the knowledge base and the IS research. Although used to great effect in IS research, it is also shown by Plomp and Nieveen (2013) that educational design research is a valid approach to developing curricula and learning artefacts. The framework of DSR used is shown in Fig. 1.

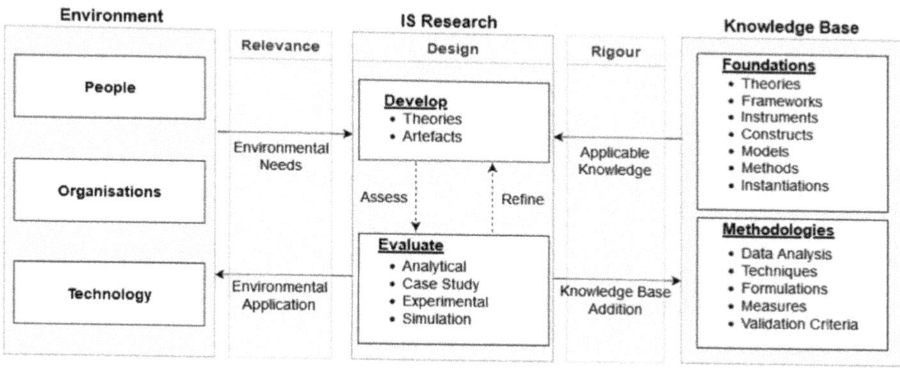

Fig. 1. Design science research cycles adapted from Hevner et al. (2004)

4 Background

The initial implementation of the proposed approach was trialed in a hackathon environment that was subject to a more open-ended project brief. A rubric was developed for evaluating submissions to the hackathon. The goal given to participants in the hackathon was to create innovative cloud solutions that address the world's toughest problems as represented by the United Nations Sustainable Development Goals. 33 teams with between one and eight members were given 48 h to develop either a solution or an idea. These were then evaluated by 15 judges of which nine were technical experts and six were not. The rubric was developed using a looser implementation of a similar technique presented in this paper – with less focus on the objectivity of the criteria. The rubric with its categories, subcategories and weight are presented in Fig. 2.

Category	Sub-Category	Weight
Global Relevancy and Impact	Global aspects consideration	3.75%
	Global impact design	3.75%
	Alignment with global initiatives	3.75%
	Multiple continents	3.75%
Technical Execution	Mockups provided	2.14%
	Working prototype provided	2.14%
	Complex or sophisticated solution	2.14%
	Emerging or advanced technology	2.14%
	Solution scalability	2.14%
	Indexed on source control	2.14%
	Stands out	2.14%
Alignment to UN Sustainable Development Goals	One or more of the development goals addressed	4.00%
	At least one development goal addressed	4.00%
	At least one sub goal addressed	4.00%
	Two or more goals addressed	4.00%
	Two or more subgoals addressed	4.00%
Cloud Technology	Cloud technology used	4.00%
	Cloud software used	4.00%
	Cloud API integration	4.00%
	More than one cloud technology used	4.00%
	Cloud used novelly	4.00%
Creativity and Innovation	Non-traditional creative concept	3.75%
	Design thinking applied	3.75%
	Innovative	3.75%
	Unexpected and interesting	3.75%
Market and Business Feasibility	Addessed business feasibility	3.75%
	Practicality	3.75%
	Appealing marketing	3.75%
	Funding model provided	3.75%

Fig. 2. Weighted Hackathon rubric (including high-level categories and criteria)

Due to the nature of a hackathon, the evaluation of submissions was a lot more open-ended and even with binary scales there was a large amount of variation in results indicated by judges due to the subjective interpretation of some of the criteria. For example, one of the subcategories was whether the submission was innovative, a characteristic that would be very desirable from a hackathon entry. This is something that would inevitably be subjective between different judges. As such, the results obtained between different judges seemed to be consistent in terms of how they marked various entries but didn't correlate well between the marks allocated by different judges for the same submission. Figure 3 presents the box whisker diagram indicating the marks scored by different judges for the different submissions to the hackathon, with specific focus on the marks awarded by Judge 14, denoted by the dots.

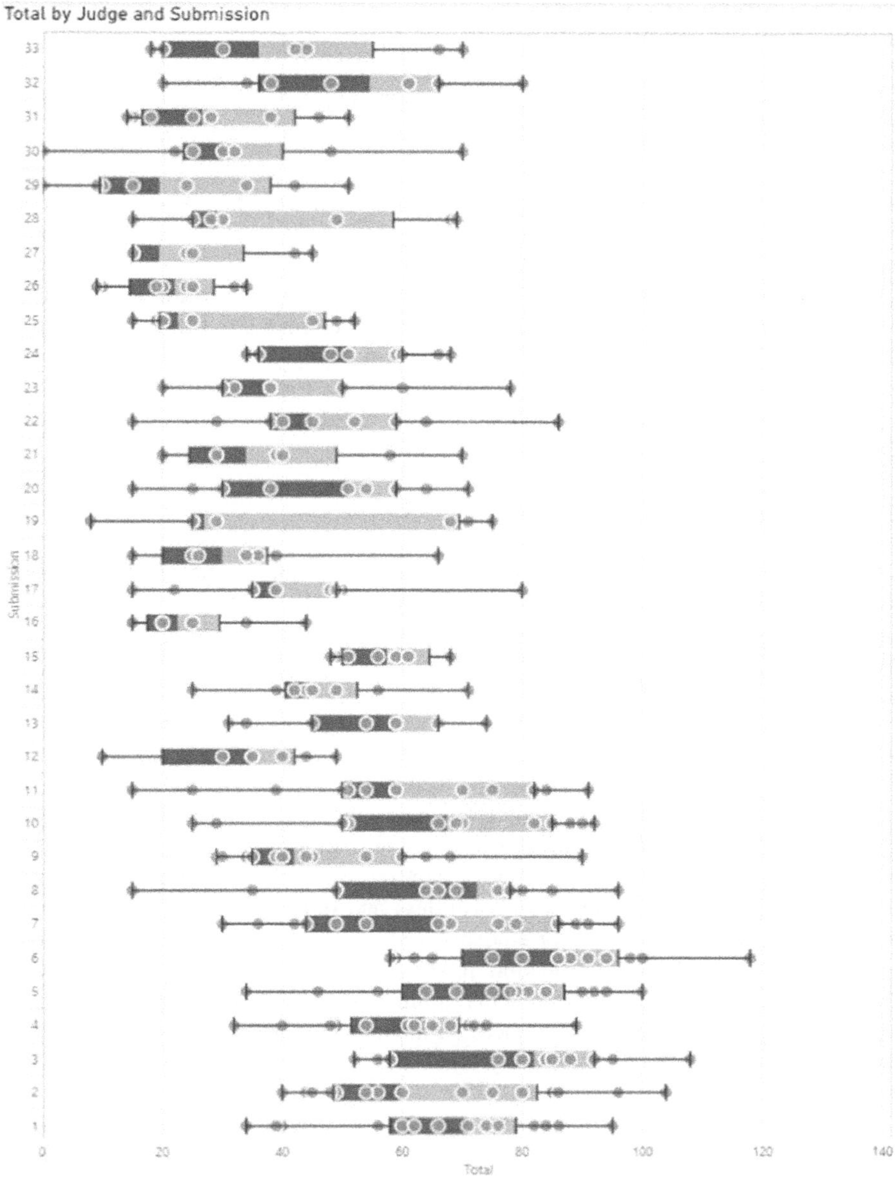

Fig. 3. Ratings by all judges on all submissions to the Hackathon

From these results it would indicate that although individual judges could be consistent in rating rubric elements the same between different submissions, there was still a large amount of subjectivity present in subcategories that were not defined precisely or with more granular and measurable detail. This also highlights the fact that even though a rubric can enable a lecturer to lessen their subjectivity, when presenting the rubric to other markers it is important to also give training to the markers as to how each element should be interpreted. Certain elements are inherently more subjective than others. The idea behind the rubric was to remain as lean as possible for ease-of-marking.

Multiple 'lessons learnt' were identified from this implementation, mainly revolving around the subjective nature of certain criteria and how dividing those criteria in ways that makes the criteria more objective would further decrease the subjective nature of an assessment. This does introduce the possibility of a longer rubric that delivers more objective evaluations.

Another observation is that due to the nature of a hackathon, very few clear outcomes are defined with the specific aim of alleviating the restriction of innovation and creativity. Modules that have defined and concise assessment, study unit and module outcomes may provide a better foundation for assessment criteria formulation. The flaws of this implementation led to the next iteration of the conceptual framework as discussed in Sect. 5.

5 Conceptual Framework

The challenge with sliding and categorical scales is maintaining consistency and objectivity while marking. Even when refining the criteria, the interpretation to degree of implementation allows subjective interpretation since there are more 'choices' available. In many university settings, lecturers deal with large groups of students for which they require assistants to assist with marking student assessments. In cases like these, some assessors may mark more strictly than others which not only jeopardise the consistency of the marks but also the objectivity of the marks. If marks were to be visualised and analysed, the marker would need to be taken into consideration as well.

The additional challenge with this approach is that students may attempt catering for a requirement simply to receive at least some marks for the attempt. With many sliding and categorical scales, the rubric criterion allows for the awarding of marks for an attempt even if the attempt was fruitless and did not contribute to a working solution. Although this is good for students, it does create a situation where students are not necessarily prepared for the kind of work (or criteria) they would be expected to execute on once they graduate which will require them to meet rigid requirements fully. In industry engagements in the ICT space contractual engagements tend to be of a nature that requirements need to be completely fulfilled before obtaining project sign-off and, in some cases, payment.

Although a pass mark for a module with a project-based assessment in it will still be 50%, it would be beneficial to the student to give them very detailed feedback on exactly which elements of the assessment they don't pass. This is especially true if that feedback can be given more frequently throughout the course of the assessment rather than only at the end. Categorical and sliding scales may obfuscate this and create a sense that not meeting requirements fully is not a problem.

The concept that forms the foundation of using binary scales to evaluate project-based assessments in Computer Science, Information Systems or Information Technology modules needs to be instilled in all elements of the assessment, from the conceptual formation of the scope through to the weighting and rubric assessment criteria.

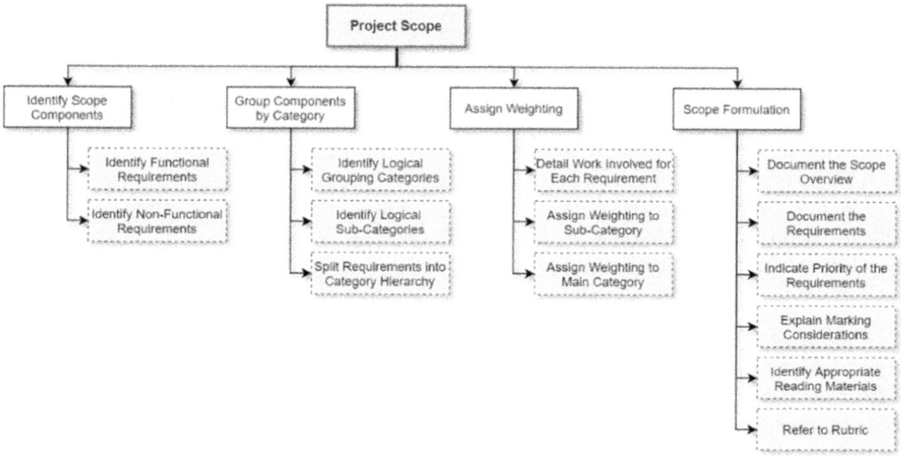

Fig. 4. Conceptual framework for creating a rubric with binary scaled elements for project based assessments in ICT programmes

There is a significant amount of prework that needs to take place in the preparation phases of the assessment before rubric criteria can be assessed using a binary scale. Figure 4 outlines the work involved and is further elaborated upon as the:

- Identification of scope components: The basis of any ICT project-based assessment is the student's ability to turn requirements into a working solution that fulfils those requirements. These requirements may be sub-divided between functional requirements and non-functional requirements. Functional requirements refer to the functionality that a system must have and how the functions should be performed whereas non-functional requirements refer to the aspects of a solution that have an impact on the quality attributes of a system (or platform). These non-functional requirements are deemed as supportive requirements to ensure that the functional requirements are implemented appropriately and according to good software practices.
- Grouping of components by category: Once the requirements have been identified, the requirements can be grouped through logical relation to form categories and sub-categories which may have an additional layer to evaluate the granular details of each requirement. The requirements would then need to be divided accordingly, into the appropriate categories and sub-categories.
- Assigning weighting: Before weighting can be applied to each requirement, the amount of work required to cater for the requirement would need to be considered. More work would mean higher weighting. It is important to also remain cognisant of the categories that are higher priority and ensure that the priority is indicated in the weighting. For example, in a core programming assessment where programmability and the use of patterns are being tested, visualisation should not contribute the highest weight to the overall project mark.
- Formulating the scope: The scope brief which should be provided to students should clearly state what is expected of them in order to achieve at least meritorious results.

The scope should provide a contextual problem which sets the tone of the assessment and helps the student understand the context for which they are trying to solve a problem. The requirements and the priority of each should be clearly defined within the scope. Marking considerations should be outlined and any additional learning materials should be provided.

Once the abovementioned work has been done, the rubric may be finalised with any additional varying factors (like group work division and assessment, bonus mark criteria, etc.) before the rubric is released to students.

5.1 Formulating a Scope

A project-based assessment within the ICT space would typically contain some form of solution design and development as well as a learning component which encapsulates any additional knowledge that students would need in order to complete the assessment, as seen in Fig. 5. These categories may differ based on the context and outcomes of the assessment.

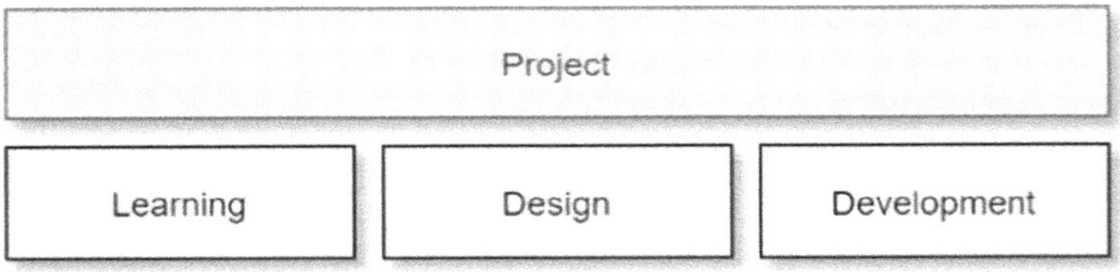

Fig. 5. Project categories

Based on the project categories defined in Fig. 5, the content of the scope of the project-based assessment would need to be expanded to cover all of the categories in greater detail. The design of the solution could be covered through providing the functional and non-functional requirements, along with the prioritisation of each as well as the errors and exceptions that should be catered for, as seen in Fig. 6.

Figure 6 illustrates that the development category should be further divided to cater for the sub-categories that would make up development. The most common sub-categories that would typically be addressed in programming assessments would be infrastructure (what tools and technologies should be used and where should they be deployed, hosted or submitted), data access (what input data should be used and what output data is expected), functionality (what is the solution expected to do, with specific reference to the functional and non-functional requirements in more technical detail), presentation/user experience (how should the interface that the user is going to interact with the solution through look), standards (what architectural patterns, coding standards, design principles and design patterns should be used) as well as testing (what tests should be performed and how are they expected to be performed).

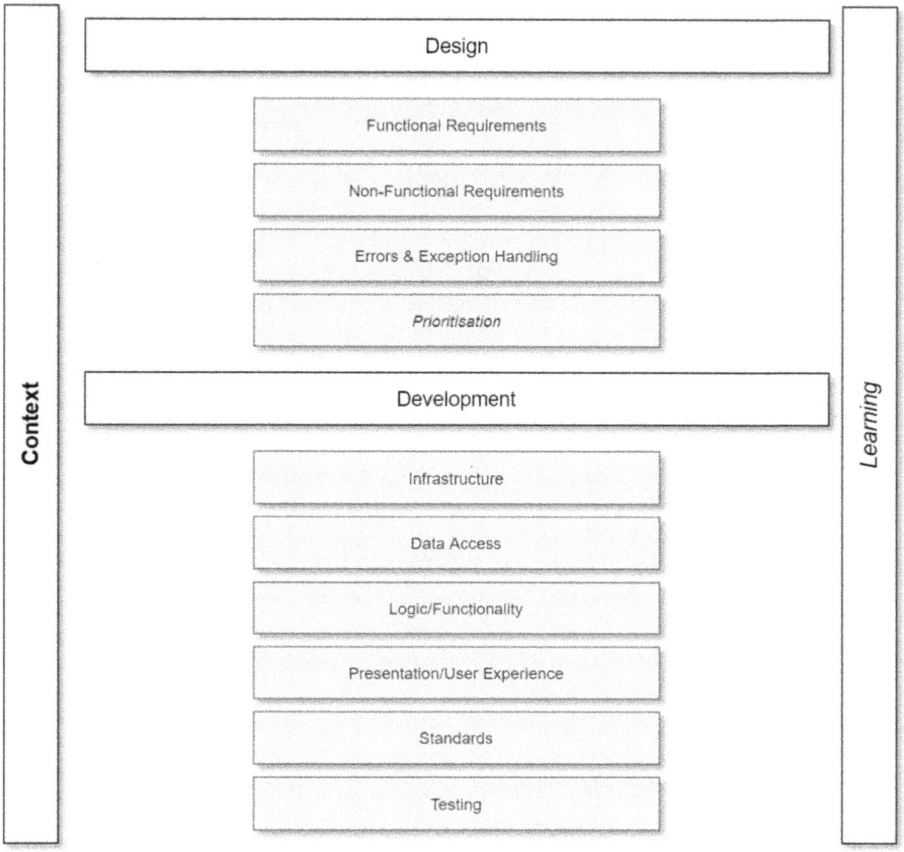

Fig. 6. Formulating a scope

The learning component, as represented in Fig. 6, would span across the design and development categories to ensure that any gaps in knowledge are bridged. The most important part of an assessment scope is the context that encapsulates all of these categories. It is important that the student understands what is expected of them, what they should achieve and what environment they are trying to achieve this in. A good way to apply context is through the use of practical and realistic industry problems. This also helps bridge the gap between industry expectation and student capability.

5.2 Formulating a Rubric

Once the scope has been defined, a rubric would need to be created to evaluate criteria which is adequately related to the content of the scope and can be evaluated using a binary scale. The content of a rubric can be broken down further, from Fig. 6, as seen in Fig. 7.

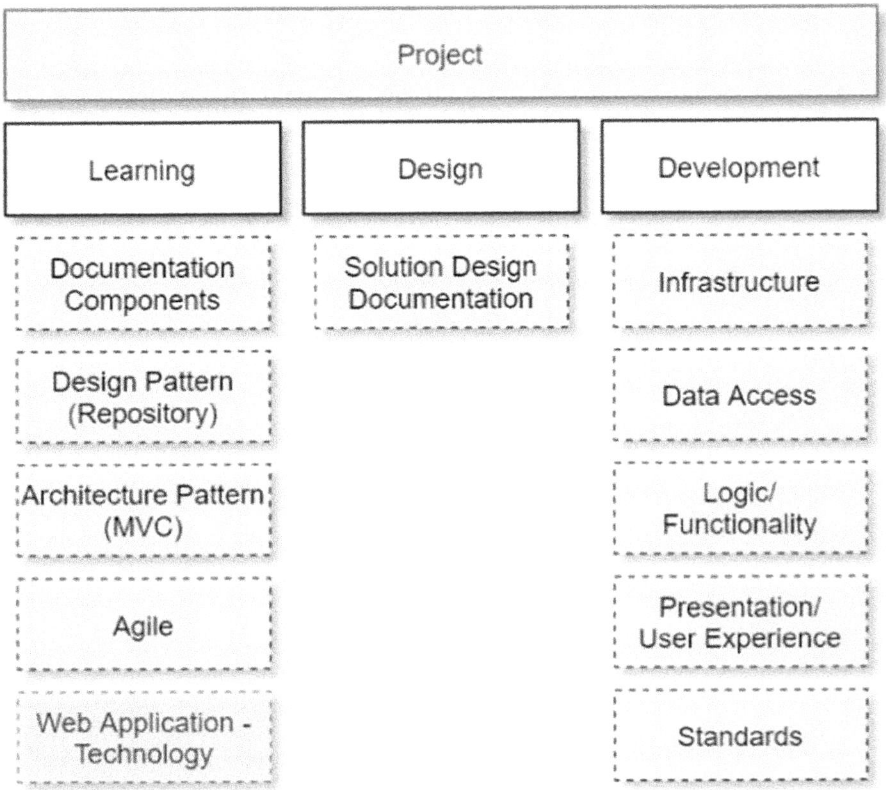

Fig. 7. Formulating a rubric

Figure 7 represents the scope categories broken down into sub-categories. Each of the sub-categories may be divided further to show how each requirement fits in and is evaluated as part of its relative sub-category and category. Criteria can then be attached to sub-categories' descriptions which clearly outline and define what is being evaluated, as seen in Fig. 8.

Once the categories, sub-categories, criteria and descriptions have been defined, weightings can be assigned and rolled up per sub-category and category. Effort and priority should be taken into account when assigning the weighting.

5.3 Assigning Weighting

Typically, projects or assessments are assigned an overall weighting to a module. The project is then further weighted on a criterial level, as seen in Fig. 9.

Category	Sub-Category	Criteria	Description
Learning	Agile	[Online test] Agile	Agile concepts tested via online test
	Design Pattern	[Online test] Design Pattern	Design pattern knowledge tested via online test
	Architecture Pattern	[Online test] Architecture Pattern	Architecture pattern knowledge tested via online test
	Document Management	[Online test] Documentation Components	Documentation components knowledge tested via online test
	Web-Application Technology	[Practical assignment] Web-Application Technology	Web Application technology to be tested via online test/assignment and practically applied as part of the project
Design	Solution Design Documentation	ERD	ERD is provided and accurately describes the data landscape
		Data Flow Diagram	Data flow diagram is present and accurately defines the flow of data between processes and agents, using the correct syntax
		Process Flow Diagram	Process flow diagram is present and accurate. It defines the flow of logic between the process and decision steps, using the correct syntax
		User Manual	User manual is present and appropriately defines how a user would use the system, with enough detail to show basic and core functions of the solution
Development	Infrastructure	Website Hosted on Cloud	The website should be accessible from any computer without having to compile and run the code on that computer
		File Storage Hosted on Cloud	The files should be stored on an online server or file storage mechanism that is secure. Files stored on a local computer and cannot be accessed from a different computer do not qualify as cloud storage
		Database Hosted on Cloud	The database should be accessible, through the site, from any computer without having the database created on that computer.

Fig. 8. Section of rubric categories, sub-categories, criteria and description

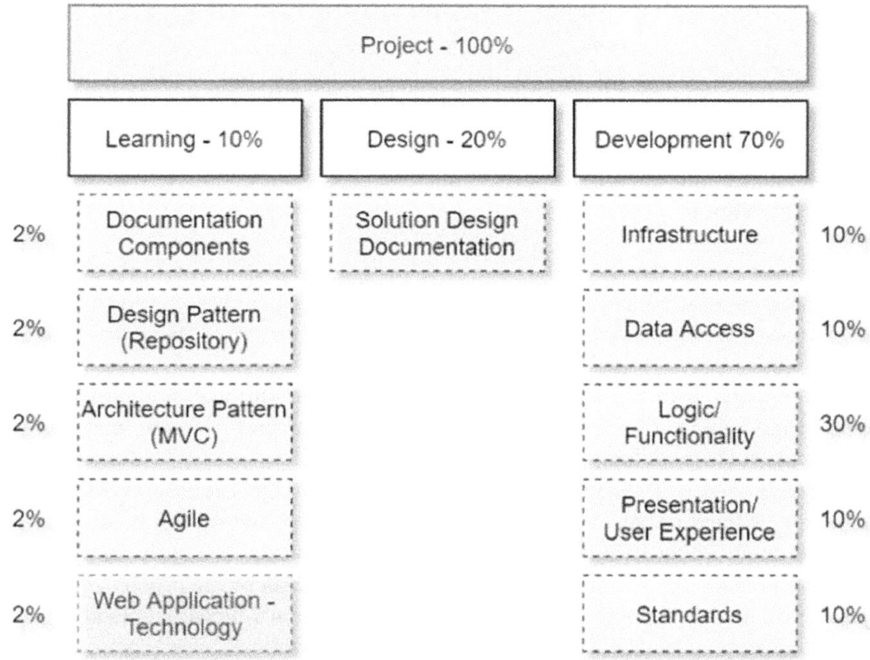

Fig. 9. Assigning weighting

Figure 10 elaborates further on the weightings defined in Fig. 9, with the binary indicator which impacts the overall mark. In a case where the weighting of a criteria is 2% and the binary indicator is '1', meaning that the criterion has been adequately fulfilled, the mark contribution increases by 2. In a case where the binary indicator is '0', meaning that the criterion has not been adequately fulfilled, the mark contribution does not increase.

Student Initials:	
Student Surname:	
Student Number:	
Examiner:	

Category	Sub-Category	Criteria	Description	Weight	Binary Indicator	Mark
Learning	Agile	[Online test] Agile	Agile concepts tested via online test	2%	1	2
	Design Pattern	[Online test] Design Pattern	Design pattern knowledge tested via online test	2%	0	0
	Architecture Pattern	[Online test] Architecture Pattern	Architecture pattern knowledge tested via online test	2%	0	0
	Document Management	[Online test] Documentation Components	Documentation components knowledge tested via online test	2%	1	2
	Web-Application Technology	[Practical assignment] Web-Application Technology	Web Application technology to be tested via online test/assignment and practically applied as part of the project	2%	1	2
Design	Solution Design Documentation	ERD	ERD is provided and accurately describes the data landscape	6%	1	6
		Data Flow Diagram	Data flow diagram is present and accurately defines the flow of data between processes and agents, using the correct syntax	4%	1	4
		Process Flow Diagram	Process flow diagram is present and accuratelt defines the flow of logic between the process and decision steps, using the correct syntax	6%	0	0
		User Manual	User manual is present and appropriately defines how a user would use the system, with enough detail to show basic and core functions of the solution	4%	1	4

Fig. 10. Section of the example weighted rubric

6 Future Work

In future iterations on this work the subjective nature of assessment criteria would need to be addressed and refined. The use of dialogistic studies could be used to formulate specific questions with very specific intent, suitable for binary assessment without any room for subjectivity.

The comparison of the approach with other, more traditional, ways of assessing students would also need to be taken into consideration as part of future work once the approach provides guidelines for less subjective criteria.

The rubrics will be expanded to consider assessment not just at the end of the project when students hand in their work at the end, but instead to measure success earlier on in projects as milestones are reached so that lecturers can establish early on when there are problems in students' abilities to meet the requirements of the project scope. This way a more data driven approach can be taken to assessment which could lead to a more dynamic teaching approach which will serve to address students' needs as soon as they become relevant.

Additionally, the binary nature of the rubric elements lend themselves to automation which could allow for some of the marking in project based work to be done using suitable automation tools. This way students don't need to wait for the lecturer to mark a batch of students' work and can instead submit partially completed work for assessment and get immediate feedback. Automating this process will also allow the lecturer to track the progress of students in real time rather than in batches.

Through the combined use of automation and analytics, this study has the potential to create a level of transparency, traceability, understanding and insight into students performance and the mapping to very specific outcomes (assessment, study unit and module).

7 Conclusion

The expectation of Computer Science, Information Systems and Information Technology degrees is that a student who completes and passes the degree has the knowledge and ability to execute on each of the module outcomes throughout the degree. These module outcomes are a rolled-up version of study unit and assessment outcomes. In the event that students cannot perform certain outcomes, feedback should be clear and immediate, which categorical and sliding scales tend to obfuscate. The use of binary scales to evaluate project-based assessments allows marking (or rubric) criteria to be specifically identified as fulfilled fully or not at all. The concept that forms the foundation of using binary scales to evaluate project-based assessments needs to be instilled in all elements of the assessment, from the conceptual formation of the scope through to the weighting and rubric assessment criteria. This approach to evaluating project-based assessments would lead to more effective, granular feedback to students that could be automated and implemented in such a way as to allow students to get feedback as they progress through their assignments rather than at the end when they have completed them leading to a more dynamic form of teaching.

Acknowledgement. The full scope of the hackathon, all data used and the template rubric for use in other projects can be obtained at https://github.com/JacquiM/The-Use-of-Binary-Scales-in-Rubrics-to-Evaluate-Computer-Science-Assessments.

References

da Alves, N.C., von Wangenheim, C.G., Hauck, J.C.R., Borgatto, A.F.: A large-scale evaluation of a rubric for the automatic assessment of algorithms and programming concepts. In: Proceedings of the 51st ACM Technical Symposium on Computer Science Education, pp. 556–562. Association for Computing Machinery, New York (2020)

Dawson, P.: Assessment rubrics: towards clearer and more replicable design, research and practice. Assess. Eval. High. Educ. **42**(3), 347–360 (2017)

Dimitrov, D.M.: An approach to scoring and equating tests with binary items: piloting with large-scale assessments. Educ. Psychol. Meas. **76**(6), 954–975 (2016)

Department of Basic Education: Curriculum Assessment Policy Statements (CAPS) (2021). https://www.education.gov.za/Curriculum/CurriculumAssessmentPolicyStatements(CAPS)/tabid/420/Default.aspx. Accessed 09 Feb 2022

Haghdoost, A.A.: Complexity of the socioeconomic status and its disparity as a determinant of health. Int. J. Prev. Med. **3**(2), 75–76 (2021)

Hevner, A.R.: A three cycle view of design science research. Scand. J. Inf. Syst. **19**(2), 1–6 (2007)

Hevner, A.R., March, S.T., Park, J.: Design science in information systems research. Manag. Inf. Syst. Q. **28**(1), 75–105 (2004)

Imbault, C., Shore, D., Kuperman, V.: Reliability of the sliding scale for collecting affective responses to words. Behav. Res. Methods **50**(6), 2399–2407 (2018). https://doi.org/10.3758/s13428-018-1016-9

Jones, D., Tadros, A.: Successful use of rubrics to assess student performance in capstone projects. In: 2010 Annual Conference & Exposition, pp. 15.1144.1–15.1144.8. ASEE, Louisville, Kentucky (2010)

Janse van Rensburg, J.T., Goede, R.: Reflecting on the use of project-based learning for 21st century competencies in an IT extended programme. In: Proceedings of the 10th Annual UNISA ISTE Conference on Mathematics, Science and Technology Education, pp. 76–84. UNISA (2019)

Lukka, K.: The constructive research approach. In: Case Study Research in Logistics. Publications of the Turku School of Economics and Business Administration, Series B, vol. 1, pp. 83–101 (2003)

Morolong, P.: Teachers' views on the challenges they experience when implementing the curriculum and assessment policy statement in the foundation phase. (Dissertation), Central University of Technology, Free State (2009)

Mustapha, A., Samsudin, N.A., Arbaiy, N., Mohamed, R., Hamid, I.R.: Generic assessment rubrics for computer programming courses. Turk. Online J. Educ. Technol. **15**(1), 53–68 (2016)

Novita, L.: The design of assessment instruments in English research. J. Engl. Educ. **3**(1), 27–30 (2017)

Park, H., Yan, X.: An investigation into rater performance with a holistic scale and a binary, analytic scale on an ESL writing placement test. Pap. Lang. Test. Assess. **8**(2), 34–64 (2019)

Simon, H.A.: The Sciences of the Artificial, 3rd edn. MIT Press, Cambridge (1996)

Plomp, T., Nieveen, N.M.: Educational Design Research, 1st edn. SLO, Enschede (2013)

Zano, K.: Exploring teachers' enactment of the Curriculum and Assessment Policy Statement (CAPS) in selected Free State Province schools. (Dissertation), UNISA, Pretoria (2015)

Teaching in Context

Guidelines for Introducing Learners to Computer Programming in a Developing Country

Jean H. Greyling(✉)

Department of Computing Sciences, Nelson Mandela University, Port Elizabeth, South Africa
Jean.Greyling@Mandela.ac.za

Abstract. The South African government has committed to the implementation of coding and robotics teaching in primary schools. This vision faces the challenge that 16,000 schools in the country do not have computer laboratories, and that most teachers are not trained to teach coding. To address this reality, the TANKS mobile app was developed at Nelson Mandela University in South Africa. It introduces introductory coding concepts without the need for a computer. The scope of the project has broadened since its initiation in 2017. Originally learners were introduced to the game, and each received a game pack. Currently coding kits with various additional resources are made available to schools, mostly after teachers are trained. Based on the evolvement of the project, generic guidelines for the introduction of computer programming in schools, are provided as the main contribution. These guidelines identify the tools to be used here, how to make the project financially sustainable, alternative methods to traditional teaching, as well as the role of training for this kind of coding instruction.

Keywords: Unplugged coding · Children coding · Coding tools · Disadvantaged schools

1 Introduction

The challenge of introducing learners to computer programming in South Africa is hampered by the harsh reality of its school landscape, where a reported 16,000 schools do not have computer laboratories [7, 32]. Furthermore, most of these schools are classified as "non-fee paying," which implies that they do not have the available budgets to spend on the installation of computer laboratories and the purchase of expensive equipment. It is estimated that, on average, it will cost one million rand per school to supply the 16,000 schools with internet-connected laboratories [7].

R. J. Barnett et al. (Eds.): SACLA 2022, CCIS 1664, pp. 75–90, 2022.
https://doi.org/10.1007/978-3-031-21076-1_5

Fig. 1. TANKS app

Robots that are often suggested as suitable for teaching coding can cost up to R7,000 each, with a maximum of only five to six learners effectively being able to interact with such a robot at one time. In addition to technological challenges, the staff members' skills at schools are a further challenge. Few teachers have adequate coding training to properly introduce learners to conventional coding languages such as HTML, Python, and Java. Although the Department of Basic Education has many training initiatives, it is argued that these are insufficient for training teachers to have the desired educational impact. A further challenge is the availability of staff with enough technical knowledge to maintain computer laboratories. The poorly managed, improperly functioning laboratories found at schools across South Africa are a stark reminder of this reality.

Considering the ongoing Fourth Industrial Revolution and the shortage of relevant skills in South Africa, its government is actively driving the introduction of coding and robotics in schools from Grade R onwards. An investigation of the published draft curricula shows a heavy reliance on the availability of computers, other technologies (e.g., robots, circuits), as well as teachers with a solid understanding of topics such as coding and electronics. While South Africa is generally described as a developing country, many of its citizens do in fact have access to the infrastructure of a modern developed country. This creates a significant challenge to the country: the danger of continuously widening the divide between the "haves" and the "have-nots." This digital divide will be addressed within this article. Any coding and robotics curricula implemented in South African schools that fail to take into consideration the above-mentioned realities will be in danger of actively widening the digital divide found among schools and learners in the country.

This article aims to find answers to the challenge of introducing learners to computer programming in a developing country by reporting on the rollout of the TANKS tangible coding app (Sect. 2), and how it evolved into a broader unplugged coding project (Sect. 3). Insights obtained from the four stages involved contribute to the provision of general guidelines (Sect. 4). Section 5 provides conclusions and future research.

2 The TANKS Coding App

The TANKS coding app was developed as an honors project at the department of computing sciences at Nelson Mandela University [2]. As shown in Fig. 1, it makes use of physical "tokens" that learners' piece together to build code without a computer. Mobile devices are needed (ideally 8 per class of 40), which are considerably less expensive than a 40 PC laboratory.

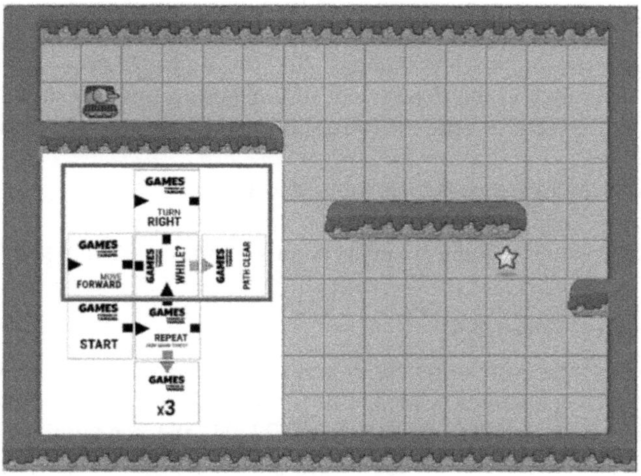

Fig. 2. Level 15 with solution

The user is given a challenge on the screen of a mobile device where a tank needs to move to a destination with obstacles in its way. The physical tokens are then used to compile the instructions to the tank, after which a photo is taken of the tokens. Using image recognition, the instructions are internalized, and then executed by moving the tank. There are 35 levels of increasing complexity. As learners progress through the levels, different coding concepts normally taught in an introductory programming module are introduced.

Various physical tokens were designed representing essential actions, including basic coding concepts. The basic tokens are used to move the tank forward and backwards and turn the tank to the left and the right. Furthermore, there are tokens that support looping (repeat) constructs such as the "for" loop and the "while" loop, as well as a conditional coding construct ("if" statement). Complexity of the challenges is increased as looping and "if" constructs are introduced, followed by nested constructs. See Fig. 2 showing Level 15 which uses nested constructs – a "while" loop within a "repeat" loop. Identifiable markers (like QR codes) are placed on each token to allow for image recognition. The game is preferably played in workshops where learners participate in groups. Its gamification concept creates an exciting, fun atmosphere. Section 3.1 provides the theoretical background behind the design of TANKS and is part of a discussion of the four stages involved in rolling out a broader unplugged coding project.

3 Stages in Rolling out the Unplugged Coding Project

With the ultimate goal to provide generic guidelines (Sect. 4), the development of the unplugged coding project from the initial implementation of the TANKS mobile app, its rollout, the extension of tools, and teacher training are discussed in this section.

3.1 Implementation of TANKS

TANKS was initially proposed in January 2017 by Byron Batteson [2] as part of his honors research project at the department of computing sciences at Nelson Mandela University. Three objectives were identified during the design phase of the project:

- apply sound pedagogical principles to the development of a coding game;
- be cost effective; and
- introduce introductory coding concepts mainly to primary school learners.

3.1.1 Pedagogical Principles

From the outset of the design process, it was decided that the features of the game as well as the targeted age groups needed to be founded upon sound principles. According to Piaget's theory of cognitive development [23–25] the *concrete operational stage* spanning the ages of seven to eleven years old is when children begin to perform mental operations such as problem-solving and arithmetic. The next stage of development is referred to as the *formal operational stage* around the ages of eleven or twelve years old when children can hypothesize different solutions to the same problem. Based on this, it was decided to set the target ages for the project at eight to twelve years of age.

A form of educational instruction called *scaffolding* is based on Vygotsky's theory and concept of the *zone of proximal development* [33]. This refers to the difference between a child's ability to learn when they receive guided supervision versus receiving no help at all. Scaffolding indicates that, although a child should receive supervision when learning, it should not be more than necessary. Scaffolding can be implemented by e.g., introducing levels of complexity to a game.

David, Triona and Williams [9] stated that a *hands-on* approach to learning could inform cognitive development via kinesthetic involvement, i.e. a transition from something concrete to something abstract. Rogers, Scaife, Gabrielli, Smith and Harris [29] suggested that allowing children to use mixed realities (virtual or physical tools) within the context of play and learning allow for uncharacteristically extended interest and reflection. This extended interest would be key to an introduction to programming concepts. Making use of tangible tokens as part of TANKS is supported by these learning theories. Marshall [20] also stated that tangible programming may increase collaboration between children, with learning on a single desktop with a mouse and keyboard resulting in one or two children taking control of the application while others may only observe.

With these ideas in mind, it was decided that the games developed needed to include the features of problem solving (intrinsic to coding), scaffolding (levels of increasing complexity), physical interaction, and group work. Physical interaction could imply the use of robots, or the concept of tangible programming, where physical components are used to compile a set of instructions.

3.1.2 Evaluation of Extant Systems

Five different extant systems were investigated and evaluated based on the pedagogical principles identified above, their cost effectiveness, and how they relate to the introduction of coding concepts.

Logo and Lego MINDSTORMS. Seymour Papert [22] developed the Logo programming language for children in 1967, and in 1985 he began a collaboration with the Lego company to create Lego MINDSTORMS. Lego MINDSTORMS satisfies the objectives of applying pedagogical principles as well as introducing coding concepts, but is unfortunately not cost effective (see introduction of Sect. 3.1).

Algoblocs. Algoblocs is a programming instruction system [30] where large electrical components connect to each other, creating a set of logical steps that allow a computer program to operate. It has controls more closely related to typical programming languages and supports a collaborative learning experience. However, it is expensive due to its use of electronic components, and how it requires a computer to run its programs.

Tern. Tern was introduced in 2007 [16] as an inexpensive coding tool that uses wood blocks the learner connects to form a program. An image is captured with a webcam from either a computer or a laptop, and the program is interpreted and executed within a virtual environment. The primary disadvantage of Tern is that it is a computer-based solution requiring a webcam.

Scratch. Scratch is a visual programming tool that was released in 2007 [28]. Scratch uses visual coding blocks on a screen to create an animation, game, or simulation. It is a vastly more powerful tool than most tangible programming systems. However, it requires a computer and does not encourage group work.

Sheets. Sheets is a promising tangible programming system developed by Tada & Tanaka [31]. It utilizes printable paper-based command objects instead of the typical command blocks and is thus a more inexpensive successor to Tern. Sheets programs are also interpreted by a computer via a webcam, requiring the need for a computer.

After evaluation of these extant systems, it was decided that the TANKS game would contain the following features:

- Allow for the construction of code, including basic introductory coding concepts such as decision making, loops, and nested constructs;
- Make use of printable tokens to construct the code; and
- Apply image recognition in a mobile application that would internalise the tangible code that would then be executed on a standard smart phone.

Since smart phones are generally available to and owned by teachers and learners, it was concluded that this would be a cost-effective way to introduce basic coding concepts without the use of desktop or laptop computers. The printable tokens would support group work. To support problem solving and scaffold learning, the game would need to have levels of increasing complexity which would add an additional feature of gamification.

3.2 Game Rollout

By the end of the research project, the TANKS game was ready to be rolled out to schools to introduce learners to computing concepts. The game's usefulness and financial sustainability were critical for this to become a reality.

3.2.1 Usefulness

To determine the usefulness of the app, nine participants took part in a formal user evaluation [2]. The results showed that all participants successfully completed the sequence-oriented levels, but were not comfortable transitioning to the more advanced tokens. Many of the participants struggled with the interpretation of the "turn left" and "turn right" command tokens, as well as whether the command was relative to their perspective or the tank's perspective. Another common concern was the direction of the arrows on the "move forwards" and "move backwards" command tokens; these had to be adapted to become less ambiguous.

Some of the participants found capturing the image of the command token sequence to be unreliable, especially among low light, multiple lights, or surfaces giving off a glare. Overall, all participants found the game enjoyable and challenging.

As a result of this initial evaluation, some of the features of the application as well as the design of the physical tokens were improved. In other cases, it was noted that certain information would need to be explained prior to starting a TANKS workshop. Some of the most important aspects included creating a correct environment (e.g. background surface and lighting), taking proper smartphone photos (e.g. distance from the tokens, keeping the smartphone vertical and stable), as well as explaining the meaning of the basic commands and how they interacted with the tank in the game itself.

3.2.2 Financial Sustainability

It was decided at the outset that the business model would mainly identify corporate sponsors, whose funding would allow for the free distribution of the games to deserving learners. This made it critical to get corporations on board to buy into the vision. In their relational framework of cause drivers for crowdfunding, Haasbroek and Ungerer [15] identify motivating factors such as making a difference, serving the greater good, and believing in the respective cause.

The first two years were used to reach as many learners as possible through direct workshops, while building up a storyline that would be attractive to media platforms. Having stories to tell and getting them told to the public became the main currency of the project during this stage. The stories told about learners enjoying the game in workshops, and the positive energy which was created regarding coding and solving problems. It was also important to show that learners from all kinds of communities were participating – especially those from disadvantaged townships and remote villages. Along with the excitement about programming came the additional educational aspects such as group work, problem solving, communication, strategizing, and dealing with mistakes.

Getting these stories told was critical for generating buy-in from corporate sponsors as well as the public. A wide range of media was utilized throughout the project. It was important to build up a positive relationship with journalists in the traditional media (print, radio, and television), and be in-tune about which stories would work for which media. Social media (Facebook and LinkedIn) became the most successful tools for giving the project momentum in the public space. LinkedIn was found to be the most effective channel for the more formal recruitment of sponsors. A valuable instrument became publishing own articles on LinkedIn, which provided more content than simple posts. While social media posts received more feedback than coverage in traditional media, traditional media is still viewed as more credible, which is why reposting traditional media coverage on social media was used as an additional strategy.

The best-accepted stories were those indicating the high quantities of learners that could be reached in schools without computers [35]; those about individuals that responded positively, and who achieved new dreams for their lives [13, 14]; as well as individuals and school teams that successfully participated in coding tournaments [19].

Although a positive public image is important for corporate sponsors, it was also important to address their more formal business expectations within this project. To do this, a partnership was formed with the Leva Foundation (a registered NPO) that could provide official Section 18A Tax Deduction Certificates for those contributing to these kinds of projects. Furthermore, documentation regarding the fact that mainly disadvantaged communities were reached was also important in terms of companies' BEE scorecards. Attempts were also made to tap into companies' skills and enterprise development CSI funding, albeit not with much success since TANKS programs to date have yet to be officially accredited.

3.2.3 Reflection

By the end of 2019, TANKS workshops had been presented to over 20,000 learners in all nine South African provinces. This was made possible through increasing buy-in from sponsors as well as the training of workshop facilitators in different regions. One of the highlights included a sponsored project in five provinces which culminated in a national event with 100 learners from 20 schools at the Sandton Convention Centre.

As part of Africa Code Week, over 70 facilitators were used in October 2019 to reach 11,000 learners in the Nelson Mandela Bay Municipality [35].

In addition to building relationships with sponsoring and media partners, the role of implementation partners became apparent. The Africa Code Week project was a partnership with a local company as well as the Nelson Mandela Bay Science & Technology Centre in Kariega [17]. Other implementation partners included the Govan Mbeki Mathematics Development Centre at the Nelson Mandela University, as well as Johannesburg libraries [27].

Although this rollout stage was successful in many aspects, as discussed in this section, challenges were also identified. Contrary to expectations, many learners, especially in rural settings, did not have phones that were modern enough play the TANKS game. Consequently, it was realized that many of the games distributed were not used at all. It thus became clear that corporate sponsorships were not well-utilized. A decision was therefore made to start focusing on schools, which resulted in the compilation of a set of tools in addition to the TANKS game.

3.3 Expanding the Project

The initial stage of interacting directly with learners was successful in giving momentum to the project, and simultaneously created challenges regarding its impact. The schools' focus necessitated the expansion of what we offered in the form of coding kits. Teachers for instance were interested in more than just a game and wanted something more formal that would effectively fit into or complement a curriculum. In addition to programming, a need was also identified to introduce computational thinking activities. And since coding is not yet officially part of their curricula, alternative ways of incorporating coding had to be explored.

3.3.1 Coding Kits

The first obvious need was for the compilation of a comprehensive TANKS coding kit that would empower teachers to introduce learners to coding. The main components of this kit are lesson plans, instructional videos on how to play the game, a solution set for the levels, and printed levels.

For the development of the set of seven lessons that could be used by teachers in class, the technology teacher Ms. Kelly Bush was approached to develop lessons that consecutively map onto every five levels in the game [3]. The following coding concepts are progressively covered here: sequential movement commands, "for" and "while" loops, optimizing code, and "if" statement decision making. Real life scenarios and physical activities are used in each lesson to introduce the different coding concepts to learners before they interact with the game.

The initial idea was that coding kits would be distributed to schools following a coding workshop attended by learners and teachers at the school. It was soon recognized that these workshops were not adequate to guide teachers through the more complex levels of the game, even though the concepts were also discussed in the lessons. In turn, eleven short instructional videos were compiled that not only introduced concepts to teachers and learners, but also assisted with issues such as troubleshooting when playing, as well as how to organize a workshop. A further important feature of the videos was that they be small enough to send via WhatsApp to learners or parents requesting them.

It was noticed during the roll-out phase that, with some of the solutions that learners came up with, although they solved a problem, they were not examples of good coding. Consequently, a compendium of suggested solutions was provided for teachers to guide learners.

A coding kit typically allows for eight groups of five learners in a class to interact with the game. In a scenario where eight phones are not available, printouts of the 35 levels are provided to the groups. They build their solutions with the tokens, with the handful of "roaming" phones in the classroom used to evaluate the solutions and provide feedback. A further advantage of providing printed levels is that teachers can better check/count how many levels are completed per lesson.

3.3.2 Computational Thinking Activities

The term "computational thinking" was first applied by Seymour Papert, and later popularized by Jeanette Wing [22, 34]. Wing described it as the thought process involved in formulating problems and their solutions. It is generally accepted that any introductory coding module at the school level should include computational thinking exercises and activities.

There are numerous resources for computational thinking exercises [12, 18, 21] which are of great value to teachers. Some of them include Code.org, CS Unplugged, and the IITPSA's Computer Olympiad. As an additional tool for the coding kits, Keith Gibson from Collegiate Girls' High School in Gqeberha developed a compendium of 40 computational thinking activities [10, 11]. This compendium is a work in progress, and more activities will continuously be added. Kelly Bush also developed a compendium of similar activities for Foundation Phase learners [5, 6].

3.3.3 Alternative Ways of Incorporating Coding

The Department of Basic Education [10] currently envisions the implementation of coding and robotics in primary schools from grade R upwards. Draft curricula were published for this in March 2021, with specific schools identified as pilot schools. This will however only become official at the earliest in 2024. Although many teachers are optimistic about the idea of incorporating coding at school, coding activities often do not occur due to the reality of other formal subjects having higher educational priority. There are several alternative options being experimented to address the lack of time for this topic during normal school hours:

Incorporating Coding into Other Subjects. In support of previous observations by educators [8], many teachers have provided feedback regarding the relevance of coding activities regarding other curriculum content. For Foundation Phase teachers, because coding is related to spatial orientation, it becomes natural to incorporate these spatial activities into teaching on concepts such as left, right, below, on top, etc. Coding is often introduced as a list of instructions which can easily contribute to lessons related to verbal communication. Teachers of older learners report that they have used coding concepts as part of mathematics lessons with positive results.

Coding Clubs. Learners voluntarily participate in other sports or cultural activities at school. Coding clubs typically take place after school, during breaks, or on weekends [13, 14]. Encouraging feedback has been received by clubs, and described as learner-driven, with the learners watching the instructional videos while they progress through the coding levels. There have also been examples of coding clubs organized by NGOs that, although not directly linked to schools, have also been successful in reaching learners.

Coding Evangelists. Teachers are often overburdened and have neither the time nor the energy to teach extracurricular coding. In certain communities it has been observed that young people (not formal staff members) introduce learners to the TANKS coding project after receiving training in how to use the game. These individuals are either compensated by the school or are part of an industry- sponsored outreach. In addition to providing a service to the school's learners, this coding evangelist concept has great potential when it comes to employment opportunities for young people.

Coding Tournaments. Because the TANKS game was designed with levels of increasing complexity, it lends itself perfectly to competitive tournaments. This principle of gamification feeds into some learners' natural competitive nature, and results in them taking control of the learning process [3]. Various tournaments have taken place regionally and nationally with great success [28]. In preparing for these tournaments, participating teams put extensive effort into finding solutions to the challenges they will encounter in their competition.

Virtual Tournaments. Due to the sometimes difficult and expensive logistics of getting teams to a shared venue, the concept of virtual tournaments is being explored, most notably considering the increased travel obstacles during the COVID-19 pandemic. The BOATS coding app, developed by the same team that produced TANKS, was adapted for learners to interact on the app from anywhere, while scores are submitted to a central database. Several virtual tournaments have taken place, with over 1,000 learners from a few hundred schools participating [19]. A current work in progress is an honors research project involving a platform that will support virtual coding tournaments for the TANKS game [1].

3.3.4 Reflection

The above-mentioned approaches have all contributed to TANKS' impact, helping it evolve into a broader-based initiative. It has now taken on the characteristics of an unplugged coding movement throughout the country. This is an umbrella term referring to any methods used to introduce learners to coding without the use of computers. Since TANKS uses only mobile phones, we take the liberty of including it under this term. In addition to TANKS, various physical, pen-and-paper, and computational thinking activities are available to teachers. Despite the extensive efforts taken here including clear lesson plans, instructional videos, and launch workshops, there were still teachers who unfortunately did not have the confidence to start this kind of project at their respective schools. This made it clear that additional training was needed.

3.4 Teacher Training

The training of teachers was implemented in 2021 over three phases: introduction to unplugged coding, physical workshops throughout the country, followed by repeating the content of the physical workshops via four online sessions. For all training activities, the assumption was made that teachers had no prior coding-related training or experience. These training interventions formed part of an international collaboration between academics from South Africa, Namibia, Mozambique, and Germany under the broader topic of resilient communities. The collaboration was referred to as the YEEES project, which was sponsored by the German Academic Exchange Service (DAAD) and the German Federal Ministry of Education and Research [36].

3.4.1 Introduction to Unplugged Coding

Acknowledging that the concept of unplugged coding is unknown to educators in South Africa, a series of online workshops was presented by educators who are actively involved in using these techniques. The topics of the workshops included:

- Laying good foundations – coding concepts in the early years [4];
- Unplugged coding tools [18];
- The need for computational thinking skills in the teaching and learning of coding [21]; and
- Developing problem solving skills informally [11].

Over 500 educators registered for the workshops that were presented over four weeks.

3.4.2 Physical Workshops on Unplugged Coding Activities

As a direct result of the four online workshops, requests from educators were for physical workshops where they could be practically introduced to the various activities referred to in the initial workshops. Here, 12 workshops were presented across South Africa and Namibia, and attended by nearly 200 educators. The main topics that were covered within four hours were:

- What is coding – introduced by practical activities;
- The importance of computational thinking activities; and
- Using the TANKS coding app to introduce different coding concepts.

Of the 192 people that attended, 105 were teachers, 49 were NGO workers, 28 were staff of the Department of Basic Education, and 10 were academics from universities. The attendance of Basic Education staff was relevant considering how the draft curricula for Coding and Robotics for Primary Schools was published during this period.

From the 58 participants who responded to a survey, the following responses were given as reasons why coding was not offered in their schools: no computer, no trained teachers, not in the curriculum and not enough time in the day. All the responses were positive (100%) regarding the usefulness of the workshops. The comments included aspects such as: coding was demystified, realization that technology was not needed, provided self-confidence to start with something, and realizing that their learners would enjoy the activities. These responses provide confirmation that the project was achieving the original objectives of the TANKS app: introduce computer programming in schools without computers, in a cost-effective way, and as a fun activity.

3.4.3 Online Workshops on Unplugged Coding Activities

Due to limited resources and time, the same content from the physical workshops was presented over four online workshops, with around 100 educators attending. All participants received the physical TANKS tokens in advance, along with electronic documents that were needed for some of the other activities. These online workshops expanded their potential reach, and opened doors for similar online workshops on various other platforms.

3.4.4 Reflection

While most participants had no prior coding experience, those attending the unplugged coding workshops found them useful. For the larger project, these workshops proved invaluable in motivating educators to get started with this kind of project by removing many of the perceived stumbling blocks. A challenge that remained for some of the delegates was the lack of time in their school day. Within the context of COVID-19 regulations, and some learners not being at school all week, this was unfortunately one of the realities we could not effectively address.

4 Guidelines

This section uses the experiences gained since 2017 (as discussed in Sect. 3) to present guidelines for introducing learners to computer programming in a developing country.

In the years since 2017, this TANKS unplugged coding project has evolved to entail more than a simple game. It continues to be supported by a successful financial model and is accompanied by effective training methods.

Rolled out in South Africa, this project is of significance for any developing country wanting to introduce its learners to coding. We provide guidelines regarding tools on how to use it and overcome any challenges that arise, alternative methods for its application, finances, and training.

4.1 Tools

Most developing countries face the reality that many of their schools lack computer laboratories, and simply lack the budgets to purchase expensive equipment such as robots. This means that the tools that are available cannot rely on access to computers or other equipment that is not readily available. It is assumed that schools and teachers do in fact have access to mobile phones. And learning activities can furthermore be supplemented by physical activities involving objects found in any classroom, as well as pen-and-paper activities.

In addition to being cost effective, tools need to apply pedagogical education principles such as problem solving, scaffolding, physical interaction, and group activities (see above). It should also be fun for the learners, taking advantage of gamification thinking [3].

Since teachers are used to formal curriculum-related activities, it is important to provide well-structured lesson plans involving the above-mentioned activities which interact with the tools provided. These lesson plans can be supplemented by short instructional videos related to their use.

Coding relies on the ability to solve problems, which means that computational thinking activities need to be provided to teachers, or they alternatively need to be directed to internet sources where these activities can be found.

4.2 Alternative Methods

Coding can often not be included in the official curricula of schools in developing countries, as a result creating the challenge of finding enough time to spend on coding during a normal school day. The first innovative way to address this is to find a relationship between coding and other curriculum content and incorporate coding into this instead. As an alternative, coding could be viewed in the same manner as sports and cultural activities, with the establishment e.g. of after-school coding clubs.

To relieve teachers from an already full schedule, coding evangelists (who are not part of staff) might represent an effective option and could rotate among schools. A further advantage of these evangelists would be the creation of employment for youth from local communities. A way to make coding activities exciting and encourage learners to participate would be to arrange coding tournaments for schools in the region [26]. Platforms allowing for virtual tournaments could extend their scope.

4.3 Training

Although the tools provided should always be as user-friendly and intuitive as possible, it needs to be acknowledged that most teachers are expected to introduce learners to concepts about which they have no prior knowledge. The concept of coding may be foreign to them, accompanied by a lack of technology to teach it in the first place, resulting in them having little confidence in even considering getting involved.

Training is required here, in either physical or online form. This training cannot assume any prior coding knowledge and must be interactive, with the teachers themselves having a positive, fun experience during the training. Presenters of the training must guard against making training too theoretical or making the teachers even more apprehensive by setting unreasonable goals.

4.4 Funding

It can generally be accepted that the schools most typically benefitting from the project will be those with limited financial resources. This means that the project's necessary tools and training must be made available to these schools at costs that are as low as possible. On the other hand, for the project to be sustainable over a long period, it needs to have finances available to develop new resources, maintain current tools, and provide quality assistance that includes training and mentoring.

For this model to be effective, the drivers of the project need to initiate and maintain healthy partnerships with corporate sponsors and their corporate social investment budgets. Sponsors finding value in this support means that they will need/look for stories that prove they are making a difference. The effective use of media is essential in achieving this, whether this is traditional media or social media platforms. A third key partnership category includes implementation partners. These include schools and other entities that could make effective use of sponsorship. On a practical level, it is important for companies to obtain tax benefits from their efforts while improving their social impact scorecards. The project as a result should preferably be driven by a registered non-profit organisation.

5 Conclusions and Future Research

Many schools in developing countries have inadequate resources to address today's challenges. One of these includes preparing learners for the job market of Fourth Industrial Revolution. In South Africa, the government is driving the introduction of coding and robotics in all schools. The problem with this vision is that most schools do not have computer laboratories, and most teachers have no prior coding training. This reality in South Africa was the motivation for the development of unplugged coding concepts.

This paper reported on the TANKS unplugged coding project that was successfully rolled out in South Africa starting in 2017. From experiences gained during this rollout, generic guidelines covering the categories of tools used, finances, alternative methods, and training have been provided. Given the focus of introducing learners to coding, it is not planned to implement further coding concepts. Developing a "tournament app" which allows for the creation of new levels will be a great improvement. Further research could investigate the longer-term effects on educational outputs and teacher training identified over the course of time. The guidelines for the introduction of computer programming in schools in developing countries could contribute to helping achieve low-cost coding training within resource-limited contexts having limited available technology. Progress in this realm could make important contributions towards preparing youth for the challenges of the Fourth Industrial Revolution.

Future research will include the process of upscaling the project by reaching all the schools in South Africa. Furthermore, the steps needed to rollout the project in different countries across Africa need to be investigated through different case studies.

References

1. Adams, T.: An Investigation into the Facilitation of a Coding Tournament Across Different Venues, Using TANKS as a Case Study. Honours Treatise, Nelson Mandela University (2021)
2. Batteson, B.: Investigation and Development of an Inexpensive Educational Tool Suite for an Introduction to Programming. Honours Treatise, Nelson Mandela University (2017)

3. Buljan, M.: Gamification for Learning: Strategies and Examples (2021). www.elearningindustry.com. Accessed 4 Aug 2022
4. Bush, K.: TANKS Lesson Plans. Hudson Park Primary School, East London (2019)
5. Bush, K.: Laying good foundations – coding concepts in the early years. CODING UNPLUGGED Series, 3 February 2021 (2021a). www.yeees-project.org. Accessed 1 Mar 2021
6. Bush, K.: Computational Thinking Lesson Ideas. Hudson Park Primary School, East London (2021b)
7. BusinessTech: Here's how many South African schools don't have the internet or a computer lab – and what it will cost to fix the problem, 18 July 2018 (2018)
8. Catapult Learning: Why All Students Should Learn How to Code in Elementary School (2016). https://catapultlearning.com/2016/09/29/students-learn-code-elementary-school/. Accessed 3 Aug 2021
9. David, K., Triona, L.M., Williams, C.: Hands on what? The relative effectiveness of physical versus virtual materials in an engineering design project by middle school children. Cognition **43**(2), 1086–1109 (2006)
10. Department of Basic Education: Proposed Ammendment to the Curriculum and Assessment Policy Statement (CAPS) to make provision for Coding and Robotics Grades R to 9 (2021). https://www.education.gov.za. Accessed 3 Aug 2021
11. Gibson, K.: Developing Problem Solving Skills Informally. CODING UNPLUGGED Series, 24 February 2021 (2021a). www.yeees-project.org. Accessed 1 Mar 2021
12. Gibson, K.: Fun Computational Thinking. Collegiate Girls' High, Gqeberha (2021b)
13. Greyling, J.: Expanding Career Horizons in Rural Eastern Cape. Published on LinkedIn, December 2020 (2020a)
14. Greyling, J.: From TANKS in Grade 7 .. to a Computer Science PhD in the Future, March 2022 (2022)
15. Haasbroek, F., Ungerer, M.: Theory versus practise: assessing reward-based crowdfunding theory through a South African case study. South Afr. J. Bus. Manag. (2020)
16. Horn, M.: Tangible Programming in the Class with Tern (2007)
17. Kuli, S., Greyling, J., Stubbs, M.: TANKS and BOATS coding apps – indigenous tools bring coding and robotics to learners in disadvantaged school. In: SAASTEC Conferences, George, November 2019 (2019)
18. Makoena, S.: Unplugged coding tools. CODING UNPLUGGED Series, 10 February 2021 (2021). www.yeees-project.org. Accessed 1 Mar 2021
19. Malonde, Z.: Eastern Cape Pupils Shine in Coding Contest. The Herald, 29 July 2020 (2020)
20. Marshall, P.: Do tangible interfaces enhance learning? TEI **2007**, 163–170 (2007)
21. Oosthuizen, L.: The need for computational thinking skills in the teaching and learning of coding. CODING UNPLUGGED Series, 17 February 2021 (2021). www.yeees-project.org. Accessed 1 Mar 2021
22. Papert, S.: Mindstorms: children, computers and powerful ideas (1980). https://doi.org/10.1017/CBO9781107415324.004
23. Piaget, J.: The Origins of Intelligence in Children. New York: International Universties Press (1952a)
24. Piaget, J.: When thinking begins. In: The Origins of Intelligence in Children, pp. 25–36. International Universties Press, New York (1952b)
25. Piaget, J.: Intellectual evolution from adolescence to adulthood. Hum. Dev. **15**(1), 1–12 (1972)
26. Preller, C.: Coding ignites Madiba magic (2022). https://www.linkedin.com/pulse/coding-ignites-madiba-magic-jean-greyling. Accessed 4 Aug 2022
27. Sun, R.: City of Johannesburg celebrates coding by awarding skilled learners. Randburg Sun, 24 October 2019 (2019)

28. Resnick, M., et al.: Scratch: programming for all. Commun. ACM **52**(11), 60–67 (2009)
29. Rogers, Y., Scaife, M., Gabrielli, S., Smith, H., Harris, E.: A conceptual framework for mixed reality environments: designing novel learning activities for young children. Presence: Teleoper. Virt. Environ. **11**(6), 677–686 (2002)
30. Suzuki, H., Kato, H.: AlgoBlock: a tangible programming language, a tool for collaborative learning. In: Proceedings of 4th European Logo Conference, June 2016, pp. 297–303 (1993)
31. Tada, K., Tanaka, J.: Tangible programming environment using paper cards as command objects. Proc. Manuf. **3**(AHFE), 5482–5489 (2015). https://doi.org/10.1016/j.promfg.2015.07.693
32. The Conversation: Coding in South African schools: what needs to happen to make it work, 31 July 2019 (2019)
33. Vygotsky, L.S.: Play and its role in the mental development of the child. Sov. Psychol. **5**(3), 6–18 (1967)
34. Wing, J.: Computational thinking. Commun. ACM (CACM) **49**(3), 33–35 (2006). https://doi.org/10.1145/1118178.1118215
35. Willemse, N.: Coding without computers reaches thousands of learners. Mail and Guardian, 22 November 2019 (2019)
36. YEEES: Yields of Evocative Entrepreneurial Approaches on Environment and Society (2021). https://yeees-project.org/

First-Year Students' IT Career Awareness

Malibongwe Twani[1], Andre P. Calitz[1(✉)], and Margaret Cullen[2]

[1] Department of Computing Sciences, Nelson Mandela University, Port Elizabeth, South Africa
{Malibongwe.Twani,Andre.Calitz}@Mandela.ac.za
[2] Business School, Nelson Mandela University, Port Elizabeth, South Africa
Margaret.Cullen@Mandela.ac.za

Abstract. The demand for Information Technology (IT) professionals has increased globally and has impacted the South African IT labour market. The IT skills in high demand include positions such as Software Developers, Data Scientists and Business Analysts. The choice of a career is usually made by a scholar early on in secondary school and various factors influence their career choice. Creating IT career awareness is important so that scholars understand the various IT career paths. First-year students have generally made a career choice and should be aware of the different job descriptions and job titles in industry. This study examined first-year IT and non-IT students' career awareness as a factor that influences first-year students choosing IT careers at the Nelson Mandela University in South Africa. A survey was completed by 405 first-year students and the data were statistically analysed, including Exploratory Factor Analysis. The results indicated that IT students were more aware of their careers prior to university enrolment than non-IT students and students over the age of 21 showed a better understanding of careers than students aged 21 years and younger. The results further indicated differences in the understanding of the job titles and job descriptions between respondents speaking different home languages. Finally, the paper presents recommendations for intervention strategies to create IT career awareness amongst scholars.

Keywords: Career awareness · Computing skills · IT and non-IT students · Career choice

1 Introduction

Heleta and Bagus [1] reason that through knowledge production and skill development, education may contribute to sustainable development and the execution of the United Nations General Assembly's Sustainable Development Goals (SDGs). However, over the past decade, one of the greatest difficulties facing the world, as well as the government of South Africa (SA), has been a skills shortage, particularly in the Information Technology (IT) sector [2]. The Fourth Industrial Revolution (4IR) is transforming the way businesses run their operations to ensure sustainability [3]. Additionally, the 4IR is driving digital skills requirements, which result in South Africa focusing on improving education and IT skills, to address the skills shortage in this sector.

R. J. Barnett et al. (Eds.): SACLA 2022, CCIS 1664, pp. 91–107, 2022.
https://doi.org/10.1007/978-3-031-21076-1_6

In South Africa, Kirlidog et al. [4] state that the IT skills shortage has resulted in the Department of Higher Education and Training's (DHET) interest in increasing enrolments in the fields leading to more students pursuing IT careers. Additionally, IT has been identified by the South African Government as the key focus for skills development and they aim to increase IT enrolments nationally. Lyon et al. [5] further add that emphasis on increasing the number of graduates can address the ongoing IT skills shortage.

Knowing what motivates scholars to pursue an IT career can assist with career awareness and recruitment, which could alleviate the IT skills shortage in South Africa [6]. Research instruments, such as the Academic Career Awareness Scale and Academic Career Interest Scale are used to measure career awareness at the tertiary education level [7]. In a study, conducted in Turkey amongst 3, 696 students from 3rd year and 4th-year undergraduates, using the abovementioned two scales, Dagyar et al. [7] found that their level of academic career awareness was low.

Other countries have seen an increase in the enrolment of students in academic institutions pursuing IT careers [8]. Several studies have shown that numerous factors influence the rate of enrolments in IT programmes namely, IT career awareness, perceptions of IT careers, gender, culture and salaries [9, 10, 13]. Parents and teachers generally do not encourage children to pursue a career in IT because of their limited knowledge of IT careers [14].

In addressing the shortage of IT professionals, this study aims to understand the IT career awareness amongst first-year students who are currently enrolled for IT (BSc CS, BSc CS&IS, BIT, NDip IT and NH Cert: IT) and non-IT (Accounting Sciences, Finance, Management, Economics) courses at the Nelson Mandela University. The layout of the paper includes a literature review (Sect. 2), followed by the research design and methodology (Sect. 3). The results are presented in Sect. 4 and Sect. 5 discusses the research findings. The conclusions and future research are presented in Sect. 6.

2 Literature Review

The global shortage of educated workers to fill jobs requiring IT skills has become a critical concern globally [5, 15]. The demand for IT skills remains unprecedented and is rising as the industry struggles to find skilled professionals to drive the demands of the transition to the 4IR and the digital economy [15]. BusinessTech [3] reported in February 2021 that, despite a small decline in the trend of businesses hiring software developers, there is still a high demand for IT skilled professionals in South Africa. Furthermore, when the supply and demand for IT jobs were compared, there remains a high demand for IT professionals.

A child's career awareness and interest vary according to knowledge and interests [16]. Children today are increasingly focused on achieving excellence in education, however, they are uncertain about the career they want to pursue [11, 16]. An incomplete understanding of the discipline or career can influence a child's career choices [17]. Limited awareness of IT careers further impacts prospective career seekers' decisions in choosing a career in IT [14].

Career awareness is the process of knowing and understanding what various career paths or career options are available to a person, based on their interest. Career awareness assists a young person to know what knowledge, training and skills they must learn and acquire to achieve success in their chosen career. Research instruments, such as the Academic Career Awareness Scale and the Academic Career Interest Scale have been used by Dagyar et al. [7] who found that under-graduate students from Akdeniz University in Turkey, had low academic career awareness, however, their level of academic career interest was above average.

2.1 IT Career Awareness

Kirlidog and Coetzee [4] allude to ignorance and lack of information on IT careers as a reason for students not enrolling for IT-related careers. Awareness can be increased through exposure and support that can provide a broader picture of IT indicating relevance to students' lives, which will increase participation in the field [18]. In their study, Kirlidog and Coetzee [4] discovered that even students in their senior years at university were unaware of IT careers and their job functions. Similar findings by Calitz et al. [19] indicated that students at the senior level lacked knowledge and awareness of IT careers.

In support, Seymour and Serumola [20] noted that while students were enrolled at university they were not exposed to Information Systems (IS), hence they did not choose to follow a career in IS. Furthermore, their findings showed that teachers did not mention IS at high school recruitment events. Govender and Khumalo [12] further found that a lack of knowledge by influencers, such as family and friends led to students not choosing to pursue IS studies.

IT career awareness at school level can be promoted and achieved through various events, such as school visits and presentations, industry talks, university IT student project open days and career events [21, 22]. In addition, IT career awareness can be created using the following approaches [6, 22, 23]:

- Exposure to working environments;
- Career days, 3rd year and Honours (4th year) project demonstration days;
- IT school and university seminars;
- Formal and informal opportunities to connect with practitioners;
- Explicit connections between academic content and related careers;
- Alumni mentorship programmes;
- Industry hackathons;
- Incorporating real-world assignments into the curriculum;
- Incorporate career development and awareness courses into programmes;
- Work-integrated learning/Work-based learning/Work placements;
- Industry speaker series;
- Partnerships between universities and industry organisations; and
- Assisting students in setting up their CVs and applying to work.

Career awareness and professional preparation should be an integral aspect of a university curriculum, as it assists students to prepare for employment and guides them to develop the necessary career skills before they enter the workforce [23]. Incorporating a course on career preparedness and education, into programmes at tertiary institutions, has been recommended to promote career awareness and development [23]. Career awareness has proven to be a factor in the work-readiness of IT graduates [22]. Academia must implement productive interventions to raise career awareness among IT students using industry participation in higher education [22].

2.2 Career Theories

Career development theories state that a career choice can be made by individuals once they know what careers are available to them. Additionally, a career seeker must have a realistic understanding of what the career entails and how to achieve goals for that career [24]. The Social Cognitive Career Theory (SCCT) focuses on understanding the outcomes of individuals who develop an interest and then decide about their education pursuits [25]. Lent et al. [26] postulate that the SCCT has developed from Bandura's general SCT theory. Alshahrani et al. [27] argue that the SCCT framework is for understanding how personal, cognitive and contextual factors influence career choices. Additionally, Lent et al. [28] state that the SCCT involves perceived social and cultural environment effects on career choices. Therefore, the SCCT is based on the development of career interests based on knowledge and awareness of existing careers for someone to make the choice.

Alshahrani et al. [27] included career perceptions, outcomes and awareness as some of the factors that influence career choices. Cohen and Parsotam [29] included perceptions and awareness of a career being closely linked with the intentions or goals to pursue a specific career choice. For this study, the Cognitive Influences factor from the SCCT theory were used, which focus on the cognitive knowledge of outcome expectations. Outcome expectations encompass the individual's self-belief in terms of competencies and capabilities. Within outcome expectations, this study investigated the career awareness knowledge of first-year students and their belief in their ability to obtain the chosen qualification and to pursue their chosen career.

3 Research Methodology

The IT skills shortage has highlighted the importance of IT career awareness, specifically amongst secondary school scholars, when choosing their school subjects. Scholars are generally not aware of IT careers, specifically in fields such as Computer Science and Information Systems [20]. The research problem investigated in this study is that first-year students' IT career awareness and knowledge have not been established and this study aimed to investigate if there is a difference in career awareness between IT and non-IT first-year students. The research question investigated in this study is as follows: *What are the differences in IT career awareness amongst first-year students and their knowledge of different job descriptions?*

A questionnaire was used, based on previous studies, matching job titles to job descriptions and measuring the career awareness of undergraduate students [14, 21, 30]. All first-year students were requested to complete the survey anonymously and online. The first-year questionnaire included the following sub-sections:

- Biographical details;
- Matching job titles to job descriptions; and
- Career awareness.

The factor, career awareness was measured using 8 items on a 5-point Likert scale. The questionnaire was captured using the online survey tool, QuestionPro. The data were collected from first-year students completing several university programmes and were divided into an IT group (Bachelor in CS, Bachelor in Science CS&IS, Bachelor IT, National Diploma: IT and National Higher Certificate: IT) and a non-IT group (Bachelors in Commerce, Accounting, Finance, Management and Economics). The data were statistically analysed using Statistica and included EFA. This study met all ethical requirements from the Nelson Mandela University Ethics Committee.

4 Results

The questionnaire was distributed to registered first-year students, during 2021 and included IT and non-IT students. The data were cleaned before statistical analysis, which resulted in 405 usable responses for the study.

4.1 Biographical Data

The respondents were requested to indicate their gender (Table 1) and 55% (n = 221) were female and 45% (n = 184) were male. The respondents were requested to indicate their race (Table 1). Most of the respondents were Black (82%; n = 332), followed by Whites (12%; n = 46), Coloured students (5%; n = 21) and six Indian students (1%).

Table 1. Biographical details (n = 405)

Gender	Male	Female	Total	
	184 (45%)	221 (55%)	405 (100%)	
Age	**18 years**	**19 years**	**20 years**	**21 + years**
	101 (25%)	111 (27%)	66 (16%)	127 (31%)
Race	**Black**	**Coloured**	**Indian**	**White**
	332 (82%)	21 (5%)	6 (1%)	46 (12%)
Home language	**English/Afrikaans**	**Sotho/Tswana/Zulu**	**Xhosa**	**Other**
	99 (24%)	75 (18%)	173 (43%)	58 (14%)
Qualification	**IT Degree**	**IT Diploma**	**Non-IT**	
	92 (22%)	181 (45%)	132 (33%)	

The respondents were requested to indicate their age. Most of the respondents (27%, n = 111), were 19 years old, followed by 25% (n = 101) 18 years, 16% (n = 66) for 20 years, 11% (n = 44) for 21 years and 20% for 21 years and above (Table 1). The respondents had to indicate the qualification they were registered for, to determine if they were in the IT or non-IT group. Sixty-one percent of the respondents spoke an African language and 24% Afrikaans or English. Further, the respondents were categorised and divided into IT and non-IT student groups. Table 1 shows that 67% (n = 273) of the respondents were IT students (IT degree & IT Diploma) and 33% (n = 132) non-IT students.

4.2 Frequency Distribution – Job Titles and Job Descriptions

The first-year students were presented with ten job titles and job descriptions in the IT and business fields. The job titles and job descriptions were used to determine career awareness amongst the first-year students. The respondents had to match seven IT job titles (Help Desk Consultant, Software Developer/Programmer, Database Administrator, Information Security Specialist, Network Engineer, Data Scientist and Business Analyst) and three business job titles (Sales and Marketing Representative, Accountant and Auditor) with their job descriptions, as shown in Table 2.

The results of the matching of correct job titles with the job descriptions are presented in Table 2. The results indicated that the first-year students understood the job by definition indicated by being matched correctly at 83% (n = 337) as Sales and Marketing Representative, followed by Help Desk and Support Consultant and Software Developer/Programmer at 76% (n = 308) and 72% (n = 292) respectively. Jobs such as Database Administrators and Information Security Specialist were matched correctly at 66% (n = 268) and 60% (n = 241). The Auditing job was the least correctly matched job at 33% (n = 34%). The results are further statistically analysed in Sect. 4.5.

Table 2. Frequency distributions: job titles and descriptions

Job descriptions	Job title	Correct	
A person who manages sales and promotional activities to increase the sales or the use of a product or service in a business and ultimately market share	Sales and Marketing representative	337	83%
A person providing IT customer support and troubleshooting daily user IT queries	Help desk and support consultant	308	76%
A person responsible for designing, writing code and testing new programmes	Software Developer/programmer	292	72%

(continued)

Table 2. (*continued*)

Job descriptions	Job title	Correct	
A person responsible for maintaining the databases and ensuring data availability in a business	Database Administrator	268	66%
A person who manages the data, information, systems, network and cloud security in an organisation	Information Security Specialist	241	60%
A person who manages the daily financial transactions and information in a business	Accountant	237	59%
A person responsible for handling LAN/WAN, network hardware, software and installations	Network Engineer	216	53%
A person working with Big data, applying statistical techniques to analyse, model and interpret the results to create actionable plans for companies	Data scientist	215	53%
A person who solves business problems by analysing and designing IT systems in the organisation	Business Analyst	160	40%
A professional person who reviews the financial statements and accounting principles of a business	Auditor	137	34%

4.3 Frequency Distribution - Career Awareness

The factor *Career Awareness* was examined, to determine whether the respondent's awareness of careers influences their chosen career. The frequency distribution of career distribution statements is shown in Table 3.

Seventy-two percent (n = 290) of the respondents indicated that they knew the job they wanted in the future. Similarly, seventy-one percent (n = 289) of the students understood the career paths available for their chosen qualifications respectively. Forty-seven percent (n = 190) of the respondents did not understand the differences between CS, IS and IT careers. Similarly, forty-six percent (n = 187) of the respondents did not understand IS careers before enrolling at university.

Table 3. Frequency distribution – career awareness

Statement	μ	Std	Disagree		Neutral		Agree	
			n	%	N	%	n	%
I do have an understanding of the career paths available for graduates with my qualifications	3,84	0,83	25	7%	91	22%	289	71%
I did have an understanding of Information Technology (IT) careers before I enrolled at university	3,36	1,13	105	26%	99	24%	201	50%
I had an understanding of Computer Science (CS) careers before I enrolled at university	2,98	1,11	155	38%	116	29%	134	33%
I did have an understanding of Information Systems (IS) careers before I enrolled at university	2,77	1,07	187	46%	114	28%	104	26%
I understand the differences between IT, CS and IS careers	2,76	1,07	190	47%	110	27%	105	26%
I know what job I want to do in the future	3,90	1,02	43	10%	72	18%	290	72%
I know which company I want to work for after I graduate	2,88	1,09	154	38%	147	36%	104	26%
I can explain the main job functions for my future job	3,47	1,04	71	18%	127	31%	207	51%

4.4 Exploratory Factor Analysis – Career Awareness

Exploratory Factor Analysis (EFA) was used to analyse the data in this study. The EFA analysis for the factor *Career Awareness,* with eight items (Table 3) resulted in a two-factor model explaining 71.9% of the total variance (Table 4). Each factor has three items that are above the minimum significant loading of .300. The two factors were named: Factor 1 - *Career Awareness – Prior to University Enrolment* and Factor 2 - *Career Awareness - Current.* The results show that there is a difference in the respondents' awareness of careers before enrolling at an academic institution compared to during the years of enrolment at an academic institution.

Table 4. EFA loadings (2-Factor model) – career awareness

Item	Factor 1	Factor 2
I had an understanding of Computer Science (CS) careers before I enrolled at university	**.893**	.138
I did have an understanding of Information Systems (IS) careers before I enrolled at university	**.871**	.108
I did have an understanding of Information Technology (IT) careers before I enrolled at university	**.860**	.061
I can explain the main job functions for my future job	.121	**.854**
I know what job I want to do in the future	.164	**.797**
I know which company I want to work for after I graduate	.044	**.760**
Explained variance	2.34	1.98
% of total variance	39.0%	32.9%
Total % of variance explained = 71.9%		

Finally, the *Career Awareness,* two factor model was tested for reliability using Cronbach's Alpha Coefficient. *Career Awareness-Prior to University Enrolment* had a reliability value of 0.86, an 'Excellent' rating and *Career Awareness-Current* had a reliability value of 0.74, a 'good' rating. Both values for *Career Awareness* indicated that the factor is important in first-year students' career choice.

4.5 One-Sample t-Test Between IT and Non-IT Groups

A one-sample t-test is used to evaluate statistically significant differences between groups [31]. The two groups were the IT group and the non-IT group. The findings of the t-test between the IT and non-IT groups are presented in Table 5.

The factor *Job Titles/Descriptions* was used to determine the respondents' knowledge of job titles and job descriptions (Table 2). In testing their knowledge, the respondents were asked to match job titles with job descriptions and the number of correct job titles and descriptions were scored.

Table 5. One sample t-test between IT (n = 273) and non-IT (n = 132)

Factor	Group	Mean	S.D	Difference	t	p (d.f. = 403)	Cohen's d
Total correct - job titles/descriptions	IT	6.11	2.37	0.49	2.02	.045	0.21
	Non-IT	5.62	2.16				Small
Career awareness - prior to university enrolment	IT	3.18	0.99	0.46	4.53	<.0005	0.48
	Non-IT	2.73	0.88				Medium
Career awareness - current	IT	3.36	0.86	−0.17	−1.90	.058	n/a
	Non-IT	3.53	0.81				

The results for the factor *Job Titles/Description* showed a non-statistically significant difference between the two groups ($p = .045$), which was below the acceptable value of $p < .05$. Additionally, Cohen's d ($d = 0.21$) showed a small practical significance (Table 8). The mean of the IT group was marginally higher than the non-IT group ($\mu = 6.11$ vs $\mu = 5.62$), therefore the results indicate that the IT group scored higher on matching and identifying the job titles and descriptions than the non-IT group.

For the factor, *Career Awareness - Prior to University Enrolment*, the IT group ($\mu = 3.18$) was more aware of careers before their studies than the non-IT group ($\mu = 2.73$). The comparison further indicates a statistical significance ($p < .0005$) with a medium practical significance (Cohen's $d = 0.48$). The results indicate that the IT group was more aware of careers when compared to the non-IT group prior to their studies. Finally, there was no statistical difference for the factor *Career Awareness-Current* in the responses, indicating that during their studies there was no difference between IT and non-IT groups in career awareness.

4.6 MANOVA Results

Statistical analyses were conducted to see if there were any statistically significant links between demographic data and characteristics that influence students' perceptions of their chosen careers. A multivariate analysis was conducted on the demographic variables and the results are presented in Table 6.

Table 6. MANOVA statistics – demographic variables

Effect	F	D.F	p
Gender	3.37	12; 390	<.0005
Age category	2.91	12; 390	.001
Home language	14.88	12; 390	<.0005

The MANOVA results verify that the demographic variables *Gender* and *Home language* ($p < .0005$), are statistically significant. Additionally, the demographic variable

Age Category ($p = .001$), indicates that the factor is statistically significant. Statistical analysis was performed to determine if there were any significant relationships between the respondents' demographics and the factors. An Analysis of Variance (ANOVA) is an exploration of statistical relationships between the demographic variables and the factors.

4.7 ANOVA Job Titles/Descriptions

A univariate ANOVA analysis was conducted on the factor *Job Titles/Descriptions* and the results are presented in Table 7.

Table 7. Univariate – ANOVA statistics – correct job title/description

Effect	F-value	D.F	p	Cohen's d
Gender	6.71	1; 401	.010	0.27 (Small)
Age category	1.21	1; 401	.273	n/a
Home language	29.20	1; 401	<.0005	0.61 (Medium)

The results of the ANOVA analysis indicated that Gender ($p = .010$; Cohen's $d = 0.027$) and Home language ($p = <.0005$; Cohen's $d = 0.061$) were statistically and practically significant. The post-hoc results (Table 8) confirmed the differences between the genders of the respondents. Female respondents were more correct in matching job titles and job descriptions ($\mu2 = 6.24$) compared with the males ($\mu1 = 5.61$). Furthermore, the post-hoc results show that there are statistical differences in languages. Students who spoke Afrikaans and English languages combined yielded more positive results ($\mu1 = 6.98$) compared to the students speaking African languages ($\mu2 = 5.62$). The results show the differences in the understanding of the job titles and job descriptions amongst genders and respondents speaking different languages. Furthermore, the results show that respondents speaking African languages do not have a thorough understanding of job titles and job descriptions.

Table 8. Post-hoc results – correct job titles and job description

Effect	Level 1	Level 2	μ_1	μ_2	t-test p	Cohen's d
Gender	Male	Female	5.61	6.24	.010	0.27 (Small)
Home language	Afrikaans/English	African	6.98	5.62	.000	0.61 (Medium)

4.8 ANOVA Career Awareness - Prior to University Enrolment

The *Career Awareness - Prior to University Enrolment* factor was analysed using the demographic data (Table 9).

Table 9. Univariate ANOVA results – career awareness – prior to university enrolment

Effect	F-value	D.F	p	Cohen's d
Gender	9.51	1; 401	.002	0.31 (Small)
Age category	0.00	1; 401	.950	n/a
Home language	12.40	1; 401	<.0005	0.41 (Small)

The results show that for *Gender,* a statistical and practical significant (p = 0.002; Cohen's d = 0.31) difference between the two groups. Additionally, for *Home Language* there is a statistical and practical significant ($p < .05$; Cohen's $d = 0.41$) difference between the two groups. Therefore, the factor *Career Awareness - Prior to University Enrolment* was further analysed and the post-hoc results are presented in Table 10.

Table 10. Post-hoc results – career awareness – prior to university enrolment

Effect	Level 1	Level 2	μ_1	μ_2	t-test p	Cohen's d
Gender	Male	Female	2.87	3.17	.002	0.31 (Small)
Home language	Afrikaans/English	African	3.33	2.94	.000	0.41 (Small)

The post-hoc results in Table 10 indicated that gender differences between the respondents, with males ($\mu_1 = 2.87$) scoring lower compared with females ($\mu_2 = 3.17$). The results indicate that female respondents' *Career Awareness - Prior to University Enrolment* was higher than male respondents. Therefore, it can be concluded that females have a higher career awareness at secondary school level.

Furthermore, the post-hoc results indicate differences between the home languages of the respondents, as students with African home languages ($\mu_1 = 2.94$) scored lower than students with Afrikaans or English home languages ($\mu 2 = 3.33$). The results indicate that respondents with Afrikaans or English as a home language have more knowledge of *Career Awareness - Prior to University Enrolment* than respondents with African home languages.

4.9 ANOVA Career Awareness – Current

Table 11 presents the results of the ANOVA analysis for the *Career Awareness – Current* factor.

The ANOVA results show both age category ($p = 0.010$) and home language ($p = 0.024$) as statistically significant. Furthermore, both age category (Cohen's $d = 0.36$) and home language (Cohen's $d = 0.33$) indicate that there is a practically significant difference between the groups in terms of their *Career Awareness-current. Career Awareness – Current* was further analysed with post-hoc results presented in Table 12.

The post-hoc results in Table 12 indicate differences in the perceptions of *Career Awareness - Current* for the two different age categories, as respondents 21 years and

Table 11. Univariate ANOVA results – career awareness - current

Effect	F-value	D.F	p	Cohen's d
Gender	1.38	1; 401	.242	n/a
Age category	6.75	1; 401	.010	0.36 (Small)
Home language	5.12	1; 401	.024	0.33 (Small)

Table 12. Post-hoc results – career awareness-current

Effect	Level 1	Level 2	μ_1	μ_2	t-test p	Cohen's d
Age category	<21 years	21+ years	3.32	3.62	.010	0.36 (Small)
Home language	Afrikaans/English	African	3.21	3.48	.024	0.33 (Small)

above ($\mu_2 = 3.62$) scored higher compared to respondents under 21 years ($\mu_1 = 3.32$). The results indicate respondents under 21 years currently have less knowledge of careers than respondents who are 21 and older. Thus, first-year students are less aware of future careers than older students.

Finally, there were differences in the means for some languages, with Afrikaans/English Home languages ($\mu_1 = 3.21$) compared with the African home languages mean ($\mu_2 = 3.48$). The results indicate that the respondents of African home languages were currently more career aware than respondents with Afrikaans/English home languages.

5 Discussion of Research Findings

Lyon et al. [5] state that it is important to build awareness among novice scholars regarding IT courses so that scholars know what to expect from courses and are prepared to handle the course. This study used EFA results for *Career Awareness,* which resulted in a 2-Factor model, which was named *Career Awareness – Prior to University Enrolment* and *Career Awareness – Current.* The combined factor explained 71.9% of the total variance. Additionally, the descriptive statistics for the *Career Awareness – Prior to University Enrolment* indicated that 37% (n = 151) and *Career Awareness – Current* 39% (n = 158) of the respondents were unaware of their career before enrolling for their studies. In support of the results, Qazi et al. [32] state that many scholars enroll for careers without being aware of the career details.

The statistical analysis of the *Careers Awareness – Prior to University Enrolment* factor, indicated a statistical and small practical differences ($p < .0005$; Cohen's d = 0.48) between the IT group ($\mu = 3.18$) and the non-IT group ($\mu = 2.73$). These results support similar findings as Wang et al. [18], as the IT group had a deeper understanding of different careers compared to the non-IT group. The Career Awareness – Current factor did not have any statistical or practical significance. Additionally, the matching of job titles with job descriptions findings showed that there is statistical and practical significance (p = 0.045; Cohen's d = 0.21) between the IT (μ = 6.11) and non-IT (μ = 5.62) groups.

The t-test results indicated a statistical and practical significance for the variables age category and home language. The differences in respondents aged 21 years and over (μ = 3.32), showed a higher current understanding of careers compared to those aged under 21 years (μ = 3.36). Aivaloglou and Hermans [8] found that age did not have any significance, however, this study's results indicated that age has a statistical significance as a student over the age of 21 showed a better understanding of careers.

The respondents who were African language speakers were more aware of careers *currently* (μ = 3.48), than Afrikaans or English language speakers (μ = 3.21). The factor, Job Title/Descriptions findings indicated the respondent's gender made a difference in understanding and matching of job titles, with females (μ = 6.24) scoring higher compared to males (μ = 5.61). The results further indicate that first-year students with Afrikaans or English as home language (μ = 6.98), scored higher than students with African home languages (μ = 5.62). Several studies compare gender and different academic groups, however not language or ethnicity [12, 17]. Govender and Khumalo [12] indicate that scholars from disadvantaged schools have limited career awareness, which the findings of this study support, as African language speakers were less aware of careers prior to their studies (μ = 2.92) than Afrikaans and English speaking first-year students (μ = 3.21).

6 Conclusions and Future Research

Career awareness is an important process for a scholar, in order to understand the various career paths or career options available to them, based on their interest and future education. Career awareness assists a scholar to know what knowledge, training and skills they must learn and acquire to achieve success in their chosen career. Career awareness differs for female and male students and changes according to their gender and academic year of study [7]. Research has highlighted the perceived benefits of involving industry in higher education to raise IT career awareness [22].

The results from this study indicate a limited understanding of job titles and job descriptions amongst respondents speaking African languages. Elias and Brian [33] indicate that IT career awareness programmes must be implemented, at the secondary school level to promote IT careers. Furthermore, Chinyamurindi et al. [34] argue that Higher Education Institutions can take an active role in assisting secondary schools through community engagement, by visiting local schools to impart information related to careers. Emphasis should be placed on the distinction between the business-oriented IT careers, which requires communication and interpersonal skills and traditional Information Technology, Computer Science and Engineering careers [14, 35].

It is important for academic departments as custodians of computing qualifications, to distinctly show the different career paths to scholars, parents and teachers. As custodians of computing qualifications, this will allow scholars to receive the correct information regarding IT qualifications. The study shows career awareness as an important aspect of career choice for scholars. In addressing the aim of this study, the study was grounded in the SCCT theory that included the factor perceptions, which investigated career awareness of existing careers. The study examined the understanding of job titles and job descriptions, which indicated that IT students had a better understanding of specific job titles and job descriptions. Parents need to be more informed with career information to assist their children in their career decision process [36].

The study recommends the implementation of an IT career awareness programme at secondary schools in the Nelson Mandela Metropolitan Bay to improve the knowledge and awareness of scholars, teachers and parents regarding IT careers and qualifications. In addition, intervention strategies at the undergraduate level, such as industry talks, industry and Alumni talks and mentorship programmes are recommended. Future research will evaluate the success of the interventions.

References

1. Heleta, S., Bagus, T.: Sustainable development goals and higher education: leaving many behind. High. Educ. **81**(1), 163–177 (2020). https://doi.org/10.1007/s10734-020-00573-8
2. Schofield, A., Dwolatzky, B.: 2019 JCSE-IITPSA ICT Skills Survey the Tenth Edition. https://www.iitpsa.org.za/wp-content/uploads/2019/09/2019-JCSE-IITPSA-ICT-Skills-Survey-v1.pdf
3. BusinessTech: The most in-demand job skills in South Africa right now. https://businesstech.co.za/news/business/468298/the-most-in-demand-job-skills-in-south-africa-right-now-5/
4. Kirlidog, M., Van der Vyver, C., Zeeman, M., Coetzee, W.: Unfulfilled need: reasons for insufficient ICT skills in South Africa. Inf. Dev. **34**(1), 5–19 (2018). https://doi.org/10.1177/0266666916671984
5. Lyon, L.A., Schatz, C., Toyama, Y.: Torres, D: Computer science intensive intervention to prepare and engage underrepresented novice students at community college. Community Coll. J. Res. Pract. **46**, 1–13 (2021). https://doi.org/10.1080/10668926.2021.1894508
6. Liebenberg, J., Huisman, M., Mentz, E.: The relevance of software development education for students. IEEE Trans. Educ. **58**(4), 242–248 (2015). https://doi.org/10.1109/TE.2014.2381599
7. Dagyar, M., Kasalk, G., Ugurlu, N.: Academic career awareness and academic career interest among Turkish undergraduate students. Cypriot J. Educ. Sci. **15**(5), 937–954 (2020). https://doi.org/10.18844/cjes.v15i5.5123
8. Aivaloglou, E., Hermans, F.: Early programming education and career orientation: the effects of gender, self-efficacy, motivation and stereotypes. SIGCSE **19**, 679–685 (2019)
9. Arcidiacono, P., Hotz, V.J., Kang, S.: Modeling college major choices using elicited measures of expectations and counterfactuals (2012). https://doi.org/10.1016/j.jeconom.2011.06.002
10. Becerra-fernandez, I., Elam, J., Clemmons, S.: Reversing the landslide in computer-related degree programs. Commun. ACM **53**, 127–133 (2010). https://doi.org/10.1145/1646353.1646387
11. Carrico, C., Matusovich, H.M., Paretti, M.C.: A qualitative analysis of career choice pathways of college-oriented rural central Appalachian high school students. J. Career Dev. **46**(2), 94–111 (2019). https://doi.org/10.1177/0894845317725603
12. Govender, I., Khumalo, S.: Reasoned action analysis theory as a vehicle to explore female students' intention to major in information systems. J. Commun. **5**(1), 35–44 (2014)
13. Alexander, P.M., et al.: Factors affecting career choice: comparison between students from computer and other disciplines. J. Sci. Educ. Technol. **20**, 300–315 (2011). https://doi.org/10.1007/s10956-010-9254-3
14. Twani, M.: Factors influencing first-year students' career decisions to pursue an IT career. M.Com Dissertation. Department of Computing Sciences, Nelson Mandela University, South Africa (2021)

15. BusinessTech: 10 critical skills needed in South Africa right now. https://businesstech.co.za/news/business/479723/here-are-the-10-critical-skills-needed-in-south-africa-right-now/
16. Jusoh, Z., Said, R.R., Kiram, N.M.: Career awareness in the study of Malay language program. Int. J. Lang. Educ. **5**(June), 89–101 (2021). https://doi.org/10.26858/ijole.v5i2.16357
17. Wang, H.-H., Chen, H.-T., Hong, Z.-R., Yore, L.D.: An investigation of Taiwanese college students' personality traits and self-worth. J. Happiness Stud. **5**, 1593–1613 (2015). https://doi.org/10.1007/s10902-014-9579-3
18. Wang, J., Ravitz, J., Ivory, M., Hong, H.: Gender differences in factors influencing pursuit of computer science and related fields. In: ITICSE, pp. 117–122 (2015). https://doi.org/10.1145/2729094.2742611
19. Calitz, A.P., Cullen, M., Fani, D.: The influence of culture on women's IT career choices. In: Hattingh, M., Matthee, M., Smuts, H., Pappas, I., Dwivedi, Y.K., Mäntymäki, M. (eds.) I3E 2020. LNCS, vol. 12067, pp. 345–357. Springer, Cham (2020). https://doi.org/10.1007/978-3-030-45002-1_30
20. Seymour, L.F., Serumola, T.: Events that lead university students to change their major to Information Systems: a retroductive South African case. S. Afr. Comput. J. **28**(1), 18–43 (2016). https://doi.org/10.18489/sacj.v28i1.367
21. Calitz, A.P., Greyling, J.H., Cullen, M.: ICT career track awareness amongst ICT graduates. In: Proceedings of the South African Institute of Computer Scientists and Information Technologists Conference on Knowledge, Innovation and Leadership in a Diverse, Multidisciplinary Environment, pp. 59–68 (2011). https://doi.org/10.1145/2072221.2072229
22. Janse van Rensburg, J.T., Goede, R.: Promoting career awareness among IT students in a South African context. High. Educ. Ski. Work. Learn. **10**(3), 541–565 (2020). https://doi.org/10.1108/HESWBL-09-2019-0110
23. Chu, J., Morreale, P., Press, M.: Workforce and career readiness for computing and technology students. J. Comput. Sci. Coll. **35**(8), 76–86 (2020)
24. Patton, W.: McMahon, M: Career Development and Systems Theory: Connecting Theory and Practice. Sense Publishers, Rotterdam/Boston/Taipei (2014)
25. Lent, R.W., Brown, S.D.: Integrating person and situation perspectives on work satisfaction: a social-cognitive view. J. Vocat. Behav. **69**, 236–247 (2006). https://doi.org/10.1016/j.jvb.2006.02.006
26. Lent, R.W., Brown, S.D., Hackett, G.: Toward a unifying social cognitive theory of career and academic interest, choice, and performance. J. Vocat. Behav. **45**(1), 79–122 (1994). https://doi.org/10.1006/JVBE.1994.1027
27. Alshahrani, A., Ross, I., Wood, M.I.: Using social cognitive career theory to understand why students choose to study computer science. In: Proceedings of ACM ICER Conference, vol. 10 (2018). https://doi.org/10.1145/3230977.3230994
28. Brown, D.: Career Choice and Development, 4th edn. Jossey-Bass, San Francisco (2002)
29. Cohen, J.F., Parsotam, P.: Intentions to pursue a career in information systems and technology: an empirical study of South African students. In: Reynolds, N., Turcsányi-Szabó, M. (eds.) KCKS 2010. IAICT, vol. 324, pp. 56–66. Springer, Heidelberg (2010). https://doi.org/10.1007/978-3-642-15378-5_6
30. Esterhuyse, A., Calitz, A.P., Cullen, M.: Post-graduate CS and IS students' career awareness. In: SACLA 2019, Drakensberg, South Africa (2019)
31. Gravetter, F.J., Wallnau, L.B.: Statistics for Behavioral Sciences, 8th edn. CA Wadsworth, Belmont (2009)
32. Qazi, M.A., Russell, M., Shannon, D.M.: A state-wide effort to provide access to authentic computer science education to underrepresented populations. In: Proceedings of the 51st SIGCSE Technical Symposium on Computer Science Education, pp. 839–844 (2020). https://doi.org/10.1145/3328778.3372679

33. Elias, S., Brian, A.: Race, friends, and college readiness: evidence from the high school longitudinal study. Race Soc. Probl. **7**, 150–167 (2015). https://doi.org/10.1007/s12552-015-9146-5
34. Chinyamurindi, W.T., Hlatywayo, C.K., Mhlanga, T.S., Marange, C.S., Everson, T.C.: Career decision-making amongst high school learners: a descriptive-exploratory study from South Africa. Cypriot J. Educ. **16**(1), 129–147 (2021). https://doi.org/10.18844/cjes.v16i1.5516
35. Babin, R., Grant, K.A., Sawal, L.: Identifying influencers in high school student ICT career choice. Inf. Syst. Educ. J. **8**(June), 1–18 (2010)
36. Uleanya, M., Naidoo, G., Rugbeer, Y., Rubeer, H.: The role of career awareness and guidance programmes for first-year university students. J. Gender Inf. Dev. Afr. **8**(2), 197–221 (2019). https://doi.org/10.31920/2050-4284/2019/8n2a11

Innovative Teaching

Gamification to Increase Undergraduate Students' Teamwork Skills

Tafadzwa Nyahuye and Adriana Aletta Steyn(✉)

University of Pretoria, Pretoria, South Africa
Riana.steyn@up.ac.za

Abstract. Historically, education is a highly competitive environment, where an individual is deemed successful based on high marks attained individually. The ability to work effectively in teams is an important learning objective for final-year undergraduate students. When undertaking group projects, undergraduate students are expected to collaborate effectively and solve real-world problems in groups of three or more individuals. Teamwork skills are among the highly desired soft skills recruiters struggle to find among many university graduates. The purpose of this study is to evaluate whether gamification can aid in developing teamwork skills in undergraduate students. Following the design science research methodology, two games were developed. The first game is a computer-based cycling game for a single player, with concepts related to teamwork skills forming part of the in-play questions. The second game is a computer-based King of the Mountain-type game, played as a team. In order to move from one level of the Mountain to the next, players would need to answer general trivia questions, in addition to applying teamwork skills to specific questions. Each team was encouraged to come up with its own strategy to achieve the best results. There was no limit to the number of attempts players made in each game. Data was collected during play and via a questionnaire administered upon completion of the games. The results show that students found the games to be engaging and enjoyable. After a few attempts, a number of students noted that they felt part of the team and perceived that the games would enhance their teamwork skills. Participants felt that the games enhanced their team dynamics and that their desire to see their team succeed increased the more they played together. The results show potential for utilising gamification as a means to enhance students' teamwork skills.

Keywords: Gamification · Teamwork · Teamwork skills · Team · Undergraduate teaching · Higher education · Computer-aided learning

1 Introduction

University students are taught the theoretical aspects of teamwork skills, such as effective leadership, time–management, communication, conflict resolution, problem-solving and accountability, but they never effectively develop these skills [1, 2]. In several modules, students undertake group assignments or projects in the anticipation that they would learn teamwork skills as they participate in the teams. Unfortunately, most students finish their

R. J. Barnett et al. (Eds.): SACLA 2022, CCIS 1664, pp. 111–128, 2022.
https://doi.org/10.1007/978-3-031-21076-1_7

group assignments or projects without learning how to work effectively in teams [3]. Many students consider group work risky, with it potentially resulting in lower grades as individual students lose control over the project outcomes [1, 4]. The prevalence of free riders who rely on work done by others, the reluctance to be responsible for work by the group, and the challenges of organising time and space for teamwork are some of the negative perceptions, students have towards teamwork [3, 5, 6]. Education has historically been about the success of the individual. Mutually beneficial collaboration is mostly prevalent at masters or doctoral research levels. The benefits of teamwork for students include higher levels of motivation, greater retention and comprehension of material, greater resilience when facing challenges, wider views, improved self-efficacy and improved attitudes towards future team projects [1, 4, 6].

Over the last two decades, many companies are moving away from the hierarchical organisational structure to flatter structures involving teams [1, 2]. Companies spend a lot of time and money on teambuilding exercises in an effort to increase productivity by developing teamwork skills in their employees. Employing university graduates who possess teamwork skills would ease their integration into work teams, over and above empowering them to effectively collaborate with their team members [1, 4, 6].

Teamwork can be defined as the integration of inputs and resources that work in harmony to attain a well-defined set of goals. Every team member's role must be set, challenges must be faced equally and improvements must be continually sought [2]. Teamwork skills are social competencies that enhance an individual's ability to collaborate and cooperate with other members of the team in order to effectively complete team tasks and goals [1, 6]. Teamwork skills may be developed using teambuilding exercises and following an interpersonal approach and the adventure learning method in the form of improvisational activities such as games, drama and painting [1]. A tool that is explored in this paper is the use of gamification to increase teamwork skills.

Gamification involves "the use of game designs (game elements, game thinking, game methodologies, game techniques and game frameworks) in a non-game context" [7, 8]. The game designs include ranks, avatars, levels, competition, a two- or three-dimensional (2D or 3D) environment, time pressures and communication systems [9]. Gamification is meant to increase the fun or usefulness of a game in a work environment. The games must be differentiated from other contests by creating an immersive feeling of play [10, 11]. The player must acquire the given skills directly or indirectly, while enjoying the gamification experience. Using the design science research methodology, the following sections identify the problem and the objectives of the given solution and why it is important [12].

In the following section, a comprehensive literature review surrounding gamification and education will be conducted, followed by the methodology, quantitative data analysis and highlights of the findings. Based on the findings, the viability of gamification is explored to increase students' teamwork skills, after which conclusions are drawn and directions provided for future research.

2 Literature Review

2.1 Gamification

The concept of gamification was first used in the early 2000s, but the first documented use of the word was around 2008 [13]. From a psychological point of view, games induce a state of flow (a state of gratification, immersion in the experience), which is ideal for optimum learning, creativity and performance [11–13].

The use of games in education has been widely accepted as a means to increase student engagement, as well as to deliver content [14, 15]. Gamification can be grouped into two broad types: structural gamification and content gamification. Structural gamification refers to the application of game elements to guide learners through the subject content without changing the content. This may include subject content questions in a maze game. Gamification of content refers to altering the content to make it more game-like. This involves overlaying the content with a story, a challenge, a mystery, characters, rewards or music. The two types of gamification(s) can be used together to create an even more engaging experience [8, 13].

Motivation can be defined as the psychological process that energises and directs behaviour. Motivation steers an individual's actions [16]. Researchers describe the two types of academic motivation as extrinsic and intrinsic motivation. Extrinsic motivation occurs when there is an external driver: someone or something pushing the student to learn. External drivers may also be viewed as external cues that form an outside pressure that controls someone to behave in a certain manner. These may include rewards, punishment, anticipated consequences and feelings of shame. Intrinsic motivation occurs when a student engages in learning because they enjoy it. They are learning for the sake of it. The student can work autonomously and succeed [8, 16, 17]. Autonomous motivation is viewed as the most ideal way of learning. It is also linked with better performance, persistence and psychological wellbeing; conversely, controlled motivation tends to vanish the moment the external control is removed. An increase in controlled motivation may decrease a learner's accomplishments and likely result in a loss of motivation once the external control is removed [16]. Gamification needs to be designed in a way that offers students more intrinsic motivation than extrinsic motivation. It must tap into the psychological needs of the learner by offering the learner a feeling of autonomy (no external pressure), a desire for competence (a desire to feel that one can attain a goal) and the need for relatedness (to feel part of a group leading to sense of 'self' value) [16, 18, 19]. The three psychological needs form what is known as the Self Determination Theory (SDT). The SDT is a broad framework that describes the fundamental needs that are essential to human motivation and engagement. When these needs are satisfied, an environment of effective learning is created [16, 20]. Extrinsic motivation reduces autonomy, while it creates a controlled setting. This may produce positive results, but may be accompanied by negative emotions of pressure to deliver. Competence is linked to extrinsic motivation, while relatedness and autonomy increase intrinsic motivation [16, 20]. This study explores gamification to increase teamwork skills, while it is cognisant of the implications of both the intrinsic and extrinsic motivation of the student.

Gamification can also be characterised by two elements: game mechanics and game dynamics. Game mechanics is composed of the rules and benefits that make up the game.

They allow the player to have control of the game and guide the player's actions [14]. The game designers decide on the game mechanics, i.e., the goals, the settings, the rules and the types of permissible interactions. The mechanics are usually constant. They determine the key parties, how the parties interact, how the player wins or loses, and where and when the gamification experience occurs [14, 15, 21]. Game mechanics, when successfully combined, can drive a specific behaviour, tapping into human emotions that may be useful to motivate learning. Gamification must progressively adapt to the player's skill and offer challenges that keep the player engaged. Students typically get bored and tired quickly [22].

Game dynamics are the interactions the player has with the game mechanics. Game dynamics are stimulated by desires and needs. They describe the in-game behaviours that emerge and the strategic actions that the player takes. Game dynamics are unpredictable, resulting in either positive or negative unintended outcomes or behaviours. Players determine the game dynamics. Game designers try to anticipate the dynamics that may emerge and develop the mechanics that may induce the desired dynamics [14, 15, 21, 23].

Common Game Mechanics

Points – These are used as a form of reward when players finish a task or activity. Points can be publicly viewed (as a score) to stimulate competition, or they can be privately viewed to provide immediate and continuous feedback to the players. Points can also be used to stimulate participation by offering a reward system through points. The player's in-game behaviour can be measured using points [14, 18, 24]. By monitoring the gameplay, points can also be used to measure how a learner understands the content, while providing immediate feedback. This can be displayed externally and used to compare learners' skills [25].

Levels – These are used to determine if a player has attained a particular goal. Finishing one level unlocks the next level. The higher the level attained, the greater the respect and status of the player [14, 18, 21, 26]. Educators may also use levels to differentiate groups of learners [25].

Badges, trophies, medals, achievements – These represent the accomplishments of a particular challenge or mission. They indicate how the player is performing and can be used to influence behaviour by offering in-play incentives, such as simplified routes or extra points. Badges may also come with membership to an elite group that users are interested in. How to attain badges is usually known upfront [14, 18, 24, 26]. Badges provide a visual cue that a player has achieved something, that can also be shared on social media platforms, highlighting accomplishments [25].

Leadership rank, score table, ranking – These display a player's success given a particular criterion, for instance the top five highest scores. They are meant to stimulate competition and create social pressure, resulting in an increased level of effort and participation by the player [14, 18, 25, 26].

Teammates – These can be virtual or real players, but the idea is to create teams to induce competition, cooperation and conflict [14, 18, 26].

Common Game Dynamics

Rewards – The desire for a tangible or intangible reward may drive the player to behave in a certain way [14, 15].

Status – The desire to be recognised, to attain the respect of peers and prestige may drive the player's behaviour [14, 15].

Accomplishments – The desire to accomplish something can also drive a player's behaviour [14, 15].

Competition – The desire to compete, or to compare performance with others, can influence a player's behaviour [14, 15].

Psychological needs described in SDT can be attained by making use of game mechanics that, in turn, derive game dynamics from the player. Competence, i.e., the mastery (of content or game), is visible via points, levels, badges and leadership boards, driven by extrinsic motivation. A sense of autonomy can be derived from game mechanics, such as choices (degree of complexity, avatars and storyline) and volitional engagements. These are driven by intrinsic motivation. Relatedness can be derived from a sense of relevance from a shared goal with teammates or competitors and a sense of belonging to a social group. Relatedness is driven by intrinsic motivation [16, 18, 27]. The game mechanics and game dynamics implemented in this study will be highlighted in the methodology phase.

2.2 Benefits of Gamification in Education

Many researchers have been studying gamification within the education space. The following are some of the benefits that have been highlighted:

- Gamification helps convert hard and mundane tasks into more enjoyable and entertaining tasks [17, 26, 28, 29].
- Gamification increases the level of motivation and engagement in and outside the classroom [8, 30–32]. Gamification has been found to be effective in teaching mathematics to children [31]. Gamification rewards every effort the learner makes, thereby benefiting the learning experience through changing attitudes, commitment and motivation [19, 26].
- Gamification provides a safe space to repetitively learn and practice, without the fear of real-life consequences, such as failure, breaking things or being judged by peers. It effectively lowers anxiety over the consequences of not performing well [26, 31]. Brull and Finlayson [25] found that gamification allowed nurses to learn in a safe environment without physically harming their patients. Students can practice trial and error as a way of discovering the solution. Gamification offers a safe space for students to express themselves [8, 30].
- Research into human brains asserts that human brains do not distinguish learning in a simulated environment versus learning in an actual environment. Gamification offers a simulated environment that can be used to teach the brain in such a way that when the actual event occurs, the individual can respond accordingly [33].

- Practical tasks may be attempted multiple times with minimum costs, if any at all [34].
- Gamification provides timely and frequent feedback, which students require to affirm whether they are on the right track, and thus offers effective learning mechanisms [8, 29, 31]. Frequent feedback that is fair and granular also allows learners to redefine a failure and better understand their own goals [22].
- Gamification opens doors for cooperation and competition. Playing students may also learn skills such as problem-solving, critical thinking and team player's skills [25, 28, 31].
- Gamification improves intrinsic motivation in adults to learn through a flexible and convenient tool, which allows students to work at their own pace. Gamification encourages autonomous learning [11, 25, 32].
- Gamification has many emotional, cognitive and social benefits. Gamification can trigger different emotions, from joy to frustration, curiosity, satisfaction, pride and optimism, which may benefit students to face their failures and be resilient in their studies [8, 15, 31].
- Gamification takes learning out of the classroom and removes limitations of time and space [8, 25]. It offers cyclical learning, leading to the better retention of information [28, 29, 33].
- By making use of a story with the student as a character, gamification can offer the student an experience where the students remove themselves from the situation and explore the content as if they are the character. This arouses excitement and interest as students can approach a challenge from outside [34].
- Gamification may also lead to improved content retention, deeper understanding, and enhanced application and analysis skills [32, 35].

2.3 Negative Features of Gamification in Education

- In order for gamification to be applied, a game designer needs to understand the content, and use different combinations of game mechanisms to create an experience that is relevant to the content. Games cannot suit everyone. To accommodate the majority would require a lot of research and many resources [23, 31, 34].
- Some students may find gaming a meaningless exercise. Especially at university level, gaming can be considered a time-wasting exercise [23, 31, 34].
- Negative perceptions that gamification will replace educators may result in their resistance to develop or use games [34].
- Play must not be mandatory. This may remove the fun side of gamification, making the experience even harder for students. Students can also cheat in order to just finish the game [29, 31, 36].
- The fear that gaming can be addictive or result in a gambling addiction also exists [34].
- Gamification may result in undesired behaviour, for instance, students may overly focus on the game's mechanics and neglect the learning objectives. Students may also get demotivated due to excessive competition [23, 26, 31, 32].
- The gamification experience needs to be well developed and continuously improved upon using the latest technological features to remain interesting and attractive to

students. Learners' motivation and engagement may gradually decrease over time. Technological constraints may also hinder a game's successful implementation [23, 29, 31].

It is important to highlight that gamification is not meant to replace classical education methods, but rather to enhance them [25, 37].

2.4 How to Gamify in Education

The gamification of any subject is difficult, as gamification should affect behaviour and allow for learning. This is in contrast to games where the main goal is to entertain. A literature review by Morschheuser, et al. [38] and Morschheuser, et al. [39] proposes 13 design principles that may assist the process of gamification.

These principles are:

1. Understand the learner's behaviour, needs, motivation and the characteristics of the context.
2. Identify the learning objectives and define them clearly.
3. Test the gamification design ideas as early as possible using learners.
4. Use an iterative design process.
5. Incorporate people with a knowledge of human psychology and game designs.
6. Assess early if gamification is the right choice to achieve the learning objectives.
7. Stakeholders (lecturers, educators and students) and organisations must support gamification.
8. The focus must be on the learners and educators during the ideation phase.
9. Define and use metrics for monitoring and evaluating success – the psychological and behavioural effects of gamification.
10. Set up controls for cheating/gaming the system.
11. Continuously optimise gamification design.
12. Consider ethical and legal constraints in the design phase.
13. Incorporate educators and learners in the ideation and design phase.

These can further be condensed into an iterative four-step process [37].

1. Determine learners' characteristics. (What skills are required by participants? Are tasks or activities too hard or too easy? What motivation is driving the students to participate?).
2. Define the learning objectives. The learning objectives must be clear and concise. The objectives will determine the educational content and the appropriate game mechanics that will be used.
3. Create the educational content and activities for gamification. They must be interactive, engaging and rich in content multimedia elements. They must allow students to repeat and ultimately achieve the goal. The learning activities must be feasible. Potential and existing student skills must be taken into consideration. The activities must be more complex after each level. The objectives must be attainable via multiple paths, allowing students to build their own strategies to succeed.

4. Identify the game mechanics (points, levels, badges, achievements, scoreboard and teammates) and the game dynamics (rewards, social, tangible or intangible rewards and status) [37].

Gamification of learning needs to maximise educational efficiency through four mechanisms:

- It must be challenging to the student (uncertain outcomes, clear goals, appropriate levels of difficulty) [22, 40].
- It must tap into the curiosity of the learner (progressive unlocking of new levels or new content, time-based patterns, thrills, fun elements) [22, 40].
- It must incorporate fantasy (visuals, audio, storytelling) [22, 40].
- It must offer players some control over the game elements (change colours, avatars, etc.) [22].

The successful application of gamification in education depends on the pre-planning, design and development of the gamified solution. There are still gaps in the literature on the effectiveness of gamified solutions in higher education [41].

3 Research Methodology

This study followed the design science research methodology [12]. An artefact was designed and developed to see if teamwork skills can be increased through gamification. Two games were developed using an online platform called GamiLab. The first game was a single-player game and the second one is played in teams (Fig. 1).

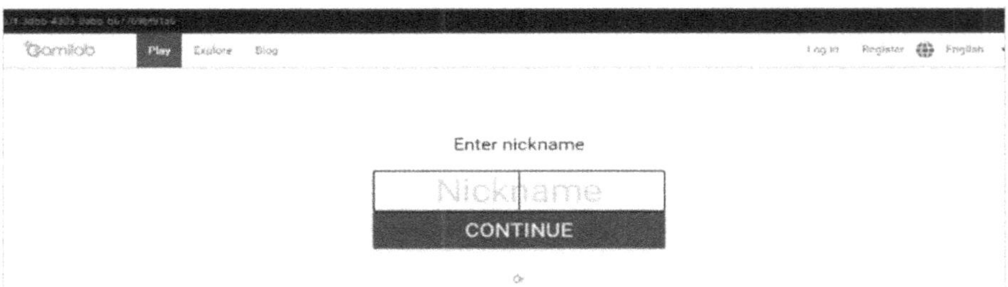

Fig. 1. The GamiLab platform, login page

To ensure that all students could access the games, they were tested on the following browsers: Google Chrome, Internet Explorer, Edge and Firefox. They were also tested on devices using both Windows 10 and Android 10 operating systems. Students were not required to sign up for GamiLab. They were asked to enter their student numbers (rather than a nickname) in order to track the individual players as the winners in each team were rewarded with a prize. Besides that, no personal information was captured or analysed.

Both games use a top five leadership board that students used to track their competition.

The games will now be briefly introduced, after which the data analysis will follow (Fig. 2).

Fig. 2. The top five leadership board

3.1 Game 1

The first game is an online 3D, single-player, cycling game with audio cues and a soundtrack. In order to gain game points, there are boxes along the way the player has to break, which open up questions. The questions are based on the team skills notes provided to the students as part of the course. Throughout the game, players must avoid obstacles to reach the end of the track in the shortest time. The points unlock game achievements in the form of added energy for the cyclist (energy increases the speed of the bike). The student with the most points at the end of the game won a shopping voucher, which was presented during the following class (Fig. 3).

Fig. 3. Game 1 - game views

3.2 Game 2

The second game is an online 2D team-based King of the Mountain-type game with audio cues and a soundtrack. At each level of the Mountain, questions are presented to the team. The team has to answer numerous questions to reach the top of the mountain in the shortest time. At each stage of the climb, the team is presented with a set of four questions. Halfway along the trail, there is a stage where failure to correctly answer all questions results in the team dropping back to the beginning of the climb. The type of questions ranges from sports to movies and team skills. The objective is to get the teams to work together and develop their own strategy to reach the top of the Mountain. The team with the highest points at the end of the game won individual shopping vouchers, which were presented during the following class (Fig. 4).

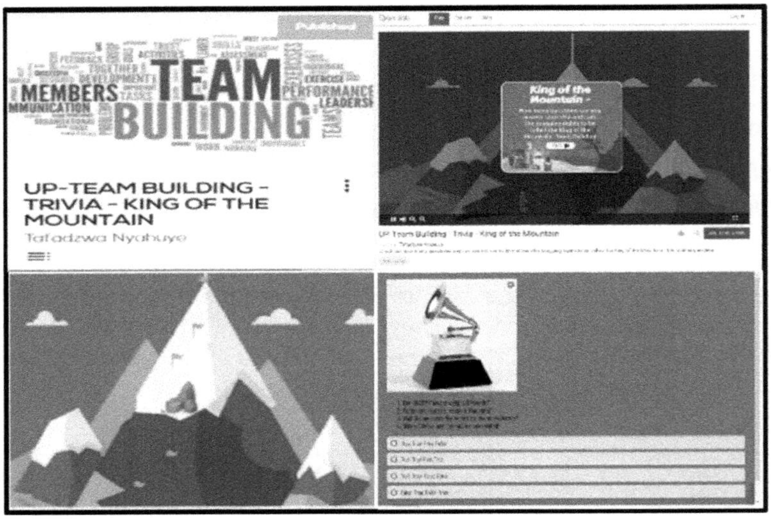

Fig. 4. Game 2 - game views

3.3 Design Principles Applied

The design principles that were applied to create the games can be viewed in Table 1.

Table 1. Design principles applied for Game 1 and Game 2

Design principle/step	Game 1	Game 2
Determine learners' characteristics	Reluctance to revise notes for Lecture 1. Students need to be able to use two fingers and should be visually able to recognise objects in a 3D environment Learners must possess basic computing skills to handle gaming using keyboard arrows or pad touches on a smart phone or tablet Target is third-year IT students; it is assumed they possess some basic gaming skills	Reluctance to cooperate, failure to apply content in final-year projects. Students need to be visually able to recognise objects in a 2D environment Learners must possess basic computing skills to handle gaming using keyboard arrows or pad touches on a smart phone or tablet Target is third-year IT students; it is assumed they possess some basic gaming skills
Define the learning objectives	Students are to individually learn the key teamwork skills from the notes for Lecture 1	Application of the theory learnt. Get students to apply the teamwork skills. Students are to learn skills indirectly by working as a team
Educational content and activities	Teamwork skills questions; theory, definitions and application questions. Questions get progressively harder	Application of teamwork skills, communication, problem-solving, listening, critical thinking, collaboration and leadership
Game mechanics	Points, level, scoreboard, achievements	Points, level, scoreboard, achievements, teammates
Game dynamics	Reward, status	Reward, status

3.4 Self Determination Theory and Motivation Applied

SDT as well as the motivation theory, and how they were applied in both games, can be viewed in Table 2.

The game mechanics and game dynamics used were determined in part by what was available on the GamiLab online platform, as well as what was consistent with the literature reviewed.

Table 2. SDT and motivation applied for Game 1 and Game 2

	Game 1	Game 2
Psychological need Motivation	Competence (points, level, scoreboard, achievements) Extrinsic motivation	Competence (points, level, scoreboard, achievements) Extrinsic motivation
Psychological need Motivation	Relatedness (shopping voucher reward, status) Autonomous (single-player game) Intrinsic motivation	Relatedness (shopping voucher reward, status) Intrinsic motivation

4 Data Analysis and Discussion

There were 210 students enrolled for the third-year Team Building and Team Dynamics module at an urban university. These students were all given access to the games as part of the demonstration and evaluation stage of the design science methodology [12]. After the games had been successfully developed, the students received a brief introduction to the games, as well as some instructions to follow while playing the games.

Of the 210 students, 89 played Game 1 voluntarily and 34 teams played Game 2. Students were given three weeks to play the games with no limit on the number of attempts. After the three-week period, the winners of both games (based on points) were announced in class and awarded their shopping vouchers. After the three weeks, students were asked to complete an online survey to evaluate their experiences.

The survey questions consisted mainly of closed questions based on literature around gamification, as discussed. Students were also requested to openly add their expectations and areas of improvement. Appendix A details the questions in the survey.

Students were not rewarded for completing the survey. A total of 44 surveys were obtained and statistically analysed using Google Forms' analysis engine. All students gave their consent to take part in the study. The data was exported to Microsoft Excel, where it was further analysed using a combination of methods: graphic representations, frequency analyses per question, cross-sectional analysis and multiple response frequency analysis.

Of the students surveyed, 70.5% were from BCom Informatics, 11.4% were from BIS Information Technology and 2.3% were from BSc Geoinformatics, BIT, BIT Information Systems, BIT Information Science and BSc IT/CS. All the students indicated that the links to access the games provided were sufficient and opened the games as expected. (Games were accessible via a URL supplied to the students.)

Students were asked about the device they had used to play the games: 75% of the students preferred to play on their laptops, while only 4.5% of students used their smart phones. No students reported switching to another device (Fig. 5).

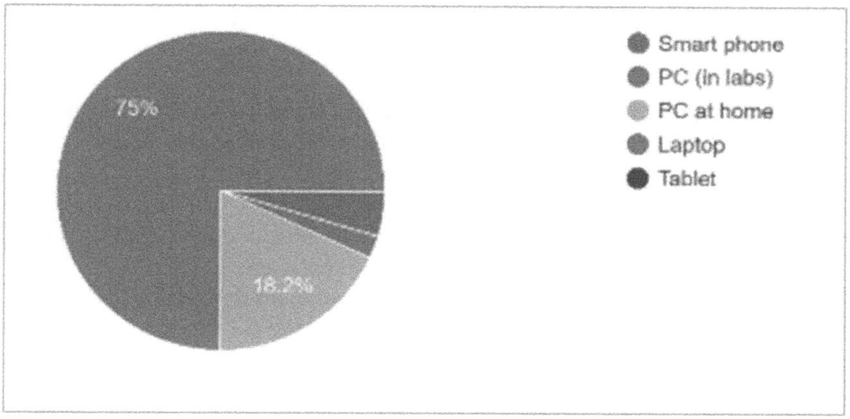

Fig. 5. Technology used to access the games

4.1 Game 1 Data and Analysis

Students were asked to play individually as often as they could find the time. More than 90% played Game 1 more than once; 50% played it more than five times and two outliers provided high values. One student played the game 25 to 30 times. The highest score was for playing the game 50 times over the three-week period. The winning player played the game five times.

Students were requested to rate the quality of Game 1 based on various variables (Fig. 6).

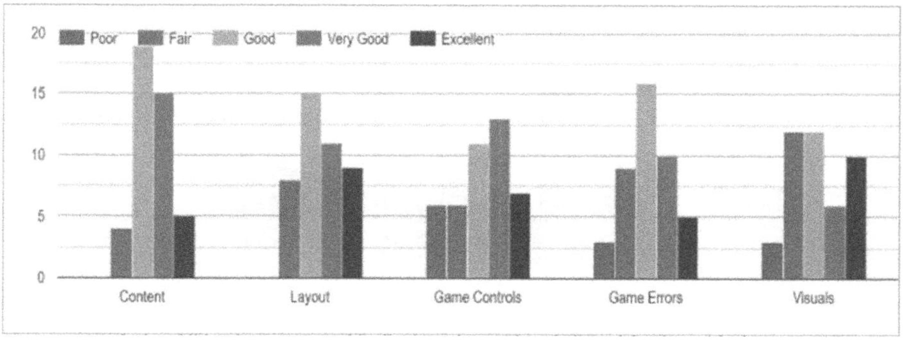

Fig. 6. Quality of Game 1

The content of Game 1 was rated highly by the majority of those surveyed. About 14% of students struggled with the game controls. Only 7% of players indicated that they had experienced some errors while playing the game and about 7% of the players indicated that they were not happy with the 3D game visuals.

Students who played on a PC at home and in the labs rated the quality higher than those who played on laptops. This is an interesting issue, which perhaps requires further interrogation.

In the additional comments and feedback section, students indicated that they wished the game had more questions and even higher and more challenging levels.

Some of the students' comments were as follows:

- "It was good for team building; maybe sub-categories could have also been good."
- "Please add a bigger pool of questions to up the challenge."
- "The graphics were a bit poor, but it was understandable as well."
- "The cycling game was fun. Maybe just improve the hit box of the road and its barriers."
- "Nothing, they were fun and educational."
- "Better visuals such as more HD graphics and maybe an option to play a different race with a different view (Game 1)."

4.2 Game 2 Data and Analysis

Students were able to play as many times as they could in their teams. Only 55% of the teams played twice or more and about 13.6% played more than twice. The highest number of plays by a team was nine. The winning team only played once.

The students were requested to rate the quality of Game 2 based on various variables (Fig. 7).

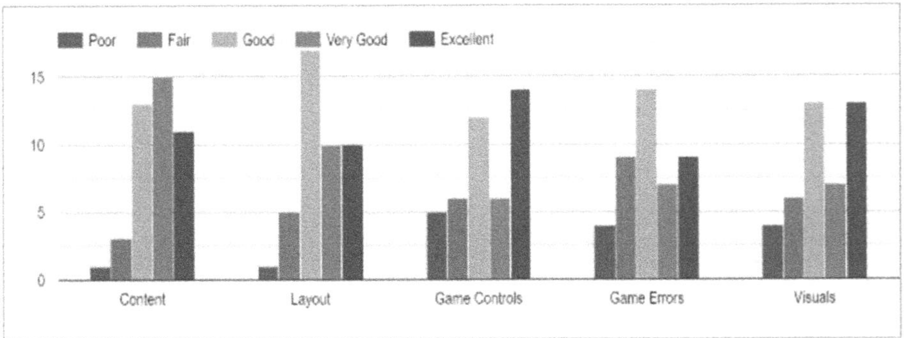

Fig. 7. Quality of Game 2

The content of Game 2 was rated the highest by the majority of students. Just over 11% of students struggled with the game controls. This was a little lower than Game 1, perhaps because it was a 2D game. Approximately 9% of the students indicated that they had experienced some errors in the game and 9% said that they found some visual issues with the game.

Similar to Game 1, students who played on a PC at home and in the labs generally rated the quality of Game 2 higher than those who played on laptops. It might be interesting for a follow-up study to determine the actual controls that were used (keyboard keys, mouse or an external controller).

A number of students were not happy with the game being a 2D game. They would have preferred the game to be a multiplayer game rather than a team game, which only allowed one team member to respond. There was also a request for a larger pool of questions and more difficulty levels.

The majority of the students found the quality of the content layouts, game controls, error handling and general look and feel good and fit for purpose. About 89% of the students found the games easy to learn and about 77% asserted that the game's objectives were clear.

Students were asked to provide feedback and any suggestions. The main issues raised highlighted design principles that the researchers had skipped. Students were not included in the design phase. There was a degree of complexity, but students expected the questions to be harder. Students requested a larger pool of questions, multi-player options and consistent graphics (Game 1 was 3D and Game 2 was 2D).

Some of the students' comments were as follows:

- "Please make multi-player mode for the team game so that all the team members can input answers on the game."
- "More communication between members should be required, maybe add in play chat."
- "I hoped to see a section where each member had to rate or comment on each other's efforts." (Table 3)

Students were asked a number of questions to determine if their teamwork skills had increased after playing both games. The results are summarised below.

About 84.1% of the participants cited that their desire to see their team succeed increased as they played the games. About 86.4% of the students indicated that all their team members had participated in the games, and that they found the games to be useful for team building. The questions in the games were clear for more than 81.4% of the participants. About 36% of the students were not sure if the games made them feel part of the team or not, and about 32% were not sure if there was a clear leader in their teams. Perhaps this may indicate that team dynamics and leadership skills need to be emphasised more in the content.

Another interesting result is that only 61.4% of students thought the games may be used to prepare for tests and exams. This perhaps indicated a need for greater depth in the content. Or perhaps it indicated that the students viewed the games as a tool that cannot be used on its own, but may only complement traditional study methods. A further study on this may be necessary to understand this observation.

Approximately 77.3% of the participants found the team games fun to play and a source to understand team dynamics. About 75% recognised the potential for the games to increase their teamwork skills. This showed a recognition by the students of the possible effectiveness of gamification to develop their teamwork skills. Further interrogation is required to determine specific teamwork skills that were developed.

Table 3. Teamwork skills survey

Teamwork skills survey questions	% Disagree	% Neutral	% Agree
A) The games made you feel part of a team	4.5	35.5	60.0
B) There was a clear leader in the team	11.4	31.8	56.8
C) All team members were involved in game 2	4.6	9.0	86.4
D) The games made you want to work in a team	6.8	29.6	63.6
E) The team goals were clear for everyone	4.5	11.4	84.1
F) The team dynamics improved during play	4.5	25.0	70.5
G) The questions in the games were clear	2.3	15.9	81.8
H) The games can be used for studying for tests and exams	20.5	18.1	61.4
I) The game made you want to work harder for the team	4.5	22.8	72.7
J) The games were useful for team building	4.5	9.1	86.4
K) Your desire to see your team succeed increased as you played	2.3	13.6	84.1
L) You would want to play games as a way to improve teamwork skills	9.1	15.9	75.0
M) Playing the games in the team was fun	4.5	18.2	77.3
N) Playing games in a team made it easier to understand team dynamics	2.3	20.4	77.3

5 Conclusion

Teamwork skills are important soft skills that recruiters are looking for in university graduates. Even though some of the skills are taught at university, getting students to master these skills is often a challenge. Gamification offers a fun and engaging way to get students to learn teamwork skills individually and in a team.

This paper explored the idea of increasing student teamwork skills through the use of gamification. It is clear from the study that gamification increases teamwork skills in students. Students certainly found the ideas envisioned in this paper worth exploring further. Future studies may require an investment into higher-quality games, a long research period, and a more quantitative analysis to determine if teamwork skills had increased and what teamwork skills the students had gained.

References

1. Marasi, S.: Team-building: developing teamwork skills in college students using experiential activities in a classroom setting. Org. Manag. J. **16**, 324–337 (2019)
2. Fapohunda, T.M.: Towards effective team building in the workplace. Int. J. Educ. Res. **1**, 1–12 (2013)

3. Oravec, J.A.: Gamification and multigamification in the workplace: expanding the ludic dimensions of work and challenging the work/play dichotomy. J. Psychosoc. Res. Cyberpsychol. **9**, 59–71 (2015)
4. Lingard, R., Barkataki, S.: Teaching teamwork in engineering and computer science. In: Frontiers in Education Conference, vol. 41ST, pp. FC1-5. ASEE/IEEE, Rapid City (2011)
5. Azizah, M.T., et al.: Improving teamwork skills and enhancing deep learning via development of board game using cooperative learning method in a Reaction Engineering course. Educ. Chem. Eng. **2**, 1–13 (2017)
6. Rudawska, A.: Students' team project experiences and their attitudes towards teamwork. J. Manag. Bus. Adm. Central Europe **25**, 78–97 (2017)
7. Loughry, M.L., Ohland, M.W., Woehr, D.J.: Assessing teamwork skills for assurance of learning using CATME team tools. J. Mark. Educ. **36**, 5–19 (2014)
8. Elshiekh, R., Butgerit, L.: Using gamification to teach students programming concepts. Open Access Libr. J. **4**, 1–8 (2017)
9. Venable, J.R., Pries-Heje, J., Baskerville, R.L.: Choosing a design science research methodology. In: Australasian Conference on Information Systems, Hobart, Australia, pp. 1–11 (2017)
10. Boskic, N., Hu, S.: Gamification in higher education: how we changed roles. In: The 9th European Conference on Games Based learning - ECGBL, Steinkjer, Norway (2015)
11. van Roy, R., Zaman, B.: Why gamification fails in education and how to make it successful: introducing nine gamification heuristics based on self-determination theory. In: Ma, M., Oikonomou, A. (eds.) Serious Games and Edutainment Applications, pp. 485–509. Springer, Cham (2017). https://doi.org/10.1007/978-3-319-51645-5_22
12. Marell-Olsson, E.: Using gamification as an online teaching strategy to develop students' 21st century skills. Interact. Des. Archit. J. **47**, 69–93 (2020)
13. Parra-González, M.E., et al.: Active and emerging methodologies for ubiquitous education: potentials of flipped learning and gamification. Sustainability **2**, 1–11 (2020)
14. Frost, R.D., Matta, V., MacIvor, E.: Assessing the efficacy of incorporating game dynamics in a learning management system. J. Inf. Syst. Educ. **26**, 59–70 (2015)
15. Da Rocha Seixas, L., Gomes, A.S., De Melo Filho, J.: Effectiveness of gamification in the engagement of students. Comput. Hum. Behav. **58**, 48–63 (2016)
16. Robson, K., et al.: Is it all a game? Understanding the principles of gamification. Bus. Horiz. **58**, 411–420 (2015)
17. Toda, A.M., Valle, P.H.D., Isotani, S.: The dark side of gamification: an overview of negative effects of gamification in education. In: Cristea, A.I., Bittencourt, I.I., Lima, F. (eds.) HEFA 2017. CCIS, vol. 832, pp. 143–156. Springer, Cham (2018). https://doi.org/10.1007/978-3-319-97934-2_9
18. Yildirim, I.: Students' perceptions about gamification of education: a Q-method analysis. Educ. Sci. **42**, 235–246 (2017)
19. Brull, S., Finlayson, S.: Importance of gamification in increasing learning. J. Continuing Educ. Nurs. **47**, 372–375 (2016)
20. Çeker, E., Özdamlı, F.: What 'gamification' is and what it's not. Eur. J. Contemp. Educ. **6**, 221–228 (2017)
21. Furdu, I., Tomozei, C., Köse, U.: Pros and cons of gamification and gaming in the classroom. Broad Res. Artif. Intell. Neurosci. **8**, 56–62 (2017)
22. Al-Azawi, R., Al-Faliti, F., Al-Blushi, M.: Educational gamification vs. game-based: comparative study. Int. J. Innov. Manag. Technol. **7**, 132–136 (2016)
23. Pektas, M., Kepceoglu, İ: What do prospective teachers think about educational gamification? Sci. Educ. Int. **30**, 65–74 (2019)
24. Miller, C.: Gamification of education. Dev. Bus. Simul. Exper. Learn. **40**, 196–200 (2013)

25. Chebotareva, I.N., Lyaskovets, A.V., Makhova, V.V.: Pros and cons of using gamification in the Russian education system. Adv. Soc. Sci. Educ. Human. Res. **505**, 775–779 (2020)
26. Dichev, C., et al.: From gamification to gameful design and gameful experience in learning. Cybern. Inf. Technol. **14**, 80–100 (2014)
27. Faiella, F., Ricciardi, M.: Gamification and learning: a review of issues and research. J. e-Learn. Knowl. Soc. **11**, 13–21 (2015)
28. Fox, G., Lyons, R.M., Lynn, T.G.: Don't make the player, make the game: exploring the potential of gamification in IS education. In: Twenty-Third Americas Conference on Information Systems, Boston, vol. August, pp. 1–10 (2017)
29. Morschheuser, B., et al.: How to design gamification? A method for engineering gamified software. Inf. Softw. Technol. **95**, 219–237 (2018)
30. Morschheuser, B., et al.: How to gamify? A method for designing gamification. In: Proceedings of the 50th Hawaii International Conference on System Sciences, pp. 1298–1307 (2017)
31. Tan, D., Ganapathy, M., Singh, M.: Kahoot! It: gamification in higher education. Pertanika J. Soc. Sci. Human. **26**, 565–582 (2018)
32. Wiggins, B.E.: An overview and study on the use of games, simulations, and gamification in higher education. Int. J. Game-Based Learn. **6**, 18–29 (2016)
33. Britton, E., et al.: Assessing teamwork in undergraduate education: a measurement tool to evaluate individual teamwork skills. Assess. Eval. High. Educ. **42**, 378–397 (2017)
34. Kiryakova, G., Angelova, N., Yordanova, L.: Gamification in education. In: 9th International Balkan Education and Science Conference, Edirne, Turkey, pp. 1–5 (2014)
35. Lister, M.C., Holland, C.: Gamification: the effect on student motivation and performance at the post-secondary level. Issues Trends Educ. Technol. **3**, 1–22 (2015)
36. Matli, W., Joubert, P.: Innovative approaches in teaching and learning: the adoption of game-based learning with information systems undergraduate first-year students. J. Manag. Adm. **2016**, 118–141 (2016)
37. Rabah, J., Cassidy, R., Beauchemin, R.: Gamification in education: real benefits or edutainment? In: Proceedings of European Conference on E-Learning Greece: Academic Conferences and Publishing International, pp. 1–12 (2018)
38. Sailer, M., et al.: How gamification motivates: an experimental study of the effects of specific game design elements on psychological need satisfaction. Comput. Hum. Behav. **69**, 371–380 (2017)
39. Strmečki, D., Bernik, A., Radosevic, D.: Gamification in e-learning: introducing gamified design elements into e-learning systems. J. Comput. Sci. **11**, 1108–1117 (2015)
40. Tu, C.-H., et al.: Gaming personality and game dynamics in online discussion instructions. Educ. Med. Int. **14**, 155–172 (2015)
41. Urha, M., et al.: The model for introduction of gamification into e-learning in higher education. Proc. – Soc. Behav. Sci. **197**, 388–397 (2015)
42. Vegt, N., et al.: Gamification in Education and Business, pp. 513–533. Springer, Cham (2015). https://doi.org/10.1007/978-3-319-10208-5

Nested-Decider: An Animation Program for Aiding Teaching and Learning of Decisions/Nested Decisions

Tlou Ramabu[1(✉)], Ian Sanders[2], and Marthie Schoeman[2]

[1] Tshwane University of Technology, Aubrey Matlala Road, Soshanguve 0152, South Africa
ramabutj@tut.ac.za

[2] University of South Africa, Florida 1034, South Africa
dr.id.sanders@gmail.com, schoema@unisa.ac.za

Abstract. Introductory programming can be challenging for teachers to teach and students to learn. Some of the learning challenges are linked to students' inadequate prior programming background. As a result, introductory programming students commit syntactical or logical errors. Animation programs have been suggested and used as aiding tools for teaching and learning introductory programming concepts. However existing animation programs for teaching introductory programming concepts are limited, tend to focus on K12 computing education and are too generic. In this study, we developed a special animation program called Nested-Decider. Nested-Decider is a teaching and learning aid program for decisions/nested decisions, especially for struggling students studying text-based programming. In order to test Nested-Decider, we adopted an action research methodology where the actual struggling introductory programming students from the university participated. We grouped struggling students into experimental and control groups, where the experimental group was taught decision-statements with Nested-Decider and the control group was taught without Nested-Decider. Through pre-teaching and post-teaching algorithm exercises, we compared the results between the two groups and found significant improvement in the experimental group.

Keywords: Teaching · Learning · Introductory programming · Animations · Decision statements · Nested decision statements · Struggling students · Comprehension

1 Introduction

Our earlier study introduced the concept of developing a physical Nested-Decider (Ramabu et al. 2021) for teaching and learning introductory programming. However, during implementation we have realised that some crucial details of the tool were not visible to students. Therefore, we developed an alternative in the form of an animated Nested-Decider. In this study, Nested-Decider can be defined as an animation program that aids teaching and learning decision statements or nested decision statements.

R. J. Barnett et al. (Eds.): SACLA 2022, CCIS 1664, pp. 129–148, 2022.
https://doi.org/10.1007/978-3-031-21076-1_8

There are similar animation programs in the literature (discussed in Sect. 2), however they are mostly designed for computer science K12 education. Some of these programs are used to inspire learners to fall in love with computing courses. Some of the programs are block-based programming like Scratch and Alice (Cooper et al. 2000; Resnick et al. 2009). Introductory programming students doing text-based programming have not been fully accommodated in the evolution of the pedagogical solution through animation programs. Therefore, we find the development of animation programs important and relevant in teaching and learning introductory programming.

Some students find programming concepts too abstract or challenging to learn (Tuparov et al. 2012; Konecki et al. 2016; Bennedsen and Caspersen 2019). These challenges continue despite various assistive tools used for teaching and learning to program (Medeiros et al. 2018). The concept of decisions/nested decisions is important in introductory programming because they are inclusive or embedded into many other subsequent programming concepts like loops, functions, arrays, classes, etc. This means that the lack of proper comprehension in this case affects the rest of the introductory programming concepts. The challenging aspects include misconceptions about short circuit operators, comparison evaluations, Boolean expression results and how the general structure of decision/nested decision works (Sirkiä and Sorva 2012; Altadmri and Brown 2015).

In this study we adopted and followed an action research methodology, to put the Nested-Decider program into practice. The test was done with actual Struggling Introductory Programming Students (SIPS) at university. In order to reveal the efficacy of Nested-Decider, SIPS were divided into two groups, an experimental and a control group. The experimental group was taught with Nested-Decider and the control group was taught without Nested-Decider. For the experimented solution to make sense this paper presents a methodology, literature review, experimental setup, results and discussions. The overall presentation of this paper is as follows: Sect. 2 presents the literature review and Sect. 3 presents the methodology. Section 4 shares the experimental setup. Section 5 shares the results. Section 6 presents the discussion then Sect. 7 concludes.

2 Literature Review

This section discusses issues of learning introductory programming and animation programs used as tools to aid teaching and learning.

2.1 Issues of Learning Introductory Programming

Programming can be both challenging to learn and to teach (Konecki et al. 2016, Bennedsen and Caspersen, 2019). This has led to high failure and attrition rates in computing or computing-related courses (Watson and Li 2014; Rum and Ismail 2017). Most of the time, these challenges revolve around misconceptions about variables, Booleans, assignments, tracing, decisions, logical operators, comparison operators, loops, arrays, functions, parameters and references (Eckerdal and Thuné 2005; Goldman et al. 2008; Schoeman et al. 2013; Brown and Altadmri 2015; Veerasamy et al. 2016; Brown and Altadmri, 2017, Grover and Basu 2017, Luxton-Reilly et al. 2018; Cetin 2020). A comprehensive study by Brown and Altadmri (2015) investigated common programming errors. The authors studied Java compilations of 250 000 novice programs across the world. Among many novice programming errors found in the study, misconceptions about decisions/nested decisions were mentioned. The following section discusses animation programs that attempt to improve comprehension in programming education.

2.2 Animation Programs in Programming Education

An animation program is computer graphics that animate or make a graphical manipulation of a programming code to enhance comprehension (Moreno et al. 2014). Animation is an important educational tool that can be featured in teaching and learning as it can give students a better mental model of program execution (Levy et al. 2003). Similar approaches like flowcharts offer static diagrams of modelling software systems, presenting a sequence or operation or algorithms (Chapin 2003; Ensmenger 2016) as compared to the versatility of animation programs. Furthermore, animation programs present an opportunity for active learning as compared to flowcharts or UML (Unified Modelling Languages) which are presented in a passive approach.

One of the animation programs in programming education is called Robomind. Robomind is a text-based programming solution with a focus on robotics-based building blocks (Faisal et al. 2017). It uses English-like commands, which interact with an animation on the right side of the application. This approach is similar to a traditional robotic game, where a physical robot is controlled through commands, however in this case a virtual robot is used. Robomind is appropriate for primary school and secondary school children (Yuana and Maryono 2016). This is because it is aimed at conceptual understanding and encouragement to pursue computing courses rather than helping a struggling student at university doing text-based programming.

Jeliot is a basic program animation that is primarily aimed at helping high school students learn computer science concepts (Haajanen et al. 1997). Jeliot 1 produces the animation to give a learner a basic understanding of computer science concepts. The latest version of Jeliot (Jeliot 3) was improved by adding features like automatic generation of animation and improvement of the interface to be more flexible. It was found that Jeliot can improve vocabulary and help build a concrete model for computer science concepts (Levy et al. 2000). However, in Moreno and Joy's (2007) experiment with Jeliot 3 with two groups of novice programmers where one group used a Jeliot 3 program and the second group did not use it, the group that used Jeliot 3 found it hard to understand the program. Jeliot 3 is also intended as a motivating factor to pursue computing in the K12 stream rather than as a tool to aid university students. Other similar animation programs suitable for K12 education or foundational courses in programming include the Scratch program, BlueJ and Alice (Cooper et al. 2000; Jadud 2005; Resnick et al. 2009; Mladenović et al. 2018). The Scratch program programming language (See Fig. 1) can be effective as a pre-computing foundation or K12 course but cannot be effective for first-year programming students at university, because Scratch and similar programs are block-based program coding. In our case, the solution is required for comprehension of text-based coding.

Osman and Elmusharaf (2014) developed a program animation called Courseware. Courseware uses various blocks of graphics that reflect program code. The tool contains

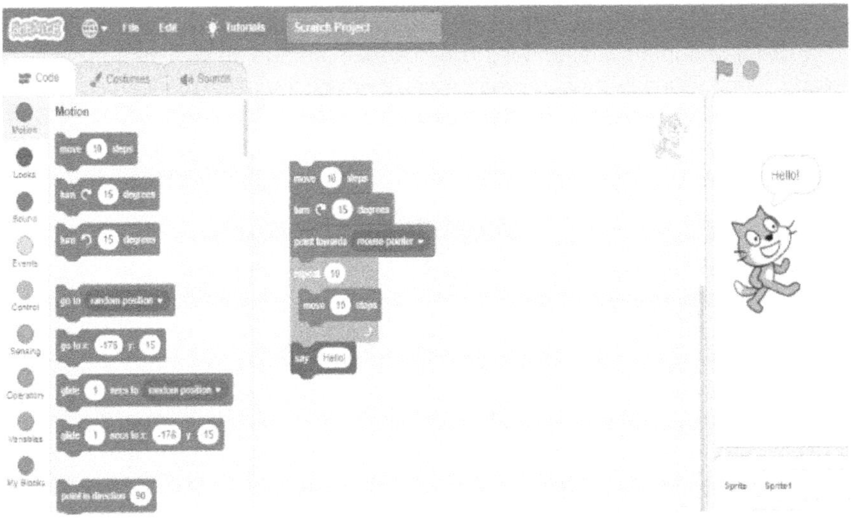

Fig. 1. Scratch program interface

many animation blocks that may distract learners' attention from learning program code. Therefore, some students may see all pieces of animation as loosely connected entities. A similar program called PlanAni was tested through control and experimental groups of learners (Sajaniemi and Kuittinen 2003; Shi et al. 2017). PlanAni contains several animations that explain the role of variables.

Végh and Stoffová (2017) developed a similar animation program to PlanAni and Courseware which uses a card that assists students to understand sorting. The application was also designed to aid teaching and learning of arrays. However, the design also contains some loosely connected graphics, which can result in knowledge that is not linked to the concept of arrays. Furthermore, the design is not a multi-view of code animation. A critical factor in our proposed animation program as compared to Végh and Stoffová (2017) is the simplicity of graphics for students to understand. Furthermore, our proposed solution simplifies teaching and learning for teachers. The following section presents the methodology followed in carrying out the study.

3 Methodology

The overall methodology followed in this study is a practical action research approach (Creswell 2002). The methodology allows teachers to reflect on their teaching approaches to continually improve teaching practices (Mills 2000). As part of the action research, we experimented with Nested-Decider in the educational environment.

In the experiment, we invited SIPS to participate in the study and the attendance was voluntary. SIPS were divided into two groups, experimental and control. The experimental group was taught with the animation program and the control group was taught without the assistance of the animation program. Both experimental and control groups were tested on the same algorithms in pre-teaching and post-teaching algorithm exercises. The teaching in the control group took place through verbal explanation and demonstration of program code through the compiler. The control group relied on verbal explanation of program code while the experimental group relied on verbal explanation with the assist of the animation program. The common factor in the control and experimental groups in that they get to see an output during code explanation and execution. We then compared the results of the pre-teaching and post-teaching algorithm exercises in order to test the efficacy of using the animation program with the experimental group. The following section further presents the experimental setup of our solution.

4 Experimental Setup

This section gives the pre-teaching and post-teaching algorithm exercises used in the experiments. The algorithm exercises were based on the concept of *decisions/nested decisions* in programming. The section further demonstrates the designed animation program and how it works.

4.1 The Pre-teaching Algorithm Exercise

Scenario

You are requested to write an algorithm that shows the process for an employee to get access into the office. An employee has to go through a gate authentication, then finally go through office door authentication. At the gate, you need to use a ***gate access card*** *or* ***identity document*** *to get in. If you get access, then in the next stage you need to use both an* ***office access card*** *and an* ***office door pin code*** *for the office door to open.*

To demonstrate how the authentication from the gate to the office will work follow the instructions below to complete the algorithm.

Prompt the user to enter the letter:

- *Y or N for the gate access card. (Y means "Yes" and N means "No").*
- *Y or N for an identity document. (Y means "Yes" and N means "No").*

If the gate access card or identity document contains the value ***Y****, then proceed by prompting the user to enter the letter (Y or N), otherwise show a message "Access into the company not granted".*

- *Y or N for an office access card. (Y means "Yes" and N means "No").*
- *Y or N for door pin. (Y means "Yes" and N means "No").*

Check if both office access card and office door pin code contain ***Y****, if so, show a message "Access into the office granted", otherwise show a message "Access into the office not granted".*

4.2 The Post-teaching Algorithm Exercise

Scenario

Write a C++ program that determines a final mark, then checks if the student has passed or failed. Prompt for a year mark and exam mark. The final mark is the average of year mark and exam mark. Show a message "You passed" if:

- *the final mark is 50 or higher and*
- *exam mark is at least 40.*

Otherwise show a message "You failed".

4.3 Animation Program (Nested-Decider)

The animation program called Nested-Decider was used as a teaching program to teach *decisions/nested decisions*. Nested-Decider was used only in the experimental group. This section explains how Nested-Decider was used.

Firstly, a console application code in Fig. 2 below is what was expected from the SIPS.

```
char gatecard, identittyC, officecard, officepin;
cout<< "Have gate card? ";
cin>> gatecard;
cout<<"Have ID card? ";
cin>> identittyC;
If (gatecard == "Y" || identittyC == "Y")
{
  cout<<"Have office card? ";
  cin>>officecard;
  cout<<"Got office door pin code correct? ";
  cin>>officepin;
     if (officecard == "Y" && officepin == "Y")
         cout<<"Access into the office granted";
     else
         cout<<"Access into the office not granted";
}
else
cout<<" Access into the company not granted";
```

Fig. 2. Pre-teaching algorithm

In the control group, the algorithm in Fig. 2 was explained without using the animation program. In the experimental group, the algorithm explanation was aided by the animation program (Nested-Decider) as in Fig. 3. The code on the right side gets executed after the user presses a start button. The animation program on the left side also starts the animation process when the start button is clicked.

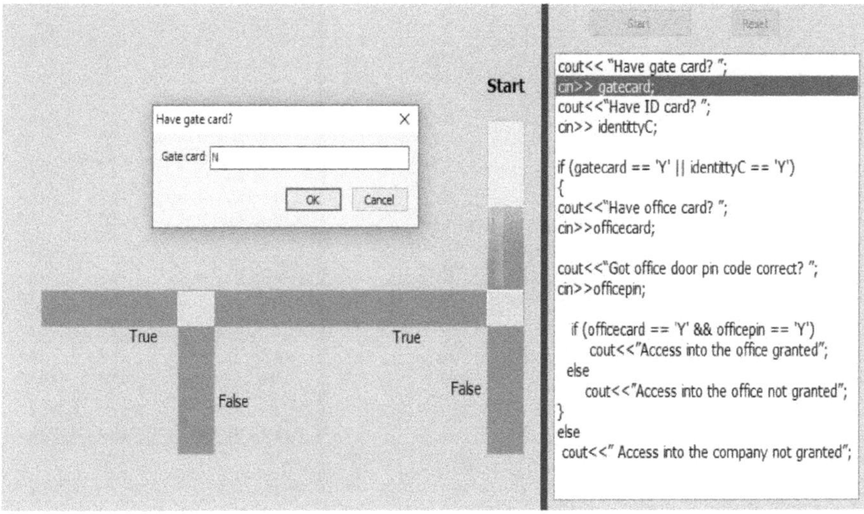

Fig. 3. Nested-Decider demo 1

More importantly, the code and the animation execute synchronously to give SIPS a better mental model of understanding the code by relating the animation with the corresponding line of code. The blue highlight in the code moves gradually from line to line, as the Nested-Decider animates accordingly with the highlighted line of the code. The green bars on the Nested-Decider represent an unexecuted flow. As the grey bar moves like a progress bar, the executed flow gradually changes from green to greyish in colour as it animates from top to bottom or left to right.

The yellow square block of the Nested-Decider is an intersection that corresponds with the *if* clause. When the blue highlight in the code reaches the *if* clause, the corresponding yellow square flickers for a few seconds to symbolise the conditional evaluation process. When the flickering stops it means the evaluation is done, then the square changes to dark-greyish and some additional text appears (See Fig. 4 below) to indicate the results of the evaluation process. In Fig. 4 additional text shows: *Have gate card? = false. Have ID document? = false. False or false = false.* The appearance of text is important as SIPS may not only rely on the teacher's narration, but can comprehend independently.

The state of Fig. 4 is as a result of *false or false* because both values gate card and identity card were "N" for No. The critical point SIPS should catch is the process of understanding the || (or short circuit operator) and how a chunk of code is jumped and the last line is executed as a result of an *else* clause. This means that SIPS would clearly see that a blue highlight that was in line 6 (See Fig. 2 for line numbers) jumped from line 7 to line 17 then highlights line 18. Similarly, SIPS would have seen that the animation bars on the left remain green which mean that the path was jumped (not executed). Furthermore, when the grey bar gradually replaced the green colour, a message with a red font is displayed "Access into the company not granted".

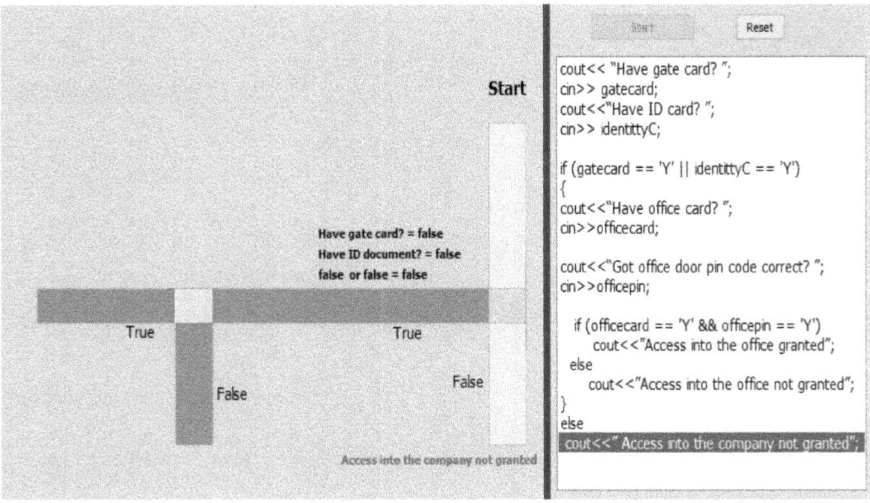

Fig. 4. Nested-Decider demo 2

The state of Fig. 5 is as a result of gate card and identity document as *false* || *true* or *true* || *false* which results in true for any of them. The prompting for the office card and checking if the office pin was correct is done before the greyish animation reaches the yellow box for another condition evaluation.

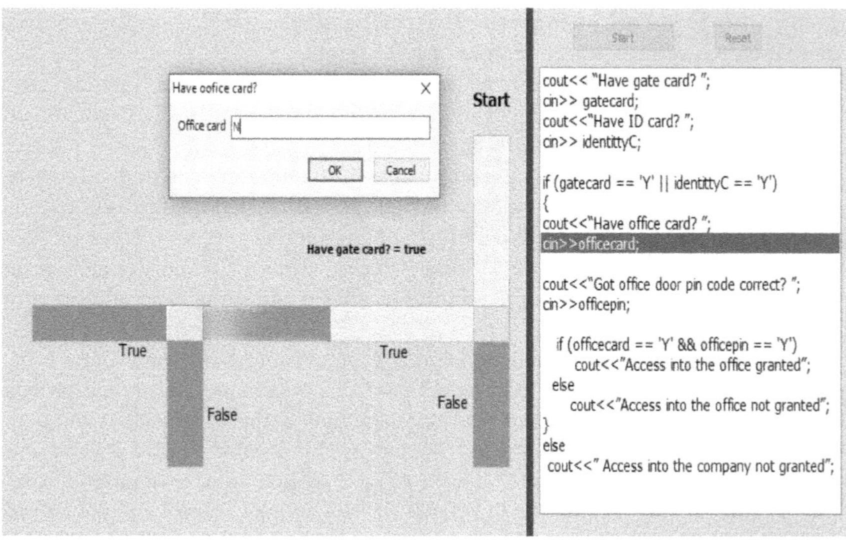

Fig. 5. Nested-Decider demo 3

Furthermore, the state of Fig. 6 represents a complete executed program where the office card and office pin are *true && false* or *false && true* which gives the result of false. In the case of Fig. 6 SIPS would have understood that the true side (green bar) is not greyish, therefore it corresponds to a jumped line (line 13 in Fig. 2).

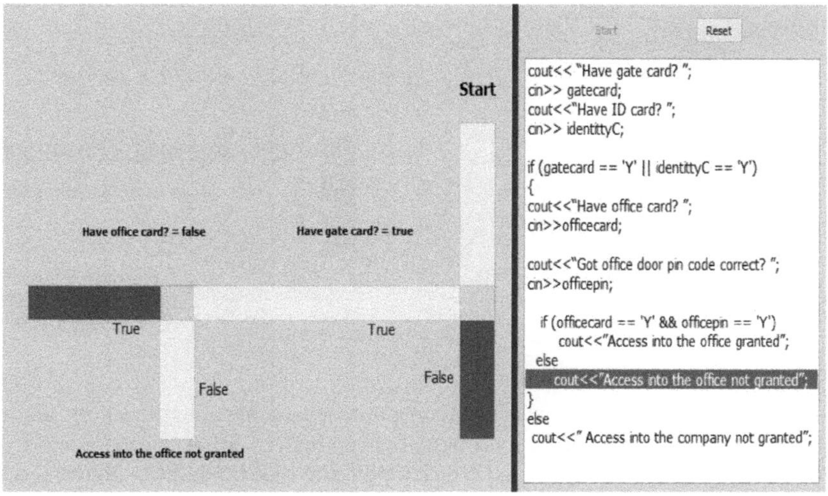

Fig. 6. Nested-Decider demo 4 (Color figure online)

Finally, Fig. 7 is as a result of an office card and office pin as *true && true* which gives the result of *true*. The corresponding text on the animation is shown as *Have office card? = true. Have office pin? = true. True and true = true.* SIPS would have understood that the true direction is executed only when the condition is *true* and *true*. Furthermore, SIPS would have understood that line number 15 (in Fig. 2) cannot be executed in case of *true* and *true* evaluation.

5 Results

This section presents comparison results between the experimental and control groups and also between pre-teaching and post-teaching algorithms.

5.1 Comparison Between Experimental and Control Groups (2021 First Semester)

In this study, Programming 1 university students who enrolled in the Computer Systems course participated in the experiments. Students were invited through an announcement on the learning management system. The invitation emphasized that is only for SIPS. This was significant in order to validate the animation program with the actual SIPS, otherwise we could not measure improvement using non-SIPS. Furthermore, with non-SIPS there

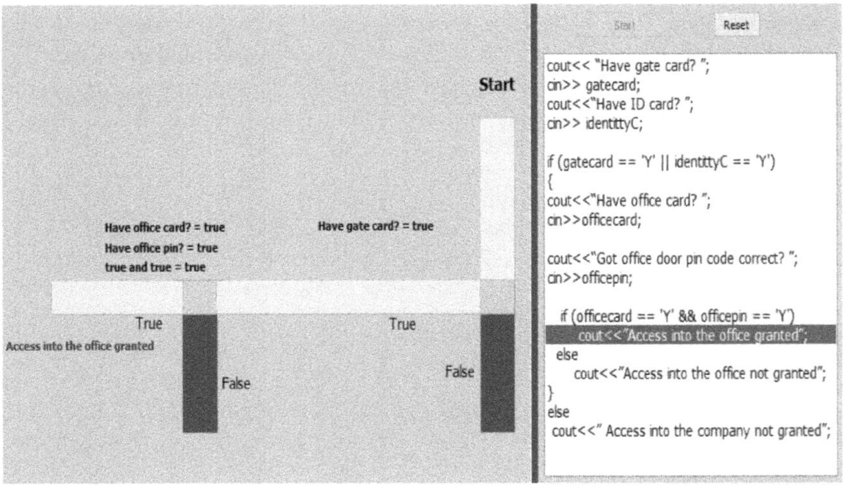

Fig. 7. Nested-Decider demo 5

was not going to be a difference between pre-teaching and post-teaching algorithm exercises for both groups. The experimental group had 16 SIPS and the control group had 15 SIPS. In order to measure the efficacy of Nested-Decider, the problem described in Sect. 4.2 was given as a pre-teaching program to solve and the expected solution (post-teaching algorithm) is depicted in Fig. 8.

Expected solution

```
float yearmark, exam_mark, final mark;
cout<<"Enter year mark"<<endl;
cin>>yearmark;
cout<<" Enter exam mark" <<endl;
cin>>exam_mark;
finalmark = yearmark + exam_mark;
finalmark = finalmark/2;
if (exam_mark > 39 && finalmark > 49)
    cout<<" You passed";
else
cout<<"You failed";
```

Fig. 8. Post-teaching solution

Table 1 below contains comparison data between the experimental and control group for the pre-teaching algorithm exercise and Table 2 for the post-teaching algorithm exercise.

Table 1. Pre-teaching algorithm results

	Experimental	Control
Correct use of ||, && and the use of *else* clause	18.75%	30.7%
Perfect working code	0	2

Table 2. Post-teaching algorithm results

	Experimental	Control
Correct use of && operator	68.75%	30.7%
Correct use of *else* clause	62.5%	38.4%
Perfect working code	8 SIPS = 50%	3 SIPS = 23.0%

The following graphs display the difference between control and experimental groups in the pre-teaching algorithms and post-teaching algorithms (Figs. 9 and 10).

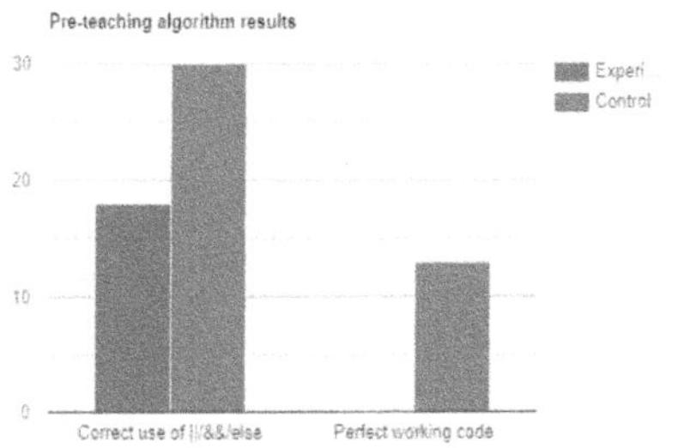

Fig. 9. Pre-teaching results

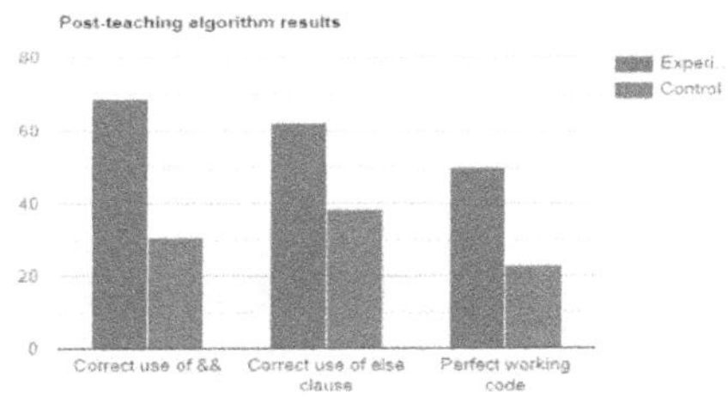

Fig. 10. Post-teaching results

5.2 Other Types of Errors that Were Found in the SIPS Programs

Amongst many errors in the SIPS program code, the following issues were found to be persistent in the post-teaching algorithm exercise for both the control and experimental groups:

- Incorrect use of || and && operators (or not used them where they are necessary)
- Swapped && and || operators
- Used || unnecessarily where is not needed
- Not used else or if-clause at all where it is necessary
- Used two separated if-statements instead of nested-if or if-else statement

Upon observation and reflection of the above errors during the first semester of 2021, the second cycle was implemented with an improved Nested-Decider. The second cycle was implemented during the second semester of 2021. The following section demonstrates components of the Nested-Decider animation which were not available in the version used in 2021 first semester.

5.3 Nested-Decider Improved

The updated Nested-Decider features the fundamentals of decision-statements. This was a critical inclusion as we have previously assumed that SIPS may have basic knowledge of decision statements. However, based on observation and errors detected in the algorithms (in cycle 1) we have noted that the Nested-Decider animation has to feature basic features like a demonstration of simple if-statement, followed by an if-else statement and then nested-if statement. The added structure or features of the animation are fixed but values are flexible as the user can enter different values and see the varied reaction of the animation. We claim that the use of these added features in Nested-Decider together with animations in Sect. 4.3 will give SIPS comprehensive knowledge about decisions/nested decisions. For demonstration purposes, we provide two graphics (the start-up graphics and completed graphics) per concept.

Simple if-statement (Fig. 11 and Fig. 12)

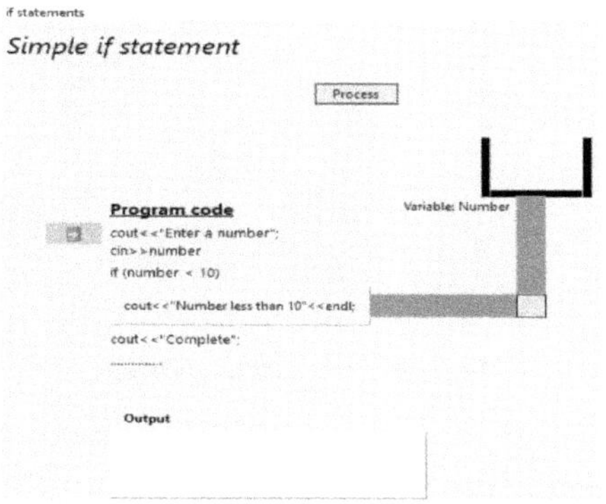

Fig. 11. Simple if statement – initial state

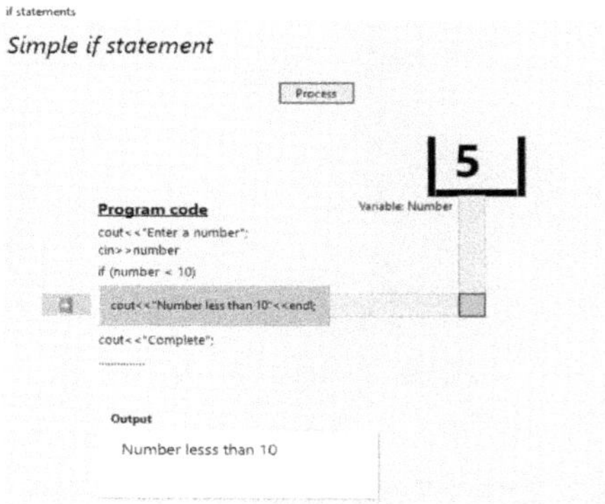

Fig. 12. Simple if statement – final state

An if-else statement (Fig. 13 and Fig. 14)

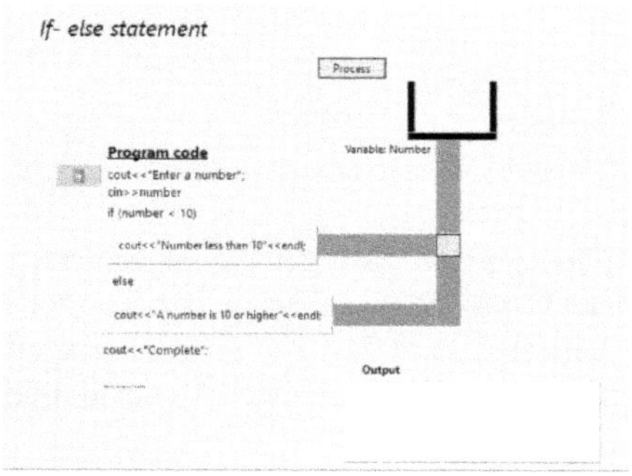

Fig. 13. An if-else statement – initial state

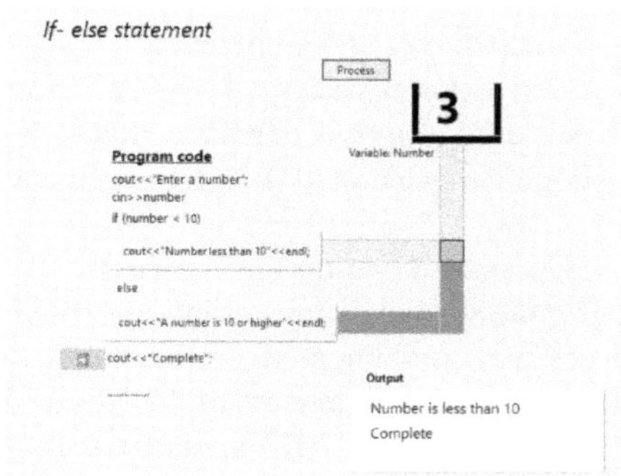

Fig. 14. An if-else statement – final state

Nesting if-else (Fig. 15 and Fig. 16)

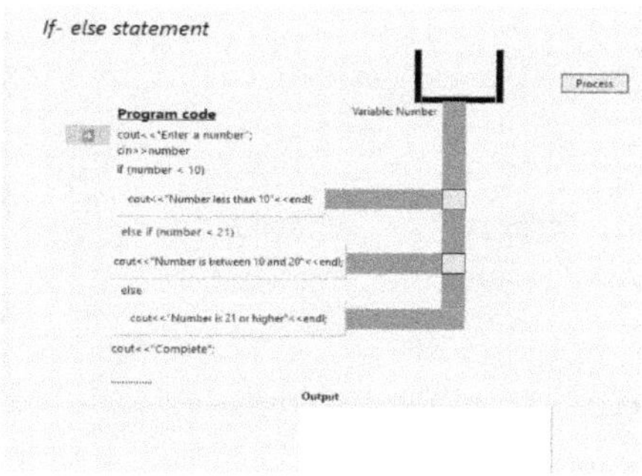

Fig. 15. Nested if-statement – initial state

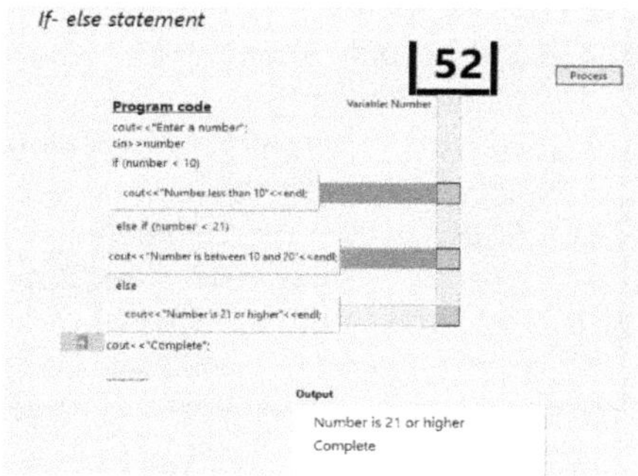

Fig. 16. Nested if-statement – final state

5.4 Comparison Between Experimental and Control Groups (2021 Second Semester)

We repeated the Nested-Decider experiment during the second semester of 2021 with another group of students who did not experience it before. The students were enrolled under the Information Technology course at the university. For more accurate analysis and comparison, we dissected both pre-teaching and post-teaching algorithms into sections for evaluation or grading purposes. Each dissected section is given a name/title for later tracing and identification purposes (See Fig. 18 and Fig. 19 below).

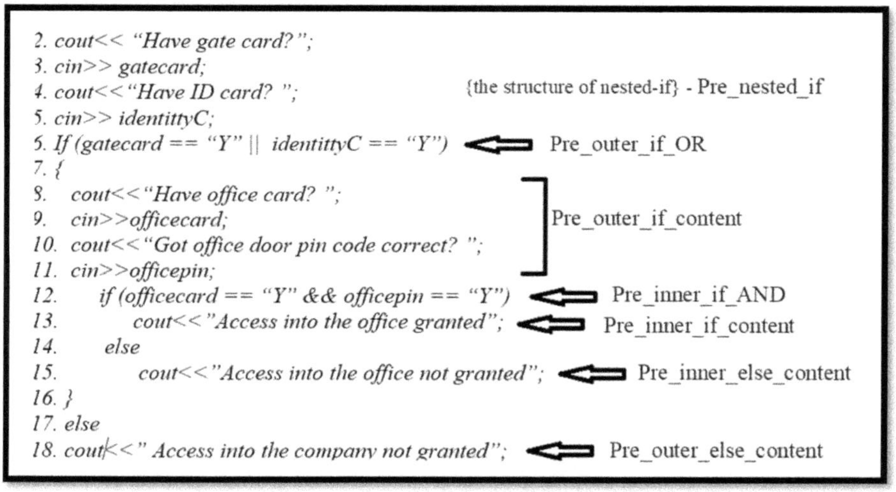

Fig. 18. Pre-teaching algorithm sections

```
float yearmark, exam_mark, final mark;
cout<<"Enter year mark"<<endl;
cin>>yearmark;
cout<<" Enter exam mark" <<endl;
cin>>exam_mark;                                   {Structure of if-else} - Post_if_else
finalmark = yearmark + exam_mark;
finalmark = finalmark/2;
if (exam_mark > 39 && finalmark > 49)   <=  Post_if_AND
     cout<<" You passed";   <=  Post_if_content
else
cout<<"You failed";   <=  Post_else_content
```

Fig. 19. Post-teaching algorithm sections

The grading of 1 is given if the section is correct and 0 is given if the section is not correct. The data in Table 3 contains grading results for the control group and Table 4 contains grading results for the experimental group.

Table 3. Control group algorithm grading

StudentNo	Pre_nested_if	Pre_outer_if_OR	Pre_outer_if_content	Pre_outer_else_content	Pre_inner_if_AND	Pre_inner_if_content	Pre_inner_else_content	Post_if_else	Post_if_AND	Post_if_content	Post_else_content
N1	0	0	0	0	0	0	0	1	1	1	1
N2	0	0	0	0	0	0	1	0	0	0	0
N3	0	1	0	0	1	0	1	1	1	1	1
N4	0	1	0	1	1	1	1	1	0	0	0
N5	0	1	0	0	0	0	0	0	0	0	0
N6	0	0	0	0	0	0	0	0	0	0	0
N7	0	0	1	1	0	0	0	1	0	1	1
N8	0	1	0	1	0	0	0	1	0	1	1
N9	1	1	1	1	1	1	1	1	0	1	0
N10	1	1	0	1	0	1	0	0	1	0	0

Table 4. Experimental group algorithm grading

StudentNo	Pre_nested_if	Pre_outer_if_OR	Pre_outer_if_content	Pre_outer_else_content	Pre_inner_if_AND	Pre_inner_if_content	Pre_inner_else_content	Post_if_else	Post_if_AND	Post_if_content	Post_else_content
N1	0	1	0	1	0	0	0	1	1	1	1
N2	0	0	0	0	0	0	0	1	1	1	1
N3	0	1	0	0	1	0	1	0	0	0	0
N4	0	0	1	0	0	0	0	1	1	1	1
N5	0	0	1	0	1	1	1	1	1	0	0
N6	1	1	0	0	1	1	0	1	1	1	1
N7	0	0	0	0	1	1	0	1	1	1	1
N8	0	1	0	0	1	0	1	1	1	1	1
N9	1	0	1	1	0	0	0	1	0	1	1
N10	1	1	1	1	0	0	1	1	1	1	1
N11	1	1	0	1	0	0	1	1	1	1	1

An improvement is noticed as 0 in the pre-teaching algorithm section and 1 in the post-teaching algorithm section. The grading outcome of 0 (pre-teaching algorithm) and 0 (post-teaching algorithm) means no improvement. The grading outcome 1 and 1 means the student was not struggling before the intervention. The outcome of 1 and 0 grading means the student may be confused and that the animation tool or teaching method might be doing more harm than good. We have paired the most closely related sections for a better and more accurate comparison. The numbers in Table 5 and Table 6 indicate the number of students according to the evaluations on 0 & 1, 0 & 0, 1 & 1 and 1 & 0.

Table 5. Control group algorithm evaluation

Sections/columns		N	0 & 1	0 & 0	1 & 1	1 & 0
Pair 1	Pre_nested_if	10	5	3	1	1
	Post_if_else					
Pair 2	Pre_inner_if_AND	10	2	5	1	2
	Post_if_AND					
Pair 3	Pre_outer_if_content	10	3	5	2	0
	Post_if_content					
Pair 4	Pre_inner_if_content	10	4	3	1	2
	Post_if_content					
Pair 5	Pre_outer_else_content	10	2	3	2	3
	Post_else_content					
Pair 6	Pre_inner_else_content	10	3	3	1	3
	Post_else_content					

Table 6. Experimental group algorithm evaluation

Sections/columns		N	0 & 1	0 & 0	1 & 1	1 & 0
Pair 1	Pre_nested_if	11	6	1	4	0
	Post_if_else					
Pair 2	Pre_inner_if_AND	11	5	1	4	1
	Post_if_AND					
Pair 3	Pre_outer_if_content	11	6	1	3	1
	Post_if_content					
Pair 4	Pre_inner_if_content	11	7	1	2	1
	Post_if_content					
Pair 5	Pre_outer_else_content	11	5	2	4	0
	Post_else_content					
Pair 6	Pre_inner_else_content	11	6	0	3	2
	Post_else_content					

This section presented comparative results collected in 2021 semester 1 and 2022 semester. In order to make results more meaningful, the following section discusses the results.

6 Discussion

In this paper, we presented an animation program called Nested-Decider. The purpose of Nested-Decider is to improve students' comprehension of *decisions/nested decisions*. The type of students that may benefit from this solution is SIPS because they find programming challenging. More importantly, Nested-Decider can be useful for students doing text-based procedural programming. Amongst various animation programs we have been developing, Nested-Decider focuses on helping students with the concept of decisions/nested decisions. Based on the experiments, we found that Nested-Decider is a crucial aid in improving SIPS comprehension. This is evident as we noted a big difference between the pre-teaching algorithm and post-teaching algorithm results for the control and experimental groups.

2021 Semester 1:
In the pre-teaching algorithm exercise for both the experimental and control groups, about 70% of SIPS did not use the ||, && and *else* properly, meaning that they confuse both or used them improperly. However, before the post-teaching algorithm exercises were written, the experimental group was taught and discussed the solution with the aid of Nested-Decider while the control group discussed the solution without the assistance of Nested-Decider. Thereafter both the control and experimental groups were given a new exercise (post-teaching algorithm exercise).

The post-teaching algorithm exercise required a learner to make use of *&&* and *else* or an alternative method in order to have a working algorithm, unlike the pre-teaching algorithm exercise where SIPS could make use of all those operators and the *else* clause to achieve a working algorithm. The assumption is that the teaching, learning and discussion that happened between the writing of pre-teaching algorithm exercises and post-teaching algorithm exercises would have improved students' understanding. A total of 68.75% of SIPS in the experimental group were able to properly choose and use the && operator or alternative nested *if-statement* to achieve the same result. A total of 62.5% of SIPS in the experimental group could also use the *else* clause properly. In the control group, only 30.7% of students were able to choose and use the && operator and *else* clause appropriately. In the experimental group, 50% of SIPS achieved perfect working algorithms whereas 23% of SIPS in the control group developed a perfect working algorithm.

In 2021 semester 2, SIPS were taught with an improved version of Nested-Decider. The following section discusses the results of the 2021 s semester.

2021 Semester 2:

The structure of the pre-teaching algorithm requires a nested if-statement (pre_nested_if) and the structure of the post-teaching algorithm requires an if-else statement (post_if_else). In the control group, 50% of students improved and in the experimental group, 54.5% improved as can be seen in pair 1 in Table 5. The differences in both control and experimental groups are similar. This means both methods of teaching are enough to instil the structure of the required decision statement in a specific algorithm. Since the other 50% that did get it right, that can also mean Nested-Decider requires some improvements on emphasising the structure of a decision statement.

Pair 2 to pair 6 (if-statement headers, compound if, contents of if-statement, contents of if-else) in the control group has less than 50% improvements. The lowest improvements (20%) in the control group are in pair 2 (using compound if/ AND operator) and pair 5 (else clause content). In the experimental group, pair 2 and pair 5 have 45% improvements, which is better than improvement in the control group. Pair 3, pair 4 and pair 6 recorded more than 50% improvements in the experimental group as compared to the control group which recorded less than 50%. The highest improvement in the experimental group is 63.6% on pair 4, while the control group recorded 40% improvements on the same pair. Pair 4 evaluates the contents of the if-statement and it means that Nested-Decider was instrumental in the comprehension of what and when certain content should be in the if-statement.

Regardless of the success in using Nested-Decider, we have noted that a few SIPS in the experimental and control group did not improve during the post-teaching algorithm exercises. We have also noted that 50% of the students in pair 2 and pair 3 of the control group did not improve. Pair 2 is about the ability to use a relevant compound operator (the && operator) or alternatively a nested if-statement, while pair 3 is about the relevant content of an if-statement. The experimental group has 10% of students who were not able to improve in the same pair 2 and pair 3. This further attests to the impact of Nested-Decider in the experimental group as compared to the control group. It is also interesting that pair 5 and pair 6 (both about relevant content of else-clause of if-statement) of the control group indicates that 30% of the students got confused or were in downward learning. The experimental group had only 1 pair (18 students in pair 6) who may potentially get confused. In the case where students get a certain pair correct in the pre-teaching algorithm, we expect the student to get the same pair correct in the post-teaching algorithm. The highest number of students who got both pre-teaching and post-teaching pairs correct is found in the experimental group (in pair 1, pair 2 and pair 5 as it has 1 & 1 evaluations). In such cases, it means that the students already knew how the pairs works and Nested-Decider intervention was not necessary or was meaningless.

7 Conclusion

The main objective of this study was to develop and test a program called Nested-Decider. Nested-Decider is an animation program that can help in teaching and learning the concept of *decisions/nested decisions* in introductory programming. The program is best suited for SIPS at university to learn text-based programming. In order to test the efficacy of the Nested-Decider, we followed an action research methodology at the university with the actual SIPS. We further divided the SIPS into two groups (experimental and control groups). The experimental group was taught with an aid of the Nested-Decider animation program and the control group was taught without the use of the Nested-Decider program. We have also developed pre-teaching and post-teaching algorithms exercises in order to compare the improvements between the two groups. In the first semester of 2021 (first cycle), we compared the pre-teaching and post-teaching algorithms of both the experimental and control groups, we noted significant improvement in the experimental group. In 2021 semester 2, we implemented the second cycle with an improved Nested-Decider. The improvements on the animation included simple-if statements, if-else statements and nested if-statement. We performed a detailed analysis in cycle 2 and generally the results in the experimental group were better than in the control group.

The experience of using Nested-Decider has provided insight into how we can further improve the program. Such improvements include a mobile-compatible app where SIPS can run the program across various platforms. Other additions can include a voice-over or an appropriate sound as a supplementary auto narration version. This can be helpful, especially since Covid19 has accelerated digital online learning. Another notable limitation is the lack of numbering in the algorithm, which helps in identifying line numbers within the algorithm. As part of our continuous action research, we keep identifying these limitations, improve the animation program and other introductory programming concepts.

References

Ramabu, T., Sanders, I., Schoeman, M.A.: Manipulatives for teaching introductory programming to struggling students: a case of nested decisions. In: Proceedings of the 13th International Conference on Computer Supported Education, pp. 505–510 (2021)

Cooper, S., Dann, W., Pausch, R.: Alice: a 3-D tool for introductory programming concepts. J. Comput. Sci. Coll. **15**(5), 107–116 (2000)

Resnick, M., et al.: Scratch: programming for all. Commun. ACM **52**(11), 60–67 (2009)

Tuparov, G., Tuparova, D., Tsarnakova, A.: Using interactive simulation-based learning objects in introductory course of programming. Procedia Soc. Behav. Sci. **46**, 2276–2280 (2012)

Konecki, M., Lovrenčić, S., Kaniški, M.: Using real projects as motivators in programming education. In: 2016 39th International Convention on Information and Communication Technology, Electronics and Microelectronics (MIPRO), pp. 883–886. IEEE (2016)

Bennedsen, J., Caspersen, M.E.: Failure rates in introductory programming: 12 years later. ACM Inroads **10**(2), 30–36 (2019)

Medeiros, R.P., Ramalho, G.L., Falcão, T.P.: A systematic literature review on teaching and learning introductory programming in higher education. IEEE Trans. Educ. **62**(2), 77–90 (2018)

Sirkiä, T., Sorva, J.: Exploring programming misconceptions: an analysis of student mistakes in visual program simulation exercises. In: Proceedings of the 12th Koli Calling International Conference on Computing Education Research, pp. 19–28 (2012)

Altadmri, A., Brown, N.C.: 37 million compilations: investigating novice programming mistakes in large-scale student data. In: Proceedings of the 46th ACM Technical Symposium on Computer Science Education, pp. 522–527 (2015)

Creswell, J.W.: Educational Research: Planning, Conducting, and Evaluating Quantitative, pp. 146–166. Prentice Hall, Upper Saddle River (2002)

Mills, G.E.: Action Research: A Guide for the Teacher Researcher. Prentice-Hall Inc., Upper Saddle River (2000)

Watson, C., Li, F.W.: Failure rates in introductory programming revisited. In: Proceedings of the 2014 Conference on Innovation & Technology in Computer Science Education, pp. 39–44 (2014)

Rum, S.N.M., Ismail, M.A.: Metocognitive support accelerates computer assisted learning for novice programmers. J. Educ. Technol. Soc. **20**(3), 170–181 (2017)

Eckerdal, A., Thuné, M.: Novice Java programmers' conceptions of object and class, and variation theory. ACM SIGCSE Bull. **37**(3), 89–93 (2005)

Goldman, K., et al.: Identifying important and difficult concepts in introductory computing courses using a Delphi process. ACM SIGCSE Bull. **40**(1), 256–260 (2008)

Schoeman, M., Gelderblom, H., Muller, H.: Investigating the effect of program visualization on introductory programming in a distance learning environment. African J. Res. Math. Sci. Technol. Educ. **17**(1–2), 139–151 (2013)

Veerasamy, A.K., D'Souza, D., Laakso, M.J.: Identifying novice student programming misconceptions and errors from summative assessments. J. Educ. Technol. Syst. **45**(1), 50–73 (2016)

Brown, N.C., Altadmri, A.: Novice Java programming mistakes: large-scale data vs. educator beliefs. ACM Trans. Comput. Educ. (TOCE) **17**(2), 1–21 (2017)

Grover, S., Basu, S.: Measuring student learning in introductory block-based programming: examining misconceptions of loops, variables, and Boolean logic. In: Proceedings of the 2017 ACM SIGCSE Technical Symposium on Computer Science Education, pp. 267–272 (2017)

Luxton-Reilly, A., et al.: Developing assessments to determine mastery of programming fundamentals. In: Proceedings of the 2017 ITiCSE Conference on Working Group Reports, pp. 47–69. ACM (2018)

Cetin, I.: Teaching loops concept through visualization construction. Inform. Educ.-An Int. J. **19**(4), 589–609 (2020)

Moreno, A., Sutinen, E., Joy, M.: Defining and evaluating conflictive animations for programming education: the case of Jeliot ConAn. In: Proceedings of the 45th ACM Technical Symposium on Computer Science Education, pp. 629–634 (2014)

Levy, R.B.B., Ben-Ari, M., Uronen, P.A.: An extended experiment with Jeliot 2000. In: Proceedings of the First International Program Visualization Workshop, Porvoo, Finland, pp. 131–140 (2000)

Haajanen, J., Pesonius, M., Sutinen, E., Tarhio, J., Terasvirta, T., Vanninen, P.: Animation of user algorithms on the web. In: Proceedings. 1997 IEEE Symposium on Visual Languages (Cat. No. 97TB100180), pp. 356–363. IEEE (1997)

Levy, R.B.B., Ben-Ari, M., Uronen, P.A.: The Jeliot 2000 program animation system. Comput. Educ. **40**(1), 1–15 (2003)

Jadud, M.C.: A first look at novice compilation behaviour using BlueJ. Comput. Sci. Educ. **15**(1), 25–40 (2005)

Mladenović, M., Boljat, I., Žanko, Ž: Comparing loops misconceptions in block-based and text-based programming languages at the K-12 level. Educ. Inf. Technol. **23**(4), 1483–1500 (2017). https://doi.org/10.1007/s10639-017-9673-3

Osman, W.I., Elmusharaf, M.M.: Effectiveness of combining algorithm and program animation: a case study with data structure course. Issues Inf. Sci. Inf. Technol. **11**, 155–168 (2014)

Sajaniemi, J., Kuittinen, M.: Program animation based on the roles of variables. In: Proceedings of the 2003 ACM Symposium on Software Visualization, p. 7-ff (2003)

Shi, N., Min, Z., Zhang, P.: Effects of visualizing roles of variables with animation and IDE in novice program construction. Telematics Inform. **34**(5), 743–754 (2017)

Faisal, M., Yuana, R., Basori, M.: Comparative study between Robomind and Scratch as programming assistance tool in improving understanding of the basic programming concepts. Atlantis-Press, pp. 787–797 (2017)

Yuana, R.A., Maryono, D.: Robomind utilization to improve student motivation and concept in learning programming. In: Proceeding of International Conference on Teacher Training and Education, vol. 1, no. 1 (2016)

Moreno, A., Joy, M.S.: Jeliot 3 in a demanding educational setting. Electron. Notes Theoret. Comput. Sci. **178**, 51–59 (2007)

Ensmenger, N.: The multiple meanings of a flowchart. Inf. Cult. **51**(3), 321–351 (2016)

Chapin, N.: Flowchart. In: Encyclopedia of Computer Science, pp. 714–716 (2003)

Pandemic Pedagogy

Student Experiences with Blended Learning at a South African University During the Pandemic

Maryam Seboa[1] and Walter F. Uys[1,2(✉)]

[1] Department of Information Systems, University of Cape Town, Cape Town 8000, WP, South Africa
Walter.Uys@uct.ac.za
[2] CITANDA, University of Cape Town, Cape Town 8000, WP, South Africa

Abstract. Online learning was introduced as a mode of delivery at most universities in South Africa during 2020 due to the pandemic. In 2021 blended learning was implemented at some Universities to cater for students who needed to attend practical tutorials and lab work as part of their degree. This trend appears to continue in 2022 with more Universities considering blended learning as a transition to the new normal. In this paper, the blended learning experiences of eleven students at a South African University was evaluated by means of online interviews. The Blended Learning Assessment framework was used as a lens to present the students readiness for blended learning and was structured around the blended learning options and their related factors. This research highlighted a number of student readiness factors and blended learning options that impacted on the quality of learning. Future research needs to expand on these factors and also examine lecturer and institutional readiness in the transitioning from online to blended learning.

Keywords: Blended learning · Online learning · Student readiness

1 Introduction

The advent of the Covid-19 pandemic caused disruptions in education on a global scale [1]. This initially resulted in many schools and universities closing worldwide [1] with some institutions rapidly pivoting to online learning to cater for social distancing [2]. The initial response of Universities to continue the academic project can be referred to as Emergency Remote Teaching (ERT) [2] which involved moving their existing courses online [3]. This includes labs, clinics, and other learning experiences [3]. ERT was seen as a temporary response to the shift to online learning due to the pandemic[2]. ERT was never intended to be a long-term response to the pandemic, and in 2021 this approach was adapted to include planned teaching and learning activities and was referred to as Physically Distanced Learning (PDL) [4].

PDL was a term used by a South African University to describe the mode of learning imposed by Health regulations that "combines online teaching and learning with selected

R. J. Barnett et al. (Eds.): SACLA 2022, CCIS 1664, pp. 151–170, 2022.
https://doi.org/10.1007/978-3-031-21076-1_9

forms of face-to-face teaching under physical distancing" [4]. PDL can be equated to Blended Learning with the option of changing modes of learning depending on the prevailing health requirements. At this University, PDL included the return to campus of some final-year medical students and students who needed to perform practical evaluations as part of their degree requirements. PDL also signalled the preparations for blended or hybrid learning for 2022 in the expectation of returning to some form of normality by combining face-to-face (F2F) activities with online lectures [4]. These approaches do not necessarily represent other South African universities' responses, as they were not surveyed as part of this research.

This research examined students' experiences with Blended Learning at the University of Cape Town during the second half of 2021. The primary research question was to understand the experience of some students who returned to campus in 2021, whilst most other courses and universities continued online.

RQ1: What was the readiness of students during the implementation of the Blended Learning approach at the University?
RQ2: How did the choice of blended learning modes affect the overall student readiness and their quality of learning?

In anticipation of the return to normal teaching for 2022, it is hoped that these experiences can provide lecturers with some insights into the kind of activities and approaches that positively impact on students learning experiences during blended learning as well as contribute to the ongoing debate of blended learning adoption in higher education.

2 Central Concepts

The following section represents a brief review of the literature related to Blended Learning at HEI's and elaborates on the chosen research framework.

2.1 Blended Learning in Higher Education

Blended learning combines the strengths of face-to-face lectures with that of online learning [5–7] and can be defined as "The appropriate use of a mix of theories, methods and technologies to optimise learning in a given context" [6]. Blended learning has a long history in higher education [8–11], however the advent of the pandemic has accelerated its implementation at some Universities [12, 13]. Blended learning is an important pedagogical tool to increase student engagement [10] and extends the student learning environment beyond the classroom to physical, virtual and online spaces [11]. A recent study [12] highlighted the importance of students' abilities to direct their own learning during this emergency transition to blended learning. They found that institutions, academia need to design curricula that are responsive to such emergent changes, as well as develop students' innate abilities to direct their own learning needs and learning strategies.

2.2 Framework for Blended Learning Assessment

The framework that we selected for situating this paper is the 'blended learning assessment (BLA) framework' as derived by Wong [14] for higher education from the OECD Business Indicator framework. Although Wong [14] tested and refined the BLA framework in their study, they did not specify individual constructs for the readiness aspect. As this framework was developed to assess the implementation of blended learning options in higher education, it is appropriate for use in our research. This framework was derived from extant adoption and use constructs in Information Systems and illustrates three phases of adoption, namely readiness, intensity and impact. The framework can be tailored to focus on each of these phases individually or can be considered linearly. According to this framework, the institution, staff and learner readiness influence the intensity of adoption in terms of the choice of the blended learning options by staff and the adoption of these by students, which then impacts the quality of learning (Table 1).

Table 1. Definition of key constructs adapted from Wong [14]

Construct	Description
Readiness	A measure of the degree to which an institution, staff or student is able to take advantage of the benefits of the blended learning environment
Intensity of Adoption	The blended learning options that are being used by the participants
Impact of options	The impact that the blended learning options have on the quality of learning, academic performance, perception and satisfaction of the participants

These separate constructs will be discussed below in terms of our research.

2.3 Readiness for Blended Learning

Although the Wong [14] framework does not explicitly evaluate the readiness construct, some aspects can be gleaned from related literature. Readiness examines the institutional, lecturer and student readiness. It can range from aspects such as provisioning the requisite infrastructure, software and technology, knowledge, skills, training, lesson design, social, cultural and personal factors to effectively learn in a blended environment [14–16].

Institutions primarily drive the decision to implement blended learning [14], especially as precipitated by Covid-19. They, therefore, need to provide relevant and timely support and training in the transition to blended learning [9, 17]. Blended learning can allow universities to maximise classroom space and resources for students [18]. Blended learning implementations by institutions need to be designed both for and with lecturers [19].

One of the main factors influencing blended learning implementation in Higher Education is the lecturers preparedness and technological readiness [20, 21]. Some lecturers are reluctant to use technology and prefer the F2F environment [14]. Academics at contact Universities in South Africa had limited training or experience in online/blended learning/pedagogy before the pandemic [22]. With BL, lecturers need to adopt more flexible delivery methods and pedagogies instead of conventional methods [18, 22]. The development of lecturers readiness appears to influence student readiness for blended learning [24] directly. Although lecturers complain about the student's behaviour during online learning, it has allowed the students to become more self-directed in their studies [23].

Student readiness further impacts the adoption of blended learning [14], as some students might not be able to adjust to the new learning process. Some students struggle to cope with the online structure of the blended learning approach [24]. In addition, many students are reluctant to work in the online environment [24] and prefer the F2F mode. Students already challenged with face-to-face learning will require additional support when transitioning to blended learning [25]. Students must also be prepared to adopt new technologies used for blended learning [14]. Blended learning is an essential aspect of students learning experience as it allows them to gain knowledge and skills required post-graduation [9].

Technology readiness also emerged as an additional concept in readiness for blended learning [9, 17, 26]. Technology readiness in education can be defined as the ability to appropriately respond to teaching and learning through new technologies and pedagogies [26]. Institutions must provide the required technology and software applications to support a blended learning environment [9, 17]. Lecturers and facilitators are responsible for developing the appropriate pedagogies and course designs for delivery in the blended learning environment [21]. Difficulties of access due to technology and other technical challenges can also influence lecturer and student technology readiness [17]. In the case of this University, lecturers were provided with extensive support from their centre of teaching and learning in transitioning courses and material to online learning. Likewise, students were provided laptops and data access where needed and additional training to access the online resources [22, 27, 28].

2.4 Blended Learning Options

Teaching and learning programs may include lectures, small group meetings as well as flexible time for students to apply their knowledge [29] either in an online, face-to-face or blended-learning format. Cronje suggests that the choice of mode, methods and technologies depend on the context and the pedagogical approach [6].

Students can be provided with online resources such as lecture notes as well as communication tools so that the students can stay in contact with their lecturers [14]. In addition, lectures can be recorded and made available for students online. However, even though the students can watch the lectures at their convenience, there is still a lack of lecturer-student interaction [14]. Students have shown to have a positive attitude towards adopting blended learning but there is still a preference towards face-to-face learning environments [14].

2.5 Quality of Learning

BL has the potential to improve the quality of education and learning outcomes through the appropriate choice of options and adoption by institutions, lecturers and students [16, 29]. Blended learning options can promote greater engagement and interaction amongst students and lecturers and may therefore create a more student-centred learning environment [18]. Offering students diverse modes of delivery affords them the opportunity to increase their chances of meeting the course requirements and outcomes and of catering for their individual learning styles [30].

Students who have other commitments such as career responsibilities are given the chance to be flexible with their studies [18]. Students that are geographically displaced from the institutions can save money on travelling expenses as they can learn from the comfort of their homes. Alternatively, students who prefer the traditional means of learning can still travel to the institutions for their studies [31].

With blended learning, there are less face-to-face interactions and exposure with the students and lecturers [32]. It's been stated that some students are more comfortable with the lecturers telling them information face-to-face [32]. With the decrease in social interactions, lecturers are no longer are able to observe whether the students are facing difficulties with the content in the blended learning environment [5]. In addition, students do not want to lose the social interaction that they have in the traditional learning environment [5]. Furthermore, students have stated that the decrease in social interactions was a disadvantage of the blended learning approach [32].

With the use of technology, lecturers can offer additional resources for the students, which positively impacts the student's confidence and competence, thus improving their quality of learning [33]. BL can also increase student engagement and enhance critical thinking that can ultimately improve learning outcomes [34]. Blended learning is also strongly linked to the student's satisfaction as to its effectiveness for learning [18]. Communication, interaction, and trust in the new learning environment are equally important and also impacts on the quality of learning. [34].

3 Methods and Materials

The research is based on a single case study of a South African University that had implemented Blended Learning as a response to the pandemic in some for their courses. A case study is appropriate for examining a particular situation with the possibility of informing general practices [35]. The case study is more appropriate for inductive, interpretive research where little is known about the factors and variables that influence the general situation [36]. The research sample was selected from students at a South African University who were required to attend some aspects of their course on campus e.g., lab or practical work.

The sampling strategy was purposeful [37] i.e. the participants needed to meet specific criteria for inclusion. The selection of participants was based on a snowball sampling technique as it was not possible during these times to approach students on campus or to interview them face-to-face due to health concerns prevalent at the time. The recruiting of participants was done using WhatsApp and Microsoft Teams and based on referral by other students.

The research questionnaire consisted of a number of open-ended questions that were derived from the extant literature and the researchers' experiences, and was designed to get students to elaborate on specific aspects of their blended learning experiences i.e.

1. How did online learning influence your readiness for blended learning?
2. Do you feel that your lecturers prepared you for the blended learning approach?
3. Would you say your institution and lecturer's preparedness for blended learning had an impact on the quality of learning?

For this research, we sampled eleven students at a South African University that were engaged with blended learning courses during 2021. The second round of interviews were conducted with six of the participants to clarify their initial responses and to advance the structure that was developed during the first round of analysis. The interviews were conducted over the period of 26th July 2021 till 20th October 2021. The students were mainly from the Department of Health Science and the Department of Commerce who participated in blended-learning activities in 2021. The transcription function of MS Teams was used for a first draft of the narrative, and a second round of corrections were made to the automated transcripts. The interview texts were then loaded into NVivo for further analysis.

The overall categories were derived from the BLA framework as adapted by Wong [14]. This framework takes into consideration not only the student but also the institution and staff readiness as well as the considerations for the implementation of the blended learning approach [17]. This paper however only focusses on the student readiness aspect. Even though this framework has been widely used in subsequent research, the constructs that make up the readiness categories have not been specified in greater detail.

The first round of coding was based on descriptive coding, with the second round using narrative coding [38]. Narrative coding is an method of analysis where the researcher aims to understand the participant experiences through their perspectives [38]. In our research we coded the blended learning options according to the different blended learning modes, i.e., Online, Blended and Face-to-face as well as the different kinds of activities, i.e., lectures, tutorial work, tests and exams and lab work. The first round of coding was performed by the first author and was coded according to these activities. This was appropriate, as these activities reflect the kinds of experiences that students had during online, blended and F2F learning i.e., attending classes, doing assignments, writing tests etc. The codes were then revisited by the second author and the student readiness and impact were identified based on the participants' experiences of these options. The results were extracted and added to the analysis table together with illustrative quotations for each aspect. These quotes were then used in writing up each aspect in the results section.

The research complied with the UCT Ethics in Research Policy. Ethics clearance was obtained from the Commerce Faculty Ethics Committee as well as permission from the executive director of student affairs to conduct the research amongst students. All the students that were interviewed were provided with an informed consent letter outlining the nature and the substance of the study. In order to protect the anonymity of the participants, a pseudonym (Participant 1–11) was used in the data analysis, and only the first researcher had access to this information.

4 Results

The interview transcripts were coded according to the three major constructs of student readiness, blended learning options and factors that contribute to the quality of learning [14]. These were then further grouped inductively to form the following factors (Fig. 1).

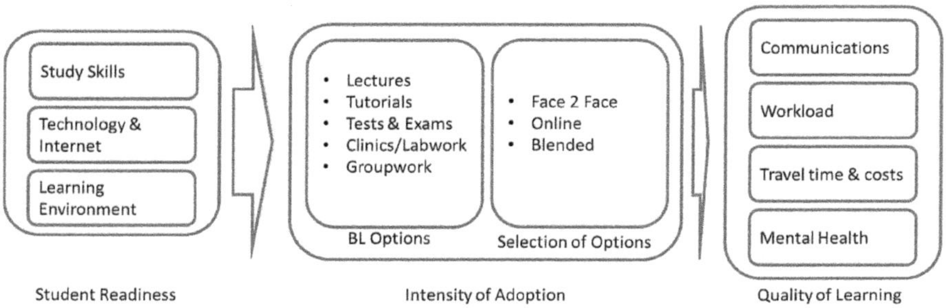

Fig. 1. Revised model for student readiness in BLE (Extended from [14]:6)

These constructs and factors will be discussed in the results section that follows.

4.1 Student Readiness

Student readiness includes all the knowledge, skills, attitudes and resources that students require to cope with the new environment. There were several aspects that students considered when transitioning to the blended learning environment. These were aspects such as taking notes, technology readiness, workload, communication, travel and mental health issues. The main factors that contributed to student readiness from our analysis were the differences between the home and campus learning environments. These aspects are discussed below. The other factors were grouped under learning outcomes.

4.1.1 Taking Notes

Before transitioning to online learning, these students were accustomed to making notes on slide handouts, course notes and their notebooks (Participants 0,2). With the advent of ERT, students were provided with notes in electronic format. In some ways, this prompted students to transition their note-taking to an online (electronic) format as well. Part of the reasons for this was that they were provided with a large volume of electronic notes, it was impractical or too costly to print them at home, and that all the material was electronic and were more accessible in an online format i.e. searchable.

> *"So now it's kind of a transition from typing and highlighting and making all your notes on PDFs and comment and making comments etc." [Participant 2]*

Returning to campus for practical work and tutorials required students to transition back to taking manual notes and supplementing that with online.pdf notes.

"You have to be writing stuff down on a continuous basis, if that's how you're going to be assessed, you have to, like, you know, be able to write quickly and be able to judge your thoughts down in like a clear, structured manner. And usually writing down your notes assisted with that a lot." [Participant 2]

Participant 0 commented on the large volume of notes that they were provided with each week, which they needed to apply to case studies, tests and exams. This also added to their academic workload. Note-taking is an essential study-skill that needs to be developed by students in higher education [39]. These skills include other academic literacy skills such as active reading, academic writing, finding information, presenting, revision and test/exam taking. Although not specifically mentioned, these skills might also have been affected by engaging in hybrid activities. For example, students were able to search for information in real time whilst they were working online; however returning to F2F activities required them to know or understand these concepts before engaging in class/clinic activities.

4.1.2 Technology Readiness

Students indicated that without technology readiness they would not have been able to cope with bended learning activities in 2021. Students also stated that they were either disadvantaged or advantaged due to their experience and knowledge of technology.

"Yes, if I. I feel like if I didn't have that readiness then I would have not been able to cope with the campus this year and last year" [Participant 5]

"It is very effective because I think that's only needed for blended learning like what I had was all I needed for blended learning. So I had all the all the technology and I think I was ready for it." [Participant 7]

"Sometimes yes, sometimes having access to the common labs would be nice because of the fact that the computers are generally a lot quicker than mine." [Participant 2]

The data collected suggests that students who used technology before the implementation of blended learning had a greater advantage than those who did not rely strongly on technology before.

4.1.3 Learning Environment

One of the main aspects that students were unprepared for was the change in their learning environment. Students indicated that the shift in their environment included the sudden transition of the traditional teaching and learning approach to online learning and blended learning.

"I've as much as I struggled with switching over from campus to home environment. Now that I'm in the swing of home environment, I wouldn't say I'm working optimally, but I've become more accustomed to it that I become kind of lazy and that since that I kind of just would rather be at home online, then go to campus just because I'm used to being at home now." [Participant 9]

In most cases, it seems like it took the students a while to adapt to working from home. Many students remarked that the lack of face-to-face interaction in 2020 with the implementation of online learning negatively impacted them. They did not feel as connected with their peers or lecturers during this time (Participant 2, 3, 7 & 9).

> *"There are some challenges that I needed to face in my environment, like the fact that I'm not close to my family and the fact that things can get lonely, and I don't feel as connected to people." [Participant 3]*

When the shift to physically distanced learning occurred in 2021, some students, especially those in the health sciences, were able to work on campus. In general, it appears as if most students preferred to study on campus (Participant 8, 9 & 10) as it provided a quiet space without distractions for them to focus on their studies whilst having access to fast computers and Wi-Fi.

> *"And I don't know if you've ever been to Health Science faculty, I mean campus, but it's very like dull kind of and everyone is working all the time. It was working all the time, but it's a good thing. As dull as it is, it's boring and that, but it's a good thing because you kind of feel forced to work...So that's why I forced myself to go to campus even on weekends. Stay there till late, even in the week getting work done." [Participant 9]*

This transition did not occur without its own challenges as Participant 3 noted.

> *"Something that was kind of a big adjustment for me was ... leaving home. I guess knowing that it's a pandemic and knowing that I'm not sure if my family will be OK, I think that emotional aspect also played a big part that I had to carry it with me to University." [Participant 3]*

The students did not note any challenges with regards to attending 'online' lectures from campus, such as finding a suitable space for them to be able to respond in class without disturbing other students around them.

4.2 Intensity of Adoption

Intensity of adoption includes both the blended-learning options as well as the modes of delivery. In this section we will first examine some of their experiences in the online environment and then contrast it with aspects of the blended learning environment such as lectures, tutorials, tests and exams, clinics and groupwork.

4.2.1 Online Learning Experiences

Interestingly, when discussing the blended learning environment, students first talked and compared it to the online environment. In 2020. The transition to emergency remote teaching (ERT) [2] was seen as a sudden but necessary shift for lecturers and students in order to complete their academic year. Some students stated that the implementation of the online learning approach felt like they were thrown in the 'deep end' and that lecturers were not well prepared for this transition.

"I found [online learning] easier because last year I feel like they still didn't have as much experience to online learning as opposed to this year. Because like last year there it was like a trial phase so people could actually give feedback what they like and what they didn't like about it." [Participant 4]

Before ERT, lectures were between 45 and 50 min with some time in between lectures to change classrooms. In the online environment, some lecturers pre-recorded their entire lecture on video and/or narrated them, whereas some lecturers split their lectures up into shorter and more manageable sessions of between 10–15 min each. Lectures and meetings were also held back-to-back as the move to online did not require any travel time between venues.

Online meetings were mainly reserved for Q&A sessions and/or discussions. In these sessions, students mostly kept their cameras off and either did not interact with the lecturer or used the chat feature to post comments.

"The communication was just terrible. Even if we video called, we didn't even really put our cameras on... so we would kind of just speak with our voices and that was it. And that's what kind of made it difficult." [Participant 9]

This experience made the online interactions very impersonal and resulted in poor engagement with the students. Transitioning to ERT in 2020 did however prepare students for using technology and tools and the University responded by providing students that were not equipped with laptops and internet access. Students recognised that they became more familiar with using these technologies as part of this transition to online learning. This also required students to become more self-directed in their use of these technologies.

"I say it would, it would have a been like if I really if I didn't know how to work my any of the Microsoft apps, uhm, I mean something as simple as Microsoft Teams. If I couldn't figure out how to work that then I think that would have delayed my learning a lot. Uhm, I wouldn't have been able to attend lectures on that" [Participant 9]

This was particularly evident in students' use of the learning management system (Vula), online meeting platforms (Zoom and MS Teams) as well as their laptops and mobile phones for studying and personal productivity.

"It used to not be as central, but it became more central and so we needed to think about learning pathways on Vula and the lessons tool and how to use that effectively." [Participant 11]

The transition to ERT was not without its own challenges, as some students struggled with data/connectivity. This was also another reason why cameras were kept off during classes, in order to save data. In some cases, it meant that students were not able to attend all their classes, took longer with their assignments and tests and struggled to collaborate with their peers. In other cases, students did most of their online work between midnight and 6am to take advantage of the additional 20Gb nightshift data that they were provided with. An initial response by UCT to cater for these challenges was to invite the most vulnerable students back to campus/res so that they could have access to a more conducive learning environment.

4.2.2 Blended Learning Options

During 2020, most face-2-face (F2F) activities were postponed. This became a challenge in 2021 with for example final year medical students who had to complete their clinical practical's as part of their qualification. Academics were also concerned with the validity of online tests and motivated for restricted access to campus for some students to write tests and exams in final year courses.

In 2021, UCT implemented physically-distanced learning (PDL). Although most students and lecturers continued their teaching and learning activities online, some students were invited back to campus for limited F2F activities. The students most affected were health-science and engineering students, although some disciplines such as accounting which require students to write a board exam also held their assessments on campus. The main F2F activities mentioned by the students that were interviewed was tutorials, clinical practice, lab work, tests and exams as well as some F2F lectures.

> *"OK, so we went to campus. I always usually when I had my blocks uh-huh and also what tutorial which is once a week. Sometimes it's online and also another lecture with two lectures on Friday which are on our campus." [Participant 6]*

> *"We had all our content delivered online through like many videos and we had to participate in quizzes but then we [had]... weekly tuts on campus and then we wrote our tests on campus." [Participant 2]*

Some students needed to go to campus once or twice a week, mainly for tutorials and practical work (clinics) and also to write tests and exams, whereas other students needed to go to campus most days of the week, even though most of the lectures and group activities were online.

> *"This semester I have two clinics, so I've been going in twice a week, but last semester it was only once a week and we would go in for tests and make use of the computers at campus to write tests and exams." [Participant 9]*

> *"For this year, [I went to campus] about three times a week." [Participant 3]*

> *"On Monday, Tuesday, Wednesday, Thursday and Friday. So it's for clinics, lectures and tutorials." [Participant 7]*

Although most students in this group found that online learning helped them prepare for blended learning, this was not always the case.

> *"Yes, I got to learn how to use like more applications such as Zoom and Microsoft Teams. But it didn't prepare me for the blended approach. It only kind of just prepared me for the online approach." [Participant 0]*

The efficacy and experiences of students varied across these different courses and learning activities, yet they felt that the implementation of blended learning was a step towards the 'new normal'.

> *"And I feel like blended learning is a step towards ... normality. I guess traditional approach still being the best in my opinion." [Participant 2]*

With this research, we did not evaluate a specific course or even a lecturers approach, so there was different ways that they implemented their blended learning approach. The students that were interviewed did however comment on five specific aspects of the blended learning approach, namely lectures, tutorials, tests and exams, clinics and groupwork.

4.2.2.1 Lectures

The formats of lectures differed amongst the students' courses. One of the students (Participant 0) reported that their lecturer repeated the same lecture for online and in person. In another case, the lecturer pre-narrated an online PowerPoint as well as hosting the same lecture F2F on the following Friday (Participant 3). Some lecturers just 'recycled' their online lectures from 2020 in F2F format in 2021 (Participant 0).

None of the participants reported on lectures being conducted simultaneously in F2F and online format (hybrid format). Although most of the classrooms on campus are equipped with video recording equipment, they (at the time) were not configured for 2-way meetings via Zoom or MS Teams. In these venues, lectures can be recorded and uploaded automatically to the LMS system and made available to the students in low, medium and high quality with optional automatic captions.

Students found that the F2F lectures were much more accessible than online lectures and felt that they had more opportunity to engage with the lecturer and the material, as well as for the lecturer to assess their level of understanding.

> *"So, with lectures, I would say the exact same thing. It's just so much easier. Yeah, in person for them to answer questions [and] for them and us to see their facial expressions. You know, it's just facial expressions, help a lot, as well as silly as it sounds, but like a lecturer, for example, can see that you're struggling with the work." [Participant 9]*

Interestingly, one of the students (Participant 10), found that the lack of interaction (social skills) during online learning in 2020 affected their ability to participate in the F2F sessions in 2021.

> *"Or maybe I'm very awkward in online learning as we go into breakout rooms in Microsoft Teams and then nobody speaks... because our social skills [have] dropped so much. On campus learning the same thing happened. It just becomes difficult to interact with each other sometimes." [Participant 10]*

Although this is not the majority perspective, it should be considered that students who are returning to F2F activities may struggle even more with social interaction due to the period of isolation in 2020 and 2021.

4.2.2.2 Tutorials

Another activity that students needed to return to campus for was tutorials. Like with lectures, tutorials were offered online in 2020. In 2021, the content was delivered online, followed by quizzes and then also weekly tutorials on campus. Although some tutorials were recorded for those who were not able to attend (Participant 2), some tutorials were even facilitated remotely. Overall, the interviewed students preferred the F2F tutorials as they were able to interact more effectively with their tutor and classmates.

> *"I do prefer going to tuts and stuff in person 100%. Cause then I [am] generally taught in smaller groups, I can ask questions more easily, right?...I guess you're a little bit more intimidated to ask questions when [online]." [Participant 2]*

Like with online learning, students found that they had to re-learn how to cope in the F2F tutorial environment as well as experienced a number of advantages in comparison to the online environment.

> *"I had to learn how to interact with people again in face to face tutorial's after we most entire of 2020 [was online]... so I feel like I had to adjust my social skills again and still learn the content." [Participant 10]*

Students also felt that the F2F environment as experienced in 2021 still allowed for cheating as the tutors were still only available online (Participant 0).

4.2.2.3 Tests and Exams

Another activity that students commented on were tests and exams. In some cases, the entire course was online except for compulsory tests and exams that had to be completed F2F. In one case (Participant 3) this was the only time that the student had any interaction with the lecturer. In general, students found that the online tests were easier than F2F (Participants 0, 9), as students were able to consult their notes/textbooks during test conditions (online exams during this period were not proctored). Returning to F2F exams also required adaptation by the students to write their answers by hand, as they had become accustomed to typing their answers and to refer to their notes.

Some academics (especially in accounting) used random MCQ's so that students were not able to share the answers with their classmates or write the exam together (Participant 11). One student (Participant 0) went so far as to say that they did not learn much in the online environment:

> *"I think it's better offline rather than online, because now that we've come back and we're being tested in person, we're realising we never learned anything in the online system. We just hoped we could pass through by memorising, which is not what our degree can do." [Participant 0]*

In a management accounting test only 7% of a class of 400 students passed (Participant 0). In another example (Participant 0), tests were written in a hybrid format, where students had to go to a test venue and write the tests on paper, yet they had to scan the script and upload it to the LMS even though they were present at the venue. This was most likely to facilitate the electronic marking of the exams remotely.

4.2.2.4 Clinics/Labwork

An important F2F activity for health sciences students was the attendance of clinical sessions. Students (Participant 9) reported that they had online clinics in 2020 where they were provided with a case-study and online activities (Participant 5). In 2021 they were required to attend F2F clinics which was significantly more challenging:

> *"And then when we came to clinics in 3rd year this year it was like I felt like we were just pushed into the deep end because…I felt like the case studies that we did online didn't really prepare us for the clinics this year. …those activities would take maybe like an hour too, but clinics are exactly the same time each week and you have to plan for each clinic and afterwards prepare a session plan management plan, assessment plan. And it's not only for 1 patient. You have two or three patients per person. So, it takes a lot more of your time, and it feels like it's a lot more draining." [Participant 5]*

This quotation indicates that the return to normal was significantly more effort than the clinical activities that they performed online in 2020.

4.2.2.5 Groupwork

Another aspect of blended learning that students commented on was groupwork (Participant 0, 3 & 9). One of the students (Participant 9) had to do a group research project and commended that this was much more effective in the F2F environment than online.

> *"Communication became terrible, so our research proposal was suffering. So now that we are able to meet in person, as a group together and sit in a room…we're working a lot better. We were able to get a lot more done and we did see a bit of an improvement in our research proposal." [Participant 9]*

Some of their challenges in the online environment were trying to get hold of their group members, scheduling meetings, planning activities and meeting deadlines as well as the different times that students worked on their groupwork. In the F2F environment they were able to communicate more effectively and get a lot more accomplished.

4.3 Quality of Learning

In addition to the online and F2F activities that students participated in, students commented on a number of related aspects that impacted the quality of their learning in the blended environment. These were aspects such as their workload, communications, travel time and costs and mental health issues. Following is a brief summary of these aspects.

4.3.1 Communications

Students commented on the poor communication during online learning that significantly improved with blended learning (Participant 0, 2, 5, 9 & 10).

> *"Last year when we had online learning, we had a few issues with lectures and their communications because sometimes they would take days to reply or they just put in reply at all. Uh, so I felt like in person was much the communication was better." [Participant 5]*

Being on campus allowed students to meet in their groups or ask questions in tutorials or practical sessions.

4.3.2 Workload

Students experienced a significant increase in their workload [Participants 0, 2 & 8] during blended learning in terms of the amount of study material, participating in a greater number of F2F and online sessions as well as in preparation and travel time.

> *"It's way harder for the fact that all are learning is now compacted into like 8 hours from each course, and we're doing six whole year courses, so that doesn't help us at all, because every day we have to also come in with our tutorials ready, but we had to do like 8 hours of learning prior to that." [Participant 0]*

The fact that lecturers did not recognise this increase in workload was frustrating for the students.

4.3.3 Travel Time and Costs

Another difference between blended learning and online learning was that students needed to travel to campus again. In some cases, buses were provided but for those who needed to travel further, there were also costs involved.

> *"Yes, it did have a big impact on transport costs. I've noticed that with blended learning or even just full online learning, the costs have dropped a lot. I have also notice that now that it is blended, learning ... I'm going to campus a lot more." [Participant 9]*

No mention was made of any challenges with accommodating travel time between classes.

4.3.4 Mental Health

One of the more detrimental impact of the transition to online learning was the adjustment to studying and working from home, which had an impact on their mental health (Participant 2, 3, 6). For some students it took a while to adust to working from home in 2020 (Participant 9) and they felt isolated, missed the social interaction and struggled to balance their studies and home life.

"one of the biggest negatives was ... your mental health. It's difficult to stay motivated. You kind of feel isolated at times. You feel it's much easier to fall into like a loop of feeling like I don't want to say depressed, but like yeah, like kind of yeah sad." [Participant 2]

The transition to blended learning appeared more positive, with students enjoying going to campus, and finding greater balance with separating their private and academic lives, even though some of them only went to campus for tutorials.

"I feel more prepared this year and I feel it is emotionally and mentally because I get to dedicate all my time to my studies. Now instead of finding a balance between doing chores at home and also my academic work so now it's just my academic work." [Participant 6]

It seems like one of the emotional challenges for students working from home [Participant 2] was the lack of change in their environment. Even though this transition occurred at the height of the pandemic, none of the students commented on any specific concerns for their physical health even though some of them were studying health sciences and needed to go to campus and even the hospital for practical work. This finding is in stark contrast with [12], where health profession students were very much concerned with testing positive/quarantine, the lack of PPE equipment and a safe environment for learning.

5 Implications

Blended learning is not a new concept, however, its implementation at contact universities in South Africa was accelerated in response to some of the challenges imposed by the pandemic and the initial transitioning to emergency remote teaching. The framework of Wong [14] gave us an appropriate framework to investigate the factors that contributed to student readiness, adoption of blended learning options, and quality of learning. From this empirical research, we derived a revised conceptual framework contributing additional factors to the framework as tabulated below (Table 2).

Student readiness was mainly influenced by study habits/factors and the ability of the student to transition between F2F activities such as note-taking by hand and memorising material versus online and blended activities such as annotating and searching online documents. The research indicates two additional factors influencing readiness: technology readiness and environmental readiness. The technology readiness aspect was identified during the literature review and is supported by [9, 17, 26]. A surprising new factor is the impact that the learning environment had on student readiness for blended learning. Students found working from home particularly challenging, especially when separating their academic, social and family lives. Returning to campus for hybrid activities in some ways negated these concerns; however, provisioning of conducive study spaces on campus became more of an issue, especially for non-residence students. These two additional factors are significant in a context such as South Africa where students may come from lower socio-demographic environments that are masked by their F2F attendance at contact universities.

Table 2. Key theoretical factors

Construct	Factor	Key findings
Readiness		
	Institutional Readiness	Not evaluated
	Staff Readiness	Not evaluated
	Student Readiness	Student needs to be equipped with the appropriate study methods for each type of option
	Technology Readiness	Ability and availability of resources for the student to participate in the blended learning options
	Environment Readiness	Conducive learning environment based on the blended learning options
Intensity of Adoption		
	F2F	Lectures, tutorials, tests & exams, clinics/labwork, groupwork
	Online	
	Blended	
Impact of options		
	Communication	Quality of communication improved in BL environment
	Workload	Workload increased in BL Environment
	Travel time and costs	Travel time and costs increased in BL environment
	Mental Health	Mental health improved in BL environment

Intensity of adoption was highlighted by the two main modes of online and blended learning of the past two years with students finding that online learning prepared them better for the blended environment. In terms of the selection of options, there was limited evidence of true blended-learning choices, with lecturers appearing to chose specific formats for specific activities i.e. F2F for clinics/labwork and tests/exams with online activities for lectures i.e. a mix of options depending on the learning activity. The format for groupwork for 2021 was left to the student/group to choose, however students favoured F2F groupwork. Some activities such as tutorials and lectures were offered in a blended mode, but it did not appear as if these were specifically designed for such a format, and that the choice was more a matter of convenience and out of necessity to accommodate students who were not resident at the campus.

The *Quality of learning* was influenced mainly by the poor communication during online learning, which improved during BL. The resultant increase in workload and greater degree of difficulty of F2F activities as well as the increase in travel time and costs further impacted on students perceptions of blended learning. A fourth factor, namely mental health, appeared to improve as a result of students engaging in F2F activities on campus.

From this research it is clear that transitioning to a blended learning environment from the online environment is able to improve the quality of learning in some aspects, however this does come at an increase in cost, time and resources. In this transition, students' technology and learning environment also needs to be taken into consideration, as well as their information literacy skills in managing digital and online resources.

6 Conclusion

In response to the call to continue the academic project at the advent of the pandemic, higher education institutions rushed to online learning platforms despite the lack of readiness of lecturers and students. The experiences of 2020 provided an opportunity to reflect on how classes are offered, both online and face-to-face. In 2021, some institutions trialled a blended approach, especially for final year health sciences students who are expected to complete some form of clinical practice. This study reports on a case where students participated in some blended-learning activities and aim to complement institutions' and academics' knowledge of the factors that may impact student readiness and the quality of learning in such a blended learning environment.

This research paper explores the experiences of eleven students who participated in a qualitative interview on their blended learning experiences during 2021. Limitations of this study are the small sample size as well as the short period during which it was conducted. We selected the blended learning assessment framework by Wong [5] for our analysis. The blended learning assessment framework [5], does not indicate factors that contribute specifically to student readiness or its impact on learning. This research identified two new readiness factors and blended learning options that impacted the overall quality of learning. These factors are technology readiness and environmental readiness. As these factors are not comprehensive due to the study's limited scope, it is suggested that they be expanded by a broader study designed to formulate a quantitative instrument. Further research needs to explore the readiness of lecturers and institutions for the blended learning environment over a longer period, as well as how the lessons learned during the past two years can be incorporated into a 'new' blended learning environment. The question remains what should be blended, by whom and by how much? Hopefully, some of the lessons learned during the past two years can be incorporated into the 'new normal' of higher education and that these learning experiences are not conveniently 'forgotten'.

Acknowledgements. We would like to thank the students who participated in the interviews, as well as the lecturers who were willing to be interviewed. This research was conducted as part of a B.Com Honours in Information Systems empirical research. The first author is the student who wrote her empirical report in partial fulfilment of the degree. The second author is her supervisor for this project and was responsible for research supervision, secondary data analysis and drafting of this paper. No funding or financial support was provided for this research.

References

1. Onyema, E.M., et al.: Impact of coronavirus pandemic on education. J. Educ. Pract. **11**, 108–121 (2020). https://doi.org/10.7176/JEP/11-13-12
2. Hodges, C., Moore, S., Lockee, B., Trust, T., Bond, A.: The difference between emergency remote teaching and online learning (2020)
3. Adedoyin, O., Soykan, E.: Covid-19 pandemic and online learning: the challenges and opportunities. Interact. Learn. Environ (2020). https://doi.org/10.1080/10494820.2020.1813180
4. Physically Distanced Learning. http://www.cilt.uct.ac.za/cilt/resources/pdl. Accessed 06 Mar 2022
5. Boelens, R., Van Laer, S., De Wever, B., Elen, J.: Blended learning in adult education: towards a definition of blended learning. Osguthorpe & Graham. (2015). https://doi.org/10.1007/s12528-013-9077-3
6. Cronje, J.: Towards a new definition of blended learning. Electron. J. e- Learn. **18**, 114–121 (2020). https://doi.org/10.34190/EJEL.20.18.2.001
7. Mahaye, N.E.: The impact of Covid-19 pandemic on South African education: navigating forward the pedagogy of blended learning (2020)
8. Vasileiou, I.: Blended Learning: the transformation of higher education curriculum. Open Educ. - J. Open Distance Educ. Educ. Technol. **5** (2009)
9. Anthony, B., et al.: Blended learning adoption and implementation in higher education: a theoretical and systematic review. Technol. Knowl. Learn. **27**, 531–578 (2020). https://doi.org/10.1007/s10758-020-09477-z
10. Nash, J.: Using blended learning to increase student engagement in a large undergraduate class. In: South African Computer Lecturers Association, pp. 7–14 (2014)
11. Keppell, M., Riddle, M.: Distributed learning spaces: physical, blended and virtual learning spaces in higher education. In: Keppell, M., Souter, K., Riddle, M. (eds.) Physical and Virtual Learning Spaces in Higher Education: Concepts for the Modern Learning Environment, pp. 1–20. IGI Publishing, Hershey (2012)
12. Singaram, V.S., Naidoo, K.L., Singh, S.: Self-Directed learning during the COVID-19 Pandemic: perspectives of South African final-year health professions students. Adv. Med. Educ. Pract. **13**, 1 (2022). https://doi.org/10.2147/amep.s339840
13. Tarigan, N.P., Nugroho, B.S., Susanty, L., Khasanah, K., Surfaifel, F.: Understanding blended learning strategy in increasing students motivation after reopening schools. e-journal.ikhac.ac.id. **4**, 685–699 (2021). https://doi.org/10.31538/nzh.v4i3.16711
14. Wong, L., Tatnall, A., Burgess, S.: A framework for investigating blended learning effectiveness. Educ. Train. **56**, 233–251 (2014). https://doi.org/10.1108/ET-04-2013-0049
15. Machado, C.: Developing an e-readiness model for higher education institutions. Br. J. Educ. Technol. **38**, 72–82 (2007)
16. Firdaus, F., Muntaqo, R., Trisnowati, E.: Analysis of student readiness for blended learning model implementation in industrial era 4.0. Indones. J. Sci. Educ. **4**, 48–56 (2020). https://doi.org/10.31002/ijose.v4i1.2309
17. Burgess, S., Bingley, S., Paguio, R., Woodley, C.: Interventions in entrepreneurial learning: blended learning and ICT capacity. Australas. J. Inf. Syst. **22**, 1–29 (2018)
18. Dzakiria, H., Don, M.S., Abdul Rahman, H.D.: Blended learning (BL) as pedagogical alternative to teach business communication course: case study of UUM executive diploma program. Turkish Online J. Distance Educ. **13**, 297–315 (2012)
19. Gachago, D., van Zyl, I., Waghid, F.: More than delivery: designing blended learning with and for academic staff. In: Creating Effective Teaching and Learning Spaces: Shaping Futures and Envisioning Unity in Diversity and Transformation. Vernon Press (2021)

20. Mulyadi, D., Arifani, Y., Wijayantingsih, T.D., Budiastuti, R.E.: Blended learning in English for specific purposes (ESP) instruction: lecturers' perspectives. Comput. Lang. Learn. Electron. J. **21**, 204–219 (2020)
21. Junus, K., Santoso, H.B., Putra, P.O.H., Gandhi, A., Siswantining, T.: Lecturer readiness for online classes during the pandemic: a survey research. Educ. Sci. **11**, 1–14 (2021). https://doi.org/10.3390/educsci11030139
22. Hedding, D., Greve, M., Breetzke, G., Nel, W., Jansen van Vuuren, B.: COVID-19 and the academe in South Africa: not business as usual. S. Afr. J. Sci. **116**, 1–3 (2020)
23. Mukhtar, K., Javed, K., Arooj, M.: Advantages, limitations and recommendations for online learning during COVID-19 pandemic era. Pakistan J. Med. Sci. (2020). ncbi.nlm.nih.gov
24. Tang, C., Chaw, L.: Readiness for blended learning: understanding attitude of university students. Int. J. Cyber Soc. **6**, 79–100 (2013). https://doi.org/10.7903/ijcse.1086
25. Sriwichai, C.: Students' readiness and problems in learning English through blended learning environment. Asian J. Educ. Train. **6**, 23–24 (2020). https://doi.org/10.20448/journal.522.2020.61.23.34
26. Geng, S., Law, K.M.Y., Niu, B.: Investigating self-directed learning and technology readiness in blending learning environment. Int. J. Educ. Technol. High. Educ. **16**(1), 1–22 (2019). https://doi.org/10.1186/s41239-019-0147-0
27. Davids, N.: UCT's approach to emergency remote teaching and learning. https://www.news.uct.ac.za/article/-2020-08-12-ucts-approach-to-emergency-remote-teaching-and-learning
28. Lange, L.: Remote teaching updates for undergraduate students—UCT News. https://www.news.uct.ac.za/article/-2020-04-30-remote-teaching-updates-for-undergraduate-students. Accessed 06 Mar 2022
29. Brodersen, R.M., Melluzzo, D.: Summary of research on online and blended learning programs that offer differentiated learning options, pp. 1–23 (2017)
30. Kaur, M.: Blended learning-its challenges and future. In: 3rd World Conference on Learning, Teaching and Educational Leadership, vol. 93, pp. 612–617 (2013)
31. Adarkwah, M.A.: "I'm not against online teaching, but what about us?": ICT in Ghana post Covid-19. Educ. Inf. Technol. **26**(2), 1665–1685 (2020). https://doi.org/10.1007/s10639-020-10331-z
32. Welker, J., Berardino, L.: Blended learning: understanding the middle ground between traditional classroom and fully online instruction. J. Educ. Technol. Syst. **34**, 33–55 (2005). https://doi.org/10.2190/67FX-B7P8-PYUX-TDUP
33. Tayebinik, M., Puteh, M.: Sense of community: how important is this quality in blended courses. In: Proceeding of the International Conference on Education and Management Innovation (2012)
34. Kumari, D., Mumthas, C.K.: Blended learning as a method of teaching mathematics for CWSN. Interdiscip. e-Journal Educ. Allied Sube. **1**, 16–20 (2020)
35. Thomas, G.: The case: generalisation, theory and phronesis in case study. Oxford Rev. Educ. **37**, 21–35 (2011). https://doi.org/10.1080/03054985.2010.521622
36. Ruddin, L.P.: You can generalize stupid! social scientists, Bent Flyvbjerg, and case study methodology. Qual. Inq. **12**, 797–812 (2006). https://doi.org/10.1177/1077800406288622
37. Coyne, I.: Sampling in qualitative research. Purposeful and theoretical sampling; merging or clear boundaries? J. Adv. Nurs. **26**, 623–630 (2008)
38. Saldaña, J.: Coding Manual for Qualitative Researchers. SAGE Publications Ltd., London (2010)
39. Fry, H., Ketteridge, S., Marshall, S. (eds.): A Handbook for Teaching and Learning in Higher Education: Enhancing Academic Practice. Routledge, Abingdon (2009)

"I Feel Like I Am Teaching Myself" - An Exploratory Study of the Factors and Implications of Online Learning

Malcolm Garbutt[1], Pitso Tsibolane[2](✉), and Tristan Pillay[2]

[1] School of IT, University of the Western Cape, Cape Town, Western Cape, South Africa
[2] Faculty of Commerce, University of Cape Town, Cape Town, Western Cape, South Africa
pitso.tsibolane@uct.ac.za

Abstract. Higher education institutions had to adapt to a new normal quickly brought about by the Covid-19 pandemic. This research set out to explore the factors impacting the adoption of online learning by students and the implications of these factors on future learning. An online survey was conducted and analysed using quantitative and qualitative methods, guided by an extended technology acceptance model. The research was necessary as online learning is anticipated to continue to be used for education by higher education institutions. The findings showed the benefits of learning flexibility of online learning. However, social isolation resulted in low motivation and perception of lowering the quality of education. The research concludes that students need reassurance that they are getting an adequate education through structured learning materials and processes with timely lecturer support. Students need access to peers and must be encouraged to engage. Furthermore, students need to find their optimal learning spaces because, as life-long learners, they need to teach themselves effectively.

Keywords: Online learning · Flexibility · Isolation · Education quality · Learning spaces · Extended technology acceptance model

1 Introduction

The Covid-19 pandemic changed how the world functions, with millions of people changing the processes they use in their daily lives. The education sector had to introduce new technologies to allow students to continue to learn. This rapidly increased the adoption of online learning, also referred to as e-learning [1]. Educational institutions and students had to adjust to these systems to ensure that students could complete the syllabus in the best manner possible [1], leading to increased use of online and blended learning [2, 3]. Although online learning was a substitute for the traditional learning method, several factors disadvantaged the students' learning [4]. A common factor was the lack of technology access in students' homes [5] and sub-optimal learning and living spaces [6]. Students found it difficult to learn without human interaction [7] productively and became distracted or suffered discomfort from sitting in front of a computer for long periods. Many students had responsibilities in their home environments [8]. Against

R. J. Barnett et al. (Eds.): SACLA 2022, CCIS 1664, pp. 171–185, 2022.
https://doi.org/10.1007/978-3-031-21076-1_10

this background, this research explored factors impacting the student experiences of the adoption of online learning during the Covid-19 pandemic. The primary purpose of exploratory research was to discover a problem and identify crucial implications of the problem [9]. Two research questions guided the research. What factors impacted higher education students' adoption of online learning due to the Covid-19 pandemic? Furthermore, what are the implications of the identified factors for online learning?

This report comprises seven sections followed by a reference list. After this introduction, the background to the research is followed by the description of the theoretical framework guiding the research. Section 4 describes the research method with the resultant findings provided in the Sect. 5. This is followed by a discussion section and, finally, the conclusion.

2 Background

Three broad categories of e-learning are distance learning, pure online learning and blended learning. Distance learning is the transition from pen and paper learning to learning through a medium such as the Internet, allowing students who cannot go to schools or universities to learn [10]. Pure online learning uses electronic resources such as computers, applications and the Internet to educate students [11]. It has become popular due to the flexibility of learning times and spaces [12]. However, online learning has disadvantages such as social isolation [12]. Blended learning combines online learning and traditional face to face learning through the use of live lectures and applications that mimic the classroom [2] to incorporate the best aspects of both for an enriched learning environment [3].

Three primary factors impacting students' adoption of online learning are technology, physical environment, and social aspects. Technological factors include digital inequity and access to adequate technology [13]. A fundamental factor is the availability of reliable, stable Internet connections [5, 8, 14]. As online learning provides limited access to physical resources such as books, notes, and hard copy documents, stable Internet connectivity is imperative for soft-copy access [14]. Many higher institutions have explored synchronous versus asynchronous learning to optimise Internet connectivity [5]. Synchronous learning allows teachers and learners to meet on an online platform that mimics the traditional learning environment allowing for real-time sharing of information [15]. In addition to requiring a stable Internet connection [5], synchronous learning is time-constrained with scheduled lessons [1]. Consequently, asynchronous learning was evaluated using recorded lecture videos that can be watched at any time [5]. Videos provide time flexibility while catering for sporadic internet connectivity [5]. Nevertheless, Internet connectivity remained a significant issue for asynchronous learning as students needed to download resources to complete assignments and submit assignments [14]. Furthermore, the technologies rely on physical factors such as a continuous supply of electricity [6]. This resulted in students using pseudo-home environments such as public libraries and internet cafés and burdening students with transport availability and costs [14]. These public spaces are only open at times and not always conducive to study [6, 16].

Due to pandemic lockdowns, many students had to relocate back to their homes and adjust to learning while living with other family members. They had responsibilities such as household chores, cooking, and care of elderly family members [8]. Students with many people living in their households had to share space with other family members [6] and share household technology [16].

Some students enjoyed the online process's flexibility, while others reported negative emotions through feeling isolated [17]. A stress factor was the financial situation of students' parents [18], as many fee-payers were retrenched, fired, or suffered from a loss of income due to the pandemic. Students also encountered boredom due to sitting for hours alone in front of computer screens [19] and the lack of social interaction experienced in the traditional learning approach. Another factor was the transition from traditional face-to-face learning to lesser structured online learning [20]. From an early age, students are groomed to follow a strict school schedule that progresses sequentially [20]. The speed and scope of the pandemic coupled with limited planning and adaptability of higher institutions to cope contributed to students' resistance to online learning [21]. A significant social impact was the gap between the online learning systems and the technology skills of the student and teacher [21]. As the effective use of the online learning systems influences the enjoyment of the online learning process [13], students and educators need to be trained to use the learning technologies as they are anticipated to provide benefits beyond the pandemic [21].

In summary, online learning has provided a method of continuing education during the Covid-19 pandemic and is expected to continue. However, students and educators have been impacted in three overarching ways: technological, physical environment, and social impact. With these impacts as a starting point, the research posed the questions of what factors impacted the adoption of online learning by higher education students due to the Covid-19 pandemic and what implications ensue from these factors.

3 Theoretical Framework

An extended technology acceptance model (TAM) derived from [4] was used to guide the research to answer the research questions. TAM is commonly used to test the acceptance and adoption of technology by monitoring factors that influence people [23]. The extended framework was built on the TAM framework of [22] adapted from [23]. The adapted model [22] comprises the variables of perceived usefulness (PU), perceived ease of use (PEU), and perceived enjoyment (PE) influencing attitude (ATT) and behavioural intention (BI), which are briefly described in Table 1. The adapted model [22] was extended by [4] and introduced three new variables, time flexibility, learning flexibility and social isolation. The added variables expand the benefits, and the disadvantages of online learning, as described in Table 2. [4], indicated that the three variables influenced PU. Nevertheless, we considered that this was mainly true for time flexibility (TF), while learning flexibility (LF) influences PEU and PE, and social isolation (SI) influences PE and ATT. The new adapted model is shown in Fig. 1.

As TAM, according to [24], is "a valid and robust model that has been widely used, but which potentially has wider applicability" (p. 740), the extended model was the ideal framework for this research. The original variables resonate with this research project's aims, while the extended variables resonate with the online learning experiences. Thus,

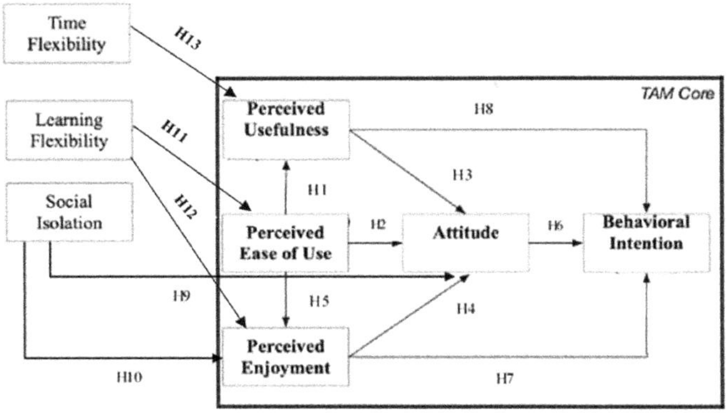

Fig. 1. Online learning research model (adapted from [4])

the extended model's three added variables helped reveal the advantages and disadvantages of online learning [4]. We determined 13 hypotheses in our adapted, extended model as listed in Table 3 and shown graphically in Fig. 1.

Table 1. Independent variables of the adapted TAM [22]

Variable	Description [22]
Perceived Usefulness (PU)	"The degree to which a person believes that using a particular system would enhance his or her performance." (p. 1097)
Perceived Ease of Use (PEU)	This variable represents how easy the online learning software, applications and methods are to use from the student's perspective
Perceived Enjoyment (PE)	"The extent to which the activity of using the computer is perceived to be enjoyable in its own right, apart from any performance consequences that may be anticipated" (p. 1099)
Attitude (ATT)	This variable represents the student's attitude towards online learning and the technology that is used, and use used to determine how the other factors affect a student's attitude

4 Research Methodology

The research hypotheses were tested with empirical data collected through a survey in a cross-sectional timeframe [25] and analysed through a positivistic deductive approach [9] using mixed methods. The target population for this research was students currently in higher education institutions. Before starting the data gathering, ethics approval was obtained from the University of Cape Town Commerce Faculty ethics committee.

Table 2. Independent variables added to the adapted TAM [22] by [4]

Variable	Description [4]
Time Flexibility (TF)	This represents the amount of time available to students and the flexibility of the students' time schedules
Learning Flexibility (LF)	This represents the learning capabilities of students and the flexibility of students learning styles
Social Isolation (SI)	This represents the social isolation that students may feel and how the students experience this isolation

Table 3. Hypotheses and sources

Hypothesis	Source
H1: PEU positively influences PU	[5, 6, 8, 21]
H2: PEU positively influences ATT	[5, 14, 17, 19]
H3: PU positively influences ATT	[5, 7, 17, 19]
H4: PE positively influences ATT	[6, 8, 17, 19]
H5: PEU positively influences PE	[7, 8, 19]
H6: ATT positively influences BI	[14, 18, 19]
H7: PE positively influences BI	[13, 19, 20]
H8: PU positively influences BI	[5, 13, 19, 20]
H9: SI negatively influences ATT	[7, 8, 17, 19]
H10: SI negatively influences PE	[7, 13, 17, 19, 20]
H11: LF positively influences PEU	[5, 6, 8, 19–21]
H12: LF positively influences PE	[5, 6, 8, 13, 19]
H13: TF positively influences PU	[5, 7, 19]

The data collection method survey comprised 29 closed questions answered through a 5-point Likert scale [26] (1-Strongly Disagree, 2-Disagree, 3-Neither agree nor disagree, 4-Agree, 5-Strongly Agree) and six open questions and was administered through the Qualtrics platform. The survey was quantitatively analysed using SPSS v25 and partial least squares structural equation modelling (PLS-SEM) in SmartPLS v3 [27]. To confirm the findings and provide further insight, qualitative analysis was undertaken in Atlas.ti v22. To test the validity and reliability of the data, the discriminant validity of the constructs was tested [28], followed by Cronbach Alpha coefficient for internal consistency [29]. Structural equation modelling (SEM) is a 'multivariate' statistical technique used to test the consistency and validity of the associations between the different factors of the framework [30]. The partial least squares (PLS) is a regression technique that involves the use of variance to test the consistency and validity of the relationship between the factors of the framework [30].

4.1 Data Analysis Method

The Qualtrics survey was piloted on a small sample population to get feedback on the questions, overall survey flow, and any issues. The feedback was taken into consideration, and the questions were revised accordingly. The data analysis started with a review of the demographics, followed by exploratory factor analysis in SPSS and PLS-SEM bootstrapping in SmartPLS to test for reliability and validity of the structural equation model and finally using the PLS algorithm to test the hypotheses. A constructive grounded theory analytical approach (CGT) [31] was used to confirm and further analyse the outcome from the structural equation model findings. This validated the quantitative findings and revealed implications for online learning.

4.2 Quantitative Data Analysis

Exploratory factor analysis was used as a data reduction method to test variable correlations and the discriminant validity of variables [28]. All variables were above the recommended acceptable value of 0.700 [32]. Consequently, the questions that make up each hypothesis were highly correlated with discriminant validity [28].

Structural Model. SmartPLS 3 software [33] was used to perform the PLS-SEM analysis of the research model [34]. After building the model shown in Fig. 2, the relationships between the model constructs were tested through bootstrapping set at 5000 bootstrap samples and 500 maximum iterations. The significance level was set at 0.05 [35]. Cronbach alpha, composite reliability and the average variance extracted techniques were performed for reliability and validity testing. Cronbach alpha calculates the variance in a construct in proportion to the true variance of the construct [29], composite reliability reflects the impact of errors of scale [36], and average variance extracted (AVE) is the amount of variance that is extracted from a construct [37]. AVE is used to test the discriminant validity of a variable and was used to test the validity of individual variables [38].

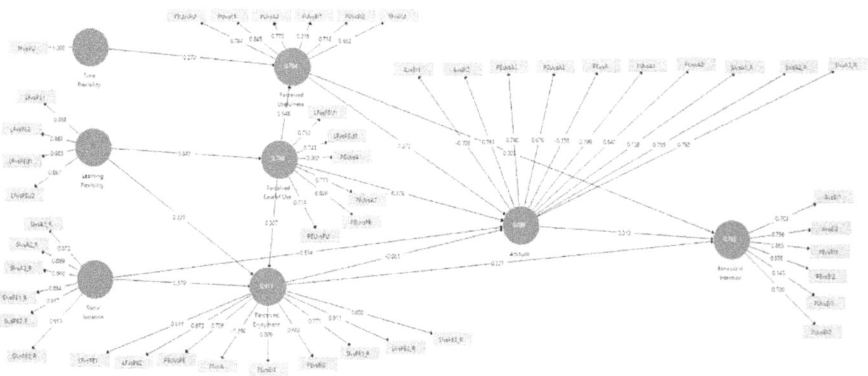

Fig. 2. Partial least squares model showing the path coefficients and weights for latent variables.

Hypotheses Testing. After bootstrap testing of the model, the PLS algorithm was run to determine the p-values, outer construct weights and inner structural path coefficients. The outer path coefficients test the relationship strength between constructs with a value greater than 0.300, indicating that the two constructs have a strong relationship [34]. The inner structural path coefficient p-values were used to test the hypotheses where p-values > 0.05 indicated rejection of the null hypothesis [9]. The weights of latent variables indicate the strength of the relationships between variables, with 0.750 indicating a strong relationship, 0.500 a moderate relationship and 0.250 a weak relationship [35].

4.3 Qualitative Data Analysis

We performed a thematic analysis (TA) of the qualitative responses based on [39] to validate the model and provide further insight into online learning. In keeping with the admonitions of [39] regarding clarity of the aims of the analysis method, we took an inductive grounded approach. Nevertheless, we had to acknowledge using the adapted online learning framework on which the greater part of this research was based. CGT [31] provided a suitable vehicle for addressing pre-existing knowledge while allowing the potential to expand the research framework as emergence in CGT allows for a (re)construction of analytical process [31, p. 408]. The six steps of [39] guided the TA process to find behavioural patterns in the data [40]. The six-step thematic analysis process began with (i) familiarising with the data, (ii) generating initial codes, (iii) searching for themes, (iv) reviewing themes, (v) defining and naming themes, and (vi) producing a manuscript [39]. The analysis for this paper was restricted to categorical semantic analysis, which restricted our approach to surface meaning [40]. Due to space constraints, we restrict the discussion to the codes and categories relevant to the quantitative model.

5 Findings

From a total of 271 surveys returned, 242 surveys were fully completed. The majority of the respondents were female (n = 144, 59%), and the most common age group was 21–30 (n = 123, 51%). The majority of respondents were undergraduates (n = 171, 71%) and at university for 1–4 years (n = 183, 76%), which indicated a balance of experiences with traditional learning techniques and online learning.

The results are depicted in Table 4 and reveal that all the values surpassed the recommended minima indicating that the model constructs were reliable and valid. All variables except BI were greater than the recommended Cronbach alpha value of 0.700 [27], and all AVE values except PU were above the recommended value of 0.500 [35]. Analysis of the weak latent variables showed that the BI latent variable AvsBI1 (boredom) had a negative weight of −0.703, and the PU latent variable PUvsBI1 (online learning is useful) had a weak weight of 0.215. Both latent variables were removed from the model and the PLS algorithm was re-run.

Table 4. Construct reliability and validity values

Construct	Number of items	Cronbach alpha	Composite reliability	Average variance extracted
Attitude	3	0,820	0,878	0,511
Behavioural intention	4	0,834	0,889	0,669
Learning flexibility	4	0,878	0,917	0,733
Perceived ease of use	3	0,856	0,893	0,582
Perceived enjoyment	3	0,826	0,878	0,505
Perceived usefulness	4	0,816	0,872	0,579
Social isolation	4	0,952	0,962	0,808
Time flexibility	4	1,000	1,000	1,000

5.1 Structural Model Evaluation

With an R^2 of 0.774, the resultant structural model explained 77% of students' intention to use online learning. Although the model explained 91% ($R^2 = 0.908$) of students' attitudes to online learning, ATT did not correlate significantly to BI. Nevertheless, PE ($\beta = 0.450$, $p < 0.001$) and PU ($\beta = 0.429$, $p < 0.001$) correlated to BI. In our adapted model, LF had a strong correlation to PEU ($\beta = 0.842$, $p < 0.001$), TF showed a weak correlation to PU ($\beta = 0.270$, $p < 0.001$), and SI had a significant but moderate correlation to PE ($\beta = 0.576$, $p < 0.001$) and ATT ($\beta = 0.537$, $p < 0.001$).

5.2 Hypotheses Testing

The findings from the hypotheses testing are shown in Table 5. All hypotheses were accepted except H4: PE influence on ATT ($\beta = -0.116$, $p > 0.05$) and H6: ATT influence on BI ($\beta = 0.050$, $p > 0.05$). Two hypotheses were below the preferred 0.300 level, namely, H12: LF influence on PE ($\beta = 0.229$, $p < 0.0001$) and H13: TF influence on PU ($\beta = 0.270$, $p < 0.0001$).

5.3 Qualitative Findings

Three themes were identified through thematic analysis – online learning experience, perceptions, and implications. However, we restrict the discussion to categories that support the quantitative findings. The most observed category relative to the research framework was SI (n = 345 occurrences), followed by TF (n = 85 occurrences) and LF (n = 42 occurrences). All three were part of the theme of online learning perception.

Table 5. Hypothesis testing with p-values and path coefficients (β).

Hypothesis	p-value	B	Accept/Reject
H1: PEU positively influences PU	0.000	0,649	**Accept
H2: PEU positively influences ATT	0.000	0,377	**Accept
H3: PU positively influences ATT	0.000	0,311	**Accept
H4: PE positively influences ATT	0.094	−0,116	Reject
H5: PEU positively influences PE	0.000	0,309	**Accept
H6: ATT positively influences BI	0.494	0,050	Reject
H7: PE positively influences BI	0.000	0,450	**Accept
H8: PU positively influences BI	0.000	0,429	**Accept
H9: SI negatively influences ATT	0.000	0,537	**Accept
H10: SI negatively influences PE	0.000	0,576	**Accept
H11: LF positively influences PEU	0.000	0,842	**Accept
H12: LF positively influences PE	0.000	0,229	**Accept
H13: TF positively influences PU	0.000	0,270	**Accept

** signifies that the p-value is less than 0.01

Social Isolation (n = 345). SI was multifaceted, with the most observed impact isolation from peers (n = 98) and lack of interaction (n = 94). *Student_130: "it very much feels like you're alone."* While lecturers (n = 34) and tutors (n = 18) were also targets of feelings of isolation, support (n = 47) was more directly felt by students. *Student_126: "it felt like there was no support as you cannot physically gauge your engagement with the work when you're not with other students."* Whereas some students differentiated isolation between peers, lecturers and tutors, others linked isolation to all three. *Student_109: "The physical interactions with students, tutors, lecturers etc. Also the ability to easily collaborate with peers."* The third most observed perception of isolation was loneliness (n = 51). *Student_107: "[I felt] Loneliness", Student_164: "Throughout ... I have felt alone."* Nevertheless, some students recognised a change in their perception of isolation (n = 3). *Student_206: "I have a study buddy ... I did not have one in the beginning and it was hard."*

Time Flexibility (n = 85). TF provided opportunities to be flexible in learning and the opportunity to attend to other chores. *Student_103: "It allows for a flexible schedule and for me to be able to structure work around the rest of my life."*

Learning Flexibility (n = 42). LF was reported half as many times as time flexibility but showed a clear link to time flexibility combined with increasing understanding. *Student_173: "I have flexibility ... allowing me to get the most important things done first." Student_191: "I have had more time to go through work, ... I am still understanding the work and doing relatively well."*

Category Co-occurrences. Category co-occurrences for SI, TF and LF were analysed to identify insights that may have been overlooked in the quantitative analysis.

Social Isolation. Analysis of category co-occurrences showed that SI affected categories across the three themes, with between 23 and 38 mentions per category. The Experiences theme (n = 23) co-occurred the least number of times and varied between challenging (n = 12), good (n = 6), and mixed experiences (n = 5). *Student_8: "It has positives and negatives. Especially when you need the physical interaction with lecturers and your colleagues."*

Overall, the most mentioned category was motivation (n = 38) in the online learning perception theme (n = 71). Low motivation (n = 18) was prevalent, followed by the need for peer motivation (n = 15). *Student_212: "I feel much less motivated than I would have been at campus." Student_104: "Seeing my peers working motivates me too."*

The second category of perception was quality of education (n = 33). Two codes equally dominated the education quality; teaching myself (n = 17) and the perception that the quality of education was low (n = 16). *Student_68: "... it was basically self-teaching ourselves." Student_34: "... you start to feel as though you're teaching yourself." Student_156: "online learning does not feel like" "real" "learning." Student_107: "... that my degree isn't real."*

The online learning implications theme (n = 152) revealed the need for a structured learning approach (n = 37), lecturer support (n = 34), constructivism (n = 29), learning spaces (n = 28), and engagement (n = 24).

Structured learning showed student appreciation for the structure and routine of campus (n = 16), workload distribution (n = 8), discipline (n = 7), and practical tutorials (n = 6). *Student_143: "... feeling lost when it is hard to figure out what exactly needs to be done/when/how." Student_181: "There are also set times for activities." Student_108: "... the workload feels greater." Student_112: "I know it is not urgent, I can do it whenever." Student_173: "... challenging trying to find the self-discipline ..." Student_212: "I feel some lecturers ... were absolutely useless with regards to responding to any inquiries."*

Lecturer support showed students' reliance on the support of the lecturers (n = 18) and the need for improved educator response times (n = 16). *Student_135: "... give us a mound of information that we need to teach ourselves, rather than being able to engage with a lecturer... it sometimes feels like I am hopelessly behind or lost." Student_187: "When you want to ask something, but lectures and tutors take long to reply to emails." Student_112: "..., it takes longer for a response. I have a very short attention span, so I tend to forget what I asked."*

The observations of constructivism showed differentiation between peer knowledge construction (n = 18) and confirming knowledge with peers (connectivism) (n = 11). *Student_156: "I was not having discussions ... to consolidate what I had learnt." Student_113: "we were not able to bond and form connections."*

Learning spaces (n = 16) were linked to SI by students motivated by peers. *Student_25: "University has a studying environment, unlike the environment at home." Student_224: "even with online learning I still go to university 5 days a week, because I find working on campus a better environment to focus in."*

Engagement (n = 24) resulted from interaction with others, constructivism with peers, and educator support. *Student_214: "my peers and fellow companions were not communicative online, and they did not participate regularly in activities or lectures." Student_158: "I feel like I don't know anything I've learnt … I only end up taking notes when I go for in person lectures."*

Time Flexibility. Time flexibility co-occurred 11 times with learning flexibility. *Student_208: "It's been quite enlightening and productive as I can work at my own pace and at my own times."* Time flexibility also co-occurred with timesaving (n = 9), convenience (n = 8) and a good online learning experience (n = 7). *Student_33: "Flexible learning and not having to travel to campus." Student_179: "Experience [was] Good. It is very convenient to work from home as I can access the work whenever I want."*

Learning Flexibility. Learning flexibility co-occurred with good online learning experience (n = 5) and the availability of lectures on video (n = 5). *Student_191: "My experience with this has been very good. I have had more time to go through work, to pause lecture videos to make notes (which cannot be done in live lectures) and my whole learning experience is relaxed."*

6 Discussion

The findings showed that TAM was appropriate for exploring online learning adoption. From the total of thirteen hypotheses, eleven were accepted. The lack of a significant correlation between PE and ATT (hypothesis 4) and ATT and BI (hypothesis 6) was theorised due to the lack of choice brought on by the Covid-19-related lockdown and the need to continue education. Although online learning did not provide a significant ATT correlation to BI, PE and PU exhibited significant correlations to BI. Thus, PE and PU were essential for the intention to use online learning. Even though PE did not significantly affect ATT, both PE and ATT were significantly impacted by SI. ATT was significantly correlated to PU and PEU, which strongly correlated to PU. This shows that PEU was important to ATT and ultimately BI for online learning. The strongest correlation in the model was between LF and PEU. Thus, LF was observed to have a meaningful impact on online learning. TF showed a significant but weak correlation to PU, which was unexpected as we hypothesised that TF would be strongly perceived as beneficial. SI was significant as expected and correlated strongly to both PE and ATT.

Examination of the qualitative responses provided insight into SI, TF, and LF. While many students generally felt isolated from their peers and educators, a perceived lack of support was common. Some students associated SI with feelings of loneliness, although some were observed to adapt to the isolation over time. The quantitative findings for SI supported the qualitative findings of a correlation to ATT and PE. TF was observed to provide opportunities for LF while providing flexibility to attend to other chores in the home due to having to spend more time there. Thus, TF supported the link to PU. LF was linked to TF and increased understanding, which resonates with the strong quantitative findings of LF correlating to PEU and weaker but significant link to PE.

The quantitative findings were further supported by an analysis of co-occurrences for SI, TF and LF with other qualitative categories. SI co-occurred across the three themes identified in the qualitative analysis. SI was linked to challenging online learning experiences, but equally to good and mixed experiences. The experiences are linked to perceptions of motivation and education quality. Motivation was the most common issue co-occurring with SI, which produced low motivation and a need for peer motivation. A concerning observation was the perception of lower quality of education whereby students felt that they were teaching themselves and that the quality of their education was being eroded.

Students provided insights into the implications of online learning in their need for structured learning, lecturer support, constructivism, learning spaces, and engagement. These implications must be borne in mind during online learning preparation. The need for structured learning showed that students appreciated the structure and routine of learning on campus, clear workload distribution, discipline, and practical tutorials. Simultaneously students need to be provided with and made aware of support from lecturers and tutors in a timely manner. Two forms of constructivism were observed. The first was the expectation of jointly increasing knowledge with peers (constructivism), and the second was confirmation of knowledge building between peers (connectivism). Students motivated by peers most noted learning spaces. Nevertheless, learning spaces are subjective, and some students prefer a home-based learning space.

Engagement resulted from the combination of interaction with peers and educators. Students expressed a need for more engagement, although our experience has found that online engagement is often limited in synchronous sessions and severely hampered in asynchronous settings.

TF and LF were connected and resulted in good online learning experiences. TF was associated with time savings and scheduling convenience, while LF was associated with the availability of lectures on video. Thus, lectures should be recorded and made available for students to review at the risk of lessened engagement due to non-attendance at live lectures. On the other hand, students raised an issue of notetaking. Asynchronous videos allow students to catch up on missed lectures and revise attended lectures, but both require good notetaking. Note-taking was mentioned by several students, predominantly in connection with the speed of taking notes. *Student_191: "[I can] pause lecture videos to make notes (which cannot be done in live lectures)." Student_230: "… couldn't take notes fast enough in class."* Thus, students need to be taught good note-taking techniques, which is a form of self-teaching.

7 Conclusion

Online learning was an emergency response to the disruptions brought about by the sudden onset of the global Covid-19 pandemic. Higher education institutions had to adapt to a new normal quickly. This research set out to explore the factors impacting the adoption of online learning by students in higher education institutions due to the Covid-19 pandemic and how these factors impacted online learning adoption. Adapting an extended TAM model [4] to underpin the research, 13 hypotheses were proposed, and an online survey was conducted and analysed using quantitative and qualitative methods.

This research was necessary as the pandemic impacts are expected to hold implications into future learning processes of higher education institutions. Although there were challenges, the findings showed that there were also benefits to online learning. In answering the first research question, the research showed that learning flexibility was the most significant factor for students' adoption of online learning. This was predominantly due to having the lecture videos available for asynchronous use. Learning flexibility is linked to a significant but weaker factor of time flexibility. Social isolation was statistically significant but not as strong as learning flexibility. Nevertheless, the qualitative analysis of social isolation provided insight into answering the second research question and provided recommendations for practice and further research.

Students were observed to have mixed experiences with online learning. While low motivation was an issue, the perception of low quality of education is concerning. Students need reassurance that they are getting an adequate education. This can be accomplished by ensuring that the students' learning materials and processes are structured, and that lecturer support is timeously available. Students need access to peers and must be encouraged to engage with peers and educators through more interactive lectures. Finally, students need to find the optimum learning spaces. These recommendations go beyond the current pandemic situation and short-term student learning. For example, being aware of their learning space [41] can extend beyond the current course to other courses, degrees, and life-long learning.

As with any research, there are limitations to this work. The most significant limitation was the small number of respondents proportional to the total number of higher education institution students. Furthermore, the qualitative analysis was predominantly semantic and restricted to categories supporting the qualitative model. Further analysis of the qualitative data may provide further insights into pandemic-induced online learning.

Further research is indicated in the findings. While note-taking was a concern for students, it is not clear if notetaking will be the same for online learning, live instruction, and blended learning. Further research into the perceptions of education quality is also indicated, while the ability to identify learning spaces for online and blended learning requires investigating. These recommendations revolve around the student's perceptions of "I feel like I am teaching myself." The challenge as lecturers is to provide scaffolding to students to become lifelong learners and learn to teach themselves knowing that they are receiving a quality education.

References

1. Eltahir, M.E.: E-learning in developing countries: is it a panacea? A case study of Sudan. IEEE Access **7**, 97784–97792 (2019)
2. Hrastinski, S.: What Do We Mean by Blended Learning? TechTrends **63**(5), 564–569 (2019). https://doi.org/10.1007/s11528-019-00375-5
3. Rasheed, R.A., Kamsin, A., Abdullah, N.A.: Challenges in the online component of blended learning: a systematic review. Comput. Educ. **144**, 103701 (2020). https://doi.org/10.1016/j.compedu.2019.103701
4. Vladova, G., Ullrich, A., Bender, B., Gronau, N.: Students' acceptance of technology-mediated teaching – how it was influenced during the COVID-19 pandemic in 2020: a

study from Germany. Front. Psychol. **12**, 636086 (2021). https://doi.org/10.3389/fpsyg.2021.636086
5. Iyer, D.G., Chapman, T.A.: Overcoming technological inequity in synchronous online learning. Commun. Assoc. Inf. Syst. **48**, 26 (2021). https://doi.org/10.17705/1CAIS.04826
6. Singh, J.B., Sharma, S.K., Gupta, P.: Physical learning environment challenges in the digital divide: how to design effective instruction during COVID-19? Commun. Assoc. Inf. Syst. **48**, 18 (2021). https://doi.org/10.17705/1CAIS.04818
7. Adnan, M., Anwar, K.: Online learning amid the COVID-19 pandemic: students' perspectives. Online Submission **2**(1), 45–51 (2020)
8. AbuJarour, S., Ajjan, H., Fedorowicz, J., Owens, D.: How working from home during COVID-19 affects academic productivity. Commun. Assoc. Inf. Syst. **48**(1), 8 (2021)
9. Bhattacherjee, A.: Scholar Commons Social Science Research: Principles, Methods, and Practices. Textbooks Collection (2012)
10. Dietrich, N., et al.: Attempts, successes, and failures of distance learning in the time of COVID-19. Am. Chem. Soc. (ACS) **97**, 2448–2457 (2020). https://doi.org/10.1021/acs.jchemed.0c00717
11. Sander, T.: What is the Definition of E-Learning? E-Student (2020). https://e-student.org/what-is-e-learning/
12. Wu, E.H., Lin, C., Ou, Y., Liu, C., Wang, W., Chao, C.: Advantages and constraints of a hybrid model K-12 E-learning assistant chatbot. IEEE Access **8**, 77788–77801 (2020). https://doi.org/10.1109/ACCESS.2020.2988252
13. Almaiah, M.A., Al-Khasawneh, A., Althunibat, A.: Exploring the critical challenges and factors influencing the E-learning system usage during COVID-19 pandemic. Educ. Inf. Technol. **25**(6), 5261–5280 (2020). https://doi.org/10.1007/s10639-020-10219-y
14. Mpungose, C.B.: Emergent transition from face-to-face to online learning in a South African University in the context of the Coronavirus pandemic. Human. Soc. Sci. Commun. **7**(1), 1–9 (2020). https://doi.org/10.1057/s41599-020-00603-x
15. Amiti, F.: Synchronous and asynchronous E-learning. Eur. J. Open Educ. E-Learn. Stud. **5**(2) (2020). http://dx.doi.org/10.46827/ejoe.v5i2.3313
16. Dwivedi, Y.K., et al.: Impact of COVID-19 pandemic on information management research and practice: transforming education, work and life. Int. J. Inf. Manag. **55**, 102211 (2020). https://doi.org/10.1016/j.ijinfomgt.2020.102211
17. Raza, S.A., Qazi, W., Khan, K.A., Salam, J.: Social isolation and acceptance of the learning management system (LMS) in the time of COVID-19 pandemic: an expansion of the UTAUT model. J. Educ. Comput. Res. **59**(2), 183–208 (2021). https://doi.org/10.1177/0735633120960421
18. Aucejo, E.M., French, J., Ugalde Araya, M.P., Zafar, B.: The impact of COVID-19 on student experiences and expectations: evidence from a survey. J. Public Econ. **191**, 104271 (2020). https://doi.org/10.1016/j.jpubeco.2020.104271
19. Irawan, A.W., Dwisona, D., Lestari, M.: Psychological impacts of students on online learning during the pandemic COVID-19. KONSELI: Jurnal Bimbingan Dan Konseling (E-J.) **7**(1), 53–60 (2020). https://doi.org/10.24042/kons.v7i1.6389
20. Aboagye, E., Yawson, J.A., Appiah, K.N.: COVID-19 and e-learning: the challenges of students in tertiary institutions. Soc. Educ. Res. **2**(1), 1–8 (2020). https://doi.org/10.37256/ser.212021422
21. Marek, M., Wu, W., Chew, C.: Teacher experiences in converting classes to distance learning in the COVID-19 pandemic. Int. J. Distance Educ. Technol. **19**(1), 89–109 (2021). https://doi.org/10.4018/IJDET.20210101.oa3
22. Lee, M.K.O., Cheung, C.M.K., Chen, Z.: Acceptance of Internet-based learning medium: the role of extrinsic and intrinsic motivation. Inf. Manag. **42**(8), 1095–1104 (2005). https://doi.org/10.1016/j.im.2003.10.007

23. Davis, F.D.: A technology acceptance model for empirically testing new end-user information systems: theory and results. Doctoral dissertation. Massachusetts Institute of Technology (1985)
24. King, W.R., He, J.: A meta-analysis of the technology acceptance model. Inf. Manag. **43**(6), 740–755 (2006)
25. Streefkerk, R.: Inductive vs. Deductive Research Approach (with Examples) (2019)
26. Joshi, A., Kale, S., Chandel, S., Pal, D.K.: Likert scale: explored and explained. Br. J. Appl. Sci. Technol. **7**(4), 396 (2015)
27. Hair, J.F., Risher, J.J., Sarstedt, M., Ringle, C.M.: When to use and how to report the results of PLS-SEM. Eur. Bus. Rev. **31**(1), 2–24 (2019). https://doi.org/10.1108/EBR-11-2018-0203
28. Rönkkö, M., Cho, E.: An updated guideline for assessing discriminant validity. Org. Res. Methods **25**, 6–14 (2020)
29. Brown, J.D.: The Cronbach alpha reliability estimate. Shiken: JALT Test. Eval. SIG Newsl. **6**(1), 17–18 (2002)
30. Samani, S.A.: Steps in research process (partial least square of structural equation modeling (PLS-SEM)). Int. J. Soc. Sci. Bus. **1**(2), 55–66 (2016)
31. Charmaz, K.: Constructionism and the grounded theory method. Handb. Constructionist Res. **1**(1), 397–412 (2008)
32. Yong, A.G., Pearce, S.: A beginner's guide to factor analysis: focusing on exploratory factor analysis. Tutor. Quant. Methods Psychol. **9**(2), 79–94 (2013)
33. Ringle, C.M., Wende, S., Becker, J.M.: SmartPLS 3. SmartPLS GmbH, Boenningstedt. J. Serv. Sci. Manag. **10**(3), 32–49 (2015)
34. Lowry, P.B., Gaskin, J.: Partial least squares (PLS) structural equation modeling (SEM) for building and testing behavioral causal theory: when to choose it and how to use it. IEEE Trans. Prof. Commun. **57**(2), 123–146 (2014). https://doi.org/10.1109/TPC.2014.2312452
35. Hair, J.F., Ringle, C.M., Sarstedt, M.: PLS-SEM: indeed a silver bullet. J. Mark. Theory Pract. **19**(2), 139–152 (2011). https://doi.org/10.2753/MTP1069-6679190202
36. Raykov, T., Grayson, D.: A test for change of composite reliability in scale development. Multivariate Behav. Res. **38**(2), 143–159 (2003)
37. dos Santos, P.M., Cirillo, M.Â.: Construction of the average variance extracted index for construct validation in structural equation models with adaptive regressions. In: Communications in Statistics-Simulation and Computation, pp. 1–13 (2021)
38. Zaiţ, A., Bertea, P.: Methods for testing discriminant validity. Manag. Mark. J. **9**(2), 217–224 (2011)
39. Braun, V., Clarke, V.: Using thematic analysis in psychology. Qual. Res. Psychol. **3**(2), 77–101 (2006)
40. Kiger, M.E., Varpio, L.: Thematic analysis of qualitative data: AMEE Guide No. 131. Med. Teach. **42**(8), 846–854 (2020)
41. Nonaka, I., Konno, N.: The concept of "Ba": building a foundation for knowledge creation. Calif. Manag. Rev. **40**(3), 40–54 (1998)

Author Index